WOMEN IN THE
CRIMINAL JUSTICE SYSTEM
SECOND EDITION

WOMEN IN THE
CRIMINAL JUSTICE SYSTEM
by
Clarice Feinman

SECOND EDITION

PRAEGER SPECIAL STUDIES • PRAEGER SCIENTIFIC

New York • Philadelphia • Eastbourne, UK
Toronto • Hong Kong • Tokyo • Sydney

Library of Congress Cataloging-in-Publication Data

Feinman, Clarice.
    Women in the criminal justice system.

    Includes bibliographies and index.
    1. Sex discrimination in criminal justice
administration—United States.   2. Female offenders—
United States.   3. Women correctional personnel—
United States.   4. Women lawyers—United States.
I. Title.
HV6791.F44   1985   364'.088042   85-16754
ISBN 0-03-000163-3 (alk. paper)
ISBN 0-03-000162-5 (pbk.: alk. paper)

Published in 1986 by Praeger Publishers
CBS Educational and Professional Publishing, a Division of CBS Inc.
521 Fifth Avenue, New York, NY 10175 USA

Printed in the United States of America on acid-free paper

INTERNATIONAL OFFICES

Orders from outside the United States should be sent to the appropriate address listed below. Orders from areas not
listed below should be placed through CBS International Publishing. 383 Madison Ave., New York, NY 10175 USA

Australia, New Zealand
Holt Saunders, Pty. Ltd., 9 Waltham St., Artarmon, N.S.W. 2064, Sydney, Australia

Canada
Holt, Rinehart & Winston of Canada, 55 Horner Ave., Toronto, Ontario, Canada M8Z 4X6

Europe, the Middle East, & Africa
Holt Saunders, Ltd., 1 St. Anne's Road, Eastbourne, East Sussex, England BN21 3UN

Japan
Holt Saunders, Ltd., Ichibancho Central Building, 22-1 Ichibancho, 3rd Floor, Chiyodaku, Tokyo, Japan

Hong Kong, Southeast Asia
Holt Saunders Asia, Ltd., 10 Fl, Intercontinental Plaza, 94 Granville Road, Tsim Sha Tsui East, Kowloon,
Hong Kong

**Manuscript submissions should be sent to the Editorial Director, Praeger Publishers, 521 Fifth Avenue,
New York, NY 10175 USA**

To
John
and to
Jonathan and Shirley

PREFACE TO THE SECOND EDITION

From a history of women in the criminal justice system we gain some understanding of U.S. values and behavior in regard to race, ethnicity, gender, and socioeconomic class. It makes us aware that the blindfold worn by Justice prevents her from seeing that the scales of justice are not balanced but, rather, are weighted in favor of some and against others. I have tried to make this point clearer in this second edition by adding a chapter on incarcerated women and by including information about minority women in all chapters. In addition, I have expanded all the chapters, bringing the information up to date, indicating the many changes that have taken place in the intervening years since the publication of the first edition in 1980. I explain why the changes occurred and what consequences have ensued from those changes. The preface to the first edition remains relevant, with the single exception that more literature exists about women throughout the criminal justice system than there was in 1980.

I would like to thank the women in the criminal justice system, for they have provided me with the incentive and information required to write this second edition. Women in police departments, courts, departments of correction, and prisons and jails in the United States, Israel, England, and Australia have been eager to discuss their experiences as professionals and as inmates. Their accents may be different, but their experiences and aspirations are similar.

I would also like to thank my editor, Lynda Sharp, for her enthusiasm about the expanded edition of the book.

PREFACE TO THE FIRST EDITION

Women in the criminal justice system (criminals, correction officers, police officers, lawyers, and judges) are poorly understood by the public. Casual and sometimes sensational exposure in the news media does not provide the kind of information that makes for understanding. Even when the behavior of women is discussed by academe or by government, explanations are often distorted by a reliance on traditional beliefs about the nature of women and their place in society. As a result there exists much misinformation, simplification, and a great tendency to rely on stereotypes and superficial theories to interpret the words and actions of women.

Unfortunately, there is still relatively little material available examining women in the criminal justice system. Information in newspapers and magazines is based on little real evidence, and usually either repeats old stereotypes or uncritically accepts new ones. Most of the scholarly literature since the 1960s focuses on women criminals and women in prison. The professionals in the system have received less attention: a few books on policewomen and lawyers, and none dealing with women as correction officers. Articles in journals cover some areas but ignore others.

This book has been written to provide a more reliable source of information on women in the criminal justice system. At the most obvious level, it gathers material from many different sources and offers a wide-ranging examination of the current situation and the historical factors that produced it. At another level, it interprets this information according to ideas more in harmony with the facts and less influenced by traditional stereotypes. It is an attempt to see women in criminal justice from a fresh perspective, outside the narrowly defined ideas that have predominated until very recently.

To some degree, this book owes a debt to the civil rights movement of the 1960s, which challenged stereotypes about black Americans and thus called into question stereotypes about other groups. It also owes much to the women's movement, which has questioned the accepted role of women. It owes most, however, to actual experiences and observations centered on the New York City Correctional Institution for Women on Rikers Island, and to conversations with prisoners; correctional personnel in jails, prisons, and departments of correction; and to police personnel, lawyers, and judges in a number of cities. For, in the final analysis, theories and statistics are valuable only if they correspond to the realities of life in prisons, police stations, and courtrooms.

CONTENTS

PART I

INTRODUCTION

That man over there says that women need to be helped into carriages, and lifted over ditches, and to have the best places everywhere. Nobody ever helps me into carriages, or over mud-puddles, or gives me any best place! And ain't I a woman? Look at me! Look at my arm! I have ploughed and planted, and gathered into barns, and no man could head me! And ain't I a woman? I could work as much and eat as much as a man—when I could get it—and bear the lash as well! And ain't I a woman? I have borne thirteen children, and seen them most all sold off to slavery, and, when I cried out with my mother's grief, none but Jesus heard me! And ain't I a woman?

(Soujourner Truth, "Ain't I a Woman?" in *Feminism: The Essential Historical Writings,* edited by Miriam Schneir [New York: Vintage Books, 1971], pp. 94–95).

1

WOMEN'S ROLE AND PLACE: A HISTORIC DEBATE

Fear of the nonconforming woman has transcended ethnic, racial, and religious bounds in almost all civilizations throughout history. The nonconforming woman can be one who questions established beliefs or practices, one who engages in activities traditionally associated with men, or one who commits a crime. Regardless of the activity, such a woman generates fear and anxiety among both women and men, and is viewed as a threat to social stability. Consequently she is subject to informal and formal sanctions and punishments intended to control her and to serve as a warning to others.

It is not surprising, then, that women in the criminal justice system are often considered as nonconformists and treated with hostility and rejection. The most obvious recipient of society's scorn is the female offender. However, the professional woman is also perceived as dangerous because she questions established beliefs about the role and place of women in society, and enters fields once considered the province of men only. As a consequence, both groups of women, offenders and professionals who seek equality with their male colleagues, continue to face the formal and informal disapproval of many women and men in the criminal justice system, and in society at large, because they are perceived as a threat to the social order and as a challenge to traditional cultural beliefs about women.

MADONNA/WHORE DUALITY

These attitudes derive in large measure from mythology and Judeo-Christian theology that present women as having one of two natures, either madonna or whore. The dual perception seems to have arisen from the two sharply different ways in which female sexuality has affected men. On the one hand, women produced children, which was good and necessary for the survival

3

of the family and community. Exactly how this was done was a mystery, although it was known somehow to relate to the equally mysterious phenomenon of menstruation. On the other hand, women inflamed men's passions and prompted them to lose control of themselves, again in ways that were often difficult to explain. Clearly women were different from men and possessed unique powers that made them both necessary and dangerous. It was therefore not surprising that men, in their effort to come to terms with female sexuality, should categorize women according to the degree to which they fit the role of either madonna or whore.[1]

Implicit in the madonna/whore duality is women's subservience to men, who assumed the role of protectors of the madonna and punishers of the whore. This is clearly stated in the Old and New Testaments. Eve was created from Adam's rib because it was "not good that the man should be alone; I will make a helpmeet for him."[2] And Paul declared that "man is not of the woman; but the woman is of the man. Neither was the man created for the woman; but the woman for the man."[3] A good woman is submissive and loyal; Ruth said, "Whither thou goest, I will go,"[4] A good woman, as in the Song of Solomon, brings life: "Thy belly is like a heap of wheat, set about with lillies."[5] A good woman is a loyal, submissive wife who serves her husband, and for this she is honored and protected.

The evil woman, on the other hand, destroys man and brings pain and ruin. Eve ate the forbidden fruit and caused the fall from Paradise. Pandora, the first woman, according to Greek mythology, could not resist the urge to open the mysterious box given to her as a marriage gift. Out of it flew all the evils of this world, leaving behind only hope. The evil woman manipulates and ruins man with lies and sex, just as Delilah robbed Samson of his strength and betrayed him. God punished Eve for her transgressions: "I will greatly multiply thy sorrow and thy conception; in sorrow thou shalt bring forth children; and thy desire shall be to thy husband and he shall rule over thee."[6] The evil woman would be redeemed only by painfully bearing children and by being controlled by her husband.

This concern with the potentially destructive and carnal nature of woman provided the basis for persistent beliefs that woman was inferior to man morally, physically, and intellectually. Zeus, for example, showed his superiority over woman by giving birth to Athena and Dionysis, usurping from female divinities their unique procreative powers.[7]

Thus did mythology and Judeo-Christain theology establish the basic principles of theories concerning women that remain so deeply engrained in the cultural perceptions and values of almost all societies. As a potential force for destruction, women had to be controlled by men and kept in their ordained role and place: to serve their husbands and bear children. If women remained within their prescribed sphere, men, families, and communities would remain orderly and safe.

WOMEN'S CRIMES AND PUNISHMENTS

The madonna/whore duality and the socioeconomic class of a woman were major factors in defining the nature of female criminal behavior and punishment. In classical Greece and Rome and medieval Europe, the primary role of a woman of the propertied class was wife and mother, and she was especially honored if she produced a legitimate male heir for the continuance of her husband's name and estate. A virgin maid was valued because, through a marriage contract, she became a medium of exchange for wealth and power. Consequently, a "spoiled" maid could be killed, banished, or confined in a convent by her father or other male guardian. Adultery was a very serious crime for a woman in a propertied marriage, since it threatened the purity, and therefore the legitimacy, of the next generation and heir. An adulterous wife could be put to death, and a husband who killed his wife and her lover *in flagrante delicto* suffered no legal penalty.[8]

Different standards prevailed among the lower-class women and among slaves, many of whom were prostitutes or "loose" women. Prostitution was condoned by Greco-Roman society as long as the women were of lower-class or slave origins. Prostitutes and mistresses were tolerated by the medieval church when titled and propertied men, whether married or unmarried, were those who kept mistresses and frequented brothels. In fact, brothels operated quite openly in many countries in medieval Europe. In England, as late as the eighteenth century, proponents of public brothels argued that such establishments would protect respectable women and their children from venereal disease if the prostitutes were examined by government medical officials. Only with the great reform movements of the Victorian era did the brothels go underground and prostitution become a crime.[9]

Unlike adultery and prostitution, which tended to follow class divisions, infanticide touched all women. In the Greco-Roman world the exposure of unwanted infants, usually in places specifically set aside for the purpose, was a legal and socially acceptable means of regulating family size and composition. The spread of Christianity, which condemned infanticide as murder, gradually did away with exposure, but new forms of infanticide arose. Studies of infanticide in England in the thirteenth and fourteenth centuries attest to the common occurrence of "overlaying," suffocation of the child being nursed when the mother rolled over on him or her. If the mother was married and living with her husband, she was rarely punished, except perhaps with a public reprimand. The unmarried mother might be labeled a witch, and could be stoned to death or buried alive.[10]

Another group of offenses affecting women emerged in the sixteenth century, as the growth of commerce and cities produced large numbers of homeless people who had no regular livelihood. Paupers moving from parish to parish and town to town created a social and financial burden, and contributed to the incidence of prostitution, theft, and more serious crimes. A common response was to make poverty a crime punishable by incarceration. In England, for example, poor laws were enacted. Vagrants and paupers with no home or employment were whipped, branded, driven from the towns, enslaved for up to two years, or placed in workhouses where they spun and carded wool or did mending. Unmarried mothers were sent to houses of correction as a punishment because their illegitimate children were charges of the parish. If they continued to have bastards, they were returned to houses of correction until they were deemed reformed. By the Act of 1661 the government authorized contractors to transport women from the workhouses to the American colonies. Some of the women were thieves and prostitutes, but others, perhaps a goodly number, were guilty only of poverty, indebtedness, or unemployment.

In contrast, during this period women of the propertied class who violated civil or criminal codes continued to be treated differently from lower-class women. They were allowed to do penance or serve the church in lieu of confinement in a workhouse and thus were able to remain free and live with their families.[11]

WOMEN REFORMERS

In addition to punishment, women offenders were subject to attempts at reform. The reformers, women of the propertied class, concentrated on the most fallen of women, the prostitutes. Basing their program on Christian teaching and exhortation, they offered their own exemplary lives as models. In order to accomplish their goals, women reformers tried to isolate the sinners from corrupt elements, primarily men. Residences were established where the women offenders could live and learn, and where unsullied women would do the reforming and teaching.

One of the earliest attempts to apply these methods of reform took place in the sixth century in the Byzantine empire. The empress Theodora initiated a plan by which over 500 prostitutes were confined in a convent called Repentance (Metanoia) for the purpose of restoring them eventually to the church and the home. Although the project failed, it did establish a precedent. Similar experiments took place in medieval Europe, and by the fourteenth century, with the encouragement of the church, there opened in Vienna a Magdalen Home where fallen but repentant women could live until they were ready to return to society as good Christians. Magdalen Homes, forerunners of present-day halfway houses, appeared in other European cities, and in 1830 the Magdalen Society established a residence in New York City.[12]

The women who helped reform the prostitutes and other women offenders acted in accord with traditional female roles. They served God and protected the family and community by reforming criminal women. Therefore, although they went beyond the singular homemaker role, they found acceptance in their home, church, and community because they fulfilled a necessary function by dealing with problems in the community. In addition, they were women beyond reproach in terms of their social class and their adherance to traditional values of womanhood.

Women reformers in the United States followed the pattern established in Europe; they were at first mostly upper-class, white, and traditional. They focused on dealing with women and children, attempting to isolate them in homes for the purpose of moral restoration. They did not seek to change the social order but, rather, to preserve it, and in so doing they gained the respect of the community. Because U.S. culture was Anglo-American, the standards set by reformers were based on values important to white Protestants; and because the reformers came from the upper class, the goals were based on the values of that class.

LAWS DEFINING WOMEN'S PLACE

Both the woman reformer and the woman offender continued to be evaluated and defined in terms of traditional attitudes, and these attitudes were reflected in law. The men who wrote and interpreted the law considered it their responsibility to secure the safety of women in order to protect the family and the community: "That God designed the sexes to occupy different spheres of action, and that it belonged to men to make, apply, and execute the laws, was regarded as an almost axiomatic truth."[13] It followed that certain areas of life could be entered by women only under carefully controlled circumstances. This was true of employment, where the principle of classification by sex was reinforced in *Muller* v. *Oregon* in 1908. The U.S. Supreme Court declared constitutional the right of states to pass labor laws for the protection of women in specific job categories. Its decision was based on the traditional belief that woman's biology, her sexual cycle, made her dependent on man. According to Justice David Brewer, "That woman's physical structure and the performance of maternal functions place her at a disadvantage in the struggle for subsistence is obvious."[14]

Recognizing that some women had to work, legislators and judges sought to protect womanhood and motherhood, but in reality they harmed women by restricting their ability to work and earn a living on an equal basis with men. Such protection made it difficult for women to have careers in criminal justice, for it reinforced traditional attitudes and thus prevented them from receiving the same work experiences, promotions, and financial rewards as men.

The belief that women had to be protected from the sordid aspects of life in order to preserve their purity led to their exclusion from jury duty, and even today automatic exemptions are available in many jurisdictions. Exclusion was based on the English common-law precedent that gave the right to serve on juries only to men. In 1879 the U.S. Supreme Court supported the common-law exclusion by deciding that states could constitutionally limit jury duty to men only. Not all states took advantage of this option; Utah gave women the legal right to serve on juries in 1898.[15]

Although women gained the right to serve on federal juries by the Civil Rights Act of 1957, states continued to impose restrictions. In 1961, in *Hoyt* v. *Florida*, the U.S. Supreme Court upheld Florida's law that "permitted" but did not "require" women to serve on juries. Justice John Harlan, delivering the opinion, wrote: "Despite the enlightened emancipation of women from the restrictions and protections of bygone years, and their entry into many parts of community life formerly considered to be reserved for men, woman is still regarded as the center of home and family life."[16] The Mississippi Supreme Court in 1966 upheld the state law "absolutely" excluding women from jury duty, despite the federal court decision that year, in *White* v. *Crook*, that held exclusion from jury duty to be a violation of women's Fourteenth Amendment right to equal protection. In the Mississippi Supreme Court's opinion, "The legislature has the right to exclude women so they may continue as mothers, wives, and homemakers, and also to protect them (in some areas they are still upon a pedestal) from the filth, obscenity and noxious atmosphere that so often pervades a courtroom during a jury trial."[17]

As of June 1975, five states provided an automatic exemption for men or women who could demonstrate that they had legal custody or care of a child. And despite the 1975 U.S. Supreme Court decision in *Taylor* v. *Louisiana* that women could not be excluded from jury duty solely because of sex, four states provided automatic exemptions for women.[18] However, in the decade that followed, states revised their laws on jury duty in compliance with federal antidiscrimination legislation and no longer excluded women from jury duty. The new laws no longer singled out women, but dealt with issues or specific reasons for exemptions that were gender-neutral. For example, persons legally responsible for the care of children could be exempted from jury duty for the period of time that was necessary to care for the children. Exemptions were to be temporary and not be meant to exclude anyone. However, in practice women could be encouraged to apply for exemptions or discouraged from taking an opportunity to apply for or accept jury duty.

Just as the proper woman, the madonna, had to be protected, so the offender, the whore, had to be punished. But the punishment had to be fitted to the unique nature of women. Thus, traditional attitudes about the nature of women influenced state laws governing the sentencing and rehabilitation of women offenders. According to these laws, women "must" be sentenced to an indeterminate term, whereas men "might" be sentenced to either an indeterminate or a determinate term upon conviction for the same type of crime under similar circumstances.

One of the best-known examples of such discriminatory legislation was the Muncy Act of Pennsylvania, which stated that any female pleading guilty to or convicted of a crime punishable by imprisonment of one year or more "must" be sentenced to the state prison for women, and that her sentence "shall be merely a general one" and the court "shall not fix or limit the duration thereof."[19] This meant that women often served longer sentences than men convicted of similar crimes, and had to wait longer before becoming eligible for parole.

The rationale for the different treatment of men and women was based on the old view of different natures. This is evident from the opinion of a lower Pennsylvania court, which, in upholding the Muncy Act, said:

> . . . the legislature reasonably could have concluded that indeterminate sentences should be imposed on women as a class, allowing the time of incarceration to be matched to the necessary treatment in order to provide more effective rehabilitation. Such a conclusion could be based on the physiological and psychological makeup of women, the type of crime committed by women, their relationship to the criminal world, their roles in society, their unique vocational skills and pursuits, and their reaction as a class to imprisonment.[20]

As long as the courts retained these traditional views of women, laws like the Muncy Act remained in force, but in the 1960s important changes occurred. In 1966 Jane Daniel was convicted in Pennsylvania of robbery, an offense that carried a maximum sentence of ten years. The judge sentenced her to one to four years in the county prison, but within a month he brought her back to court for resentencing under the Muncy Act, which required an indeterminate term of up to ten years at the state prison for women. Daniel appealed to the Pennsylvania Supreme Court and won in a precedent-setting case. The court, in *Commonwealth* v. *Daniel*, declared the Muncy Act unconstitutional.[21]

Subsequently, similar laws were proclaimed to be unconstitutional in other states. In 1971, in *State* v. *Costello*, the New Jersey Supreme Court held that "These distinctions, in essence, form the basis of defendant's claim of denial of equal protection because of discrimination on the basis of sex."[22] Mary A. Costello had argued that her constitutional right of equal protection under the Fourteenth Amendment had been violated when she was sentenced upon pleading guilty to a gambling offense. Under New Jersey law, a man convicted of the same offense would have received a sentence of not less than one year and not more than two years. Women convicted of that offense, as Costello was, received an indeterminate sentence not to exceed five years. In 1973, the New Jersey Supreme Court rejected the rationale that females were more amenable to rehabilitation and required a longer period of incarceration. The court, in *State* v. *Chambers*, stated that statutory provisions for sentencing female offenders to an indeterminate sentence when a similarly situated male would receive a minimum-maximum sentence were unconstitutional, in that they violated the equal protection clause of the Fourteenth Amendment.[23] These decisions opened the way to parole for 124 women serving indeterminate sentences at the state prison for women at Clinton.[24]

THEORETICAL REINFORCEMENT

The unquestioned existence for so many years of attitudes concerning women that permeated laws such as the Muncy Act was greatly abetted by theories promulgated by well-known researchers into human behavior. Three in particular have been important since the 1880s: Cesare Lombroso, Sigmund Freud, and Otto Pollak. Lombroso, who studied both male and female prisoners in Italy, emphasized the madonna/whore duality and the inferiority of women. The belief that woman is either good or bad is obvious in his statement, ''Her normal sister is kept in the paths of virtue by many causes, such as maternity, piety, weakness, and when these counter influences fail, and a woman commits a crime, we may conclude that her wickedness must have been enormous before it could triumph over so many obstacles''[25] He also concluded that because women are intellectually, morally, and physically inferior to men, they are less capable than men of engaging in criminal activities other than petty crimes such as prostitution. If they engage in criminal activities typically associated with men, they must certainly be ''monsters,'' abnormal even among criminal women.[26]

Freud interpreted women's behavior on the basis of personality. He asserted that women suffered from feelings of inferiority because they lacked a penis; they were incomplete persons. Because of their ''penis envy'' women had two choices of ways in which to find satisfaction and fulfillment: marriage and motherhood or neurosis and aggressive behavior.[27]

Pollak evaluated women's behavior in terms of the social roles they were expected to play. He argued that men and women have been taught that women must follow specific roles; any other path would be a betrayal of their womanhood. He inferred that women who deny their womanhood become like men, or masculine. Furthermore, women are natural deceivers who manipulate men and commit ''hidden crimes,'' but we are so steeped in the traditional view of womanhood that we refuse to admit that women would ''venture into a reserve of men'' and become criminals. In addition, according to Pollak, men are aware of women's criminality, but do little about it in order to keep women in their deceitful and inferior position so they can feel superior to women.[28]

Each writer approached the question of female criminal behavior from his own perspective. However, women's actions were never explained on the same basis as men's. Criminal actions and tendencies among men were typically explained with reference to factors such as poverty, racism, and lack of economic opportunity. Similar actions and tendencies among women were explained by resorting to the concept of the proper or natural female role. Rejection of this role, the writers argued, inevitably leads to deviance, whether as neurosis or as criminal activity. The supposed natural inferiority of women espoused by Lombroso, Freud, and Pollak only reinforced long-held beliefs in the harmful consequences if women failed to fulfill the proper female role. In this way modern writings have in theory given new strength and legitimacy to attitudes dating ultimately from ancient and medieval Europe.

The cumulative impact of theory and practice has been profound. Women in the criminal justice system, whether criminal or professional, have been taught that their one acceptable function is that of wife and mother, and their one acceptable place the home. Most women, fearing rejection by society, have accepted this role, or at least have admitted that it is a role to which they ought to aspire. Certainly this was true for U.S. women reformers who first entered the ranks of professionals in the criminal justice system. They were upper- and middle-class white women and conformed, at least outwardly, to traditional values and beliefs about women.

WOMEN'S MOVEMENT

In the past several centuries, more or less isolated voices of protest have been heard, but it is since about 1960 that widespread changes have occured in a way in which women preceive themselves, and women have become sufficiently self-conscious to have organized successful lobbies for government action against discrimination. One result has been the overturning of laws such as the Muncy Act, and another has been the opening up of a great debate on the proper roles, both public and private, of all women, in and out of the criminal justice system. This debate is the backdrop for many recent developments in law enforcement, the legal system, and corrections, affecting both female offenders and professionals, and accordingly must be taken into account in any consideration of these topics.

The women's movement is generally perceived as attempting to establish the legal right of all persons, regardless of sex, to an equal opportunity in all espects of life: work, family, and community. This principle runs counter to many of the roles traditionally ascribed to women, and in this sense the women's movement may be seen as threatening. It is commonly said, for example, that if women do not remain in their traditional mother/housewife role, children will become delinquents and husbands will not only be neglected but also diminished in manhood. Theologians, social scientists, and writers in the popular press have all stressed women's responsibility to family and community. In the nineteenth century this was embodied in the "cult of true womanhood," a view that remains enshrined even today. Then and now, women have been told that they mold the next generation and therefore should leave affairs outside the home to men.[29]

It is evident that any movement that tries to change these deeply felt values will be met with resistance and hostility, as has been true of the women's movement. Sometimes the opposition is overt, sometimes it is covert, and in many other cases it is probably unconscious. It is in the nature of fundamental values that they govern thought and action without always being clearly and consciously articulated by the affected individuals.

The women's movement has not been the only threat to traditional roles however, and it is instructive to compare previous events with those in the present. Then the question was the introduction of women into the labor force. Women have always worked, and until the invention, in the nineteenth century, of the lady of leisure, precariously perched on a pedestal, even wealthy women worked. They worked with their husbands on farms and plantations, in taverns, in newspaper offices, in retail stores, and in various other businesses; many ran the businesses in the absence of their husbands and when widowed. But by the mid nineteenth century, middle- and upper-class white women, the "ladies" of an urban, industrial society, were expected to be full-time wives and mothers. Men displayed their prowess in business or industry by being able to afford to have wives who did not have to work. The women who did work were primarily drawn from the lower class, and included many immigrants and blacks. Poor white women held low-status, low-paying jobs as domestics, salespersons, and factory and clerical workers. Poor black women worked as domestics, in laundries, and on farms.

In the nineteenth century, the madonna/whore duality became more important than ever. At that time, as long as middle- and upper-class women did not work, no violence was done to the duality, because lower-class women had never been seen as part of the madonna role. It seemed in the national interest to have available the cheap labor of these poor white and black women and eventually, of their children. The well-being of men, children, families, and the social order was not viewed as being threatened or in danger when lower-class women worked in poorly paid menial jobs.

Significant changes occured in the twentieth century as a result of wars. With the labor shortages during the two world wars, all adults, regardless of sex, race, or other distinguishing characteristics, became sought-after contributors to the common fight. Suddenly it was patriotic for women of all socioeconomic classes to leave the home and work in factories, offices, or public drives to raise money, collect scrap, or make bandages. Suddenly it was acceptable for black women to work in factories, earning a salary on an equal basis with white women. In World War I the number of women in the work force was rather limited, but in World War II it increased dramatically as women, over 6 million of them, worked in all kinds of jobs, even in shipyards, railroads, lumber camps, and the armed forces.

The end of war brought an equally sudden demand that the new workers put down their tools and make way for the returning men. Almost overnight it became patriotic to become mothers and housewives again. As the head of the National Association of Manufacturers said: "From a humanitarian point of view, too many women should not stay in the labor force. The home is the basic American institution."[30] Sociologists took up the familiar position of the prewar years: "Women must bear and rear children; husbands must support them."[31]

Again, socioeconomic class determined which women were urged to return to their proper place and role. Lower-class women continued to work, if they could find work: white and black poor women returned to the low-paying jobs that had been available to them before the war. To a considerable degree middle- and upper-class women heeded the advice of business and labor leaders and social commentators, and left the labor force. Nevertheless, precedents had been set: and gradually, beginning in the 1950s many women with families began to work outside the home. Now, however, the women were not only lower-class, but middle- and upper-class as well. The "ladies" started to combine careers with home life and, unlike the lower-class women, began to ask for their rights, for equality. They were educated and articulate, and constituted a small, identifiable group that gradually achieved some self-awareness. These women were the core of the emerging women's movement, and their ideas provided a sense of direction and a measure of what had to be done.

As the movement grew, affecting ever larger numbers of educated women, the threat to traditional values increased. Men were confronted by a movement that seemed to be increasing the competition in the marketplace for jobs and money, by an apparently liberated female identity that reversed the old roles, and by the specter of a topsy-turvy family in which men did the dishes and women brought home the bacon. Many women who were wives and mothers felt that their roles were being threatened and that their husbands' images and livelihoods were in jeopardy. The whole situation was made even more unsettling because the women who joined the movement were too well educated to be dismissed out of hand, and too articulate and committed to be squelched. Since the movement could not be evaded, it had to be confronted, and no one who lived throught the 1960's and 1970's will forget the passion of that debate.

Women are most likely to make gains toward equality under the law and in all aspects of life during periods of social ferment and reform. Obviously their abilities are important, but their chances of breaking down the barriers of discrimination and achieving increased career opportunities are related to the intellectual and social reform climate of the time. The periods in which women have made significant gains toward equality have come during distinct reform eras in which the women's movement has flourished. The first, 1820 to 1870, was a period of antislavery crusades in which women actively participated as speakers, propagandists, petitioners, and members of the Underground Railroad. Once women argued for freedom, equality, and the right to vote for black people, the next step was to organize and seek these rights for themselves. The women's rights movement started with a meeting at Seneca Falls, New York, in 1848; women asked for equality under the law and the right to vote. They did not win the right to vote under the Fifteenth Amendment, but several states did pass laws giving women the right to own property and keep their wages.

Between 1880 and 1920 another social reform era developed, the Progressive Era, during which reformers focused on urban ills, poverty, and crime. Again women organized, and lobbied and petitioned government for reforms, including women law enforcement officers to protect women and children, and a separate prison system for women staffed by women. In doing so, they recognized their own political impotence and a second women's rights movement surfaced. This time they succeeded; the Nineteenth, or Anthony, Amendment was added to the constitution.

At last women could vote, hold elected office, and exert political pressure on judges and legislators to eliminate discrimination against them. However, between 1920 and 1960 this did not take place. Rather, the momentum generated to pass the Anthony Amendment ebbed sharply, with a resultant curtailment of efforts to obtain equality under the law for women in all aspects of life. Women had concentrated on getting the right to vote, but appeared to have lost interest in pursuing other rights once the fight was won. Certainly the preoccupation with the hardships of the depression and World War II contributed to the decline in the women's movement.

Again it took a significant social reform agent, the civil rights movement in the 1950s and 1960s, to reawaken the latent women's movement. Women organized, lobbied, and used their right to vote to pressure for court decisions and legislation to bring about the end of discrimination based on sex and to afford all women equal rights and opportunities. Congress passed anti-discrimination legislation, such as Title VII of the Civil Rights Act of 1964, and sent the Equal Rights Amendment to the states for ratification. Federal and state courts generally upheld these laws. Equality under the law appeared to be within women's grasp.

However, by the end of 1984, the women's movement faced serious problems. The Equal Rights Amendment had not been ratified and only the Democratic Party continued officially to support the amendment in its 1984 presidential campaign platform. The Republican Party platform, on which President Ronald Reagan ran and was elected to a second term, made no mention of the amendment or women's rights. Conservative forces influenced Republican Party policy, and the concept of equal rights, anathema to right-wing groups, was rejected. The political climate in the nation ceased to be conducive to the advancement of women's rights or civil rights. Institutional and societal opposition to women's rights gained strength. Even the Miss America pageant became politicized against the women's movement.

SUMMARY

Beliefs concerning women's role and place, stemming from Judeo-Christian theology, are deeply rooted in our culture. Women who conform as pure, obedient daughters, wives, and mothers benefit men and society; the madonnas are honored. Women who do not conform threaten men and society; the whores are punished. The pervasive and tenacious nature of these beliefs is evident in all areas of life and is reinforced by pronouncements from church, academe, legislature, and court. Hypocrisy in applying and enforcing these beliefs is also evident; poor and minority women have not been considered madonnas and have not been honored, only punished. The madonna/whore duality and the hypocrisy that surrounds it continue to have significant consequences for women in the criminal justice system.

NOTES

1. Sarah B. Pomeroy, *Goddesses, Whores, Wives, and Slaves: Women in Classical Antiquity* (New York: Schocken Books, 1975), pp. 8–9; Page Smith, *Daughters of the Promised Land: Women in American History* (Boston: Little, Brown, 1970), pp. 1–7.

2. Genesis, 2:18.

3. I Corinthians, 11:8–9.

4. Ruth, 1:16.

5. Song of Solomon, 7:2, 7.

6. Genesis, 3:16.

7. Pomeroy, op. cit., pp. 2–3.

8. Ibid., pp. 20–23, 33–35, 62–65, 81–82, 86–88, 154–60; Vern L. Bullough, *The Subordinate Sex: A History of Attitudes Towards Women* (Baltimore: Penguin Books, 1974), pp. 19–120, 153–94; Julia O'Faolain and Laura Martines, eds., *Not in God's Image: Women in History from the Greeks to the Victorians* (New York: Harper Torchbook, 1973), pp. 175–78.

9. Pomeroy, op. cit., pp. 68–70, 86–87, 164–69; David J. Pivar, *Purity Crusade: Sexual Morality and Social Control, 1868–1900* (Westport, Conn.: Greenwood Press, 1973), pp. 13–17; J. Johnson, *The Laws Respecting Women* (repr. Dobbs Ferry, N.Y.: Oceana Publications, 1974), p. 300.

10. Marvin Harris, *Cannibals and Kings: The Origins of Culture* (New York: Random House, 1977), pp. 171, 183–84.

11. Johnson, op. cit., pp. 300, 302; Walter H. Blumenthal, *Brides from Bridewell: Female Felons Sent to Colonial America* (Rutland, Vt.: Charles E. Tuttle, 1962), pp. 11–26; Norman Longmate, *The Workhouse* (New York: St. Martin's Press, 1974), pp. 14–18.

12. Bullough, op. cit., pp. 161–63, 206–07; O'Faolain and Martines, op. cit., pp. 82–83; Pivar, op. cit., p. 15.

13. Leo Kanowitz, *Sex Roles in Law and Society: Cases and Materials* (Albuquerque: University of New Mexico Press, 1973), p. 44.

14. Ibid. p. 47.

15. Anne R. Mahoney, "Sexism in Voir Dire: The Use of Sex Stereotypes in Jury Selection," in *Women in the Courts*, edited by Winifred L. Hepperle and Laura Crites (Williamsburg, Va.: National Center for State Courts, 1978), p. 115.

16. Kanowitz, op. cit., p. 76.

17. Ibid., p. 59.

18. Mahoney, op. cit., p. 117; Leo Kanowitz, *Women and the Law: The Unfinished Revolution* (Alburquerque: University of New Mexico Press, 1969), p. 28.

19. Kanowitz, *Women and the Law*, p. 167.

20. Ibid., p. 168.

21. Carolyn Temin, "Discretionary Sentencing of Women Offenders," *American Criminal Law Review* 11 (1973): 357–61; *Commonwealth* v. *Daniel*, 430 Pa. 642, 243 A.2d. 400 (1968).

22. *State* v. *Costello*, New Jersey State Supreme Court 59, 1971: 343.

23. *State* v. *Chambers*, New Jersey State Supreme Court 63, 1973: 287–300.

24. Kanowitz, *Women and the Law*, p. 169; Karen DeCrow, *Sexist Justice* (New York: Vintage Books, 1975), pp. 243–45.

25. Cesare Lombroso and William Ferrero, *The Female Offender* (New York: D. Appleton, 1920), p. 152.

26. Ibid., pp. 150, 152, 205.

27. Sigmund Freud, *New Introductory Lectures on Psychoanalysis* (New York: W. W. Norton, 1933), pp. 153–85.

28. Otto Pollak, *The Criminality of Women* (Philadelphia: University of Pennsylvania Press, 1950), pp. 149, 10–29.

29. Barbara Welter, "The Cult of True Womanhood: 1820–1860," in *Our American Sisters: Women in American Life and Thought*, edited by Jean E. Friedman and William G. Shade (Boston: Allyn and Bacon, 1973), pp. 96–123; William H. Chafe, *The American Woman: Her Changing Social, Economic, and Political Role, 1920–1970* (New York: Oxford University Press, 1972), pp. 199–225; Robert W. Smuts, *Women and Work in America* (New York: Schocken Books, 1971), pp. 110–55.

30. Quoted in Chafe, op. cit., p. 176.

31. Quoted Ibid.

PART II

WOMEN CRIMINALS

Female offenders are forgotten women, except when someone chooses to make them the albatross of the women's movement. Female offenders are rarely forgiven because 'nice girls' don't commit crimes.

. . .

Those of us who sincerely care about these forgotten and unforgiven women look not at the women's movement as a cause but as a clue to a possible cure—the creation of a strong, independent woman able to make her own decisions, able to choose her own path, and able to look in the mirror and say, 'I like myself.'

(Charlotte Ginsburg, "Who Are the Women in Prison?" in *Women in Corrections*, edited by Barbara H. Olsson [College Park, Md.: American Correctional Association, 1981], p. 56.)

2

WOMEN AND CRIME: MYTHS AND REALITIES

The persistent association of the women's movement with the madonna/whore duality has major implications for women. Many have been led to believe that as women reject their proper role, more women will become criminals. Although discredited by research conducted since the 1970s and by those who work directly with female offenders, the myth persists that changes in the extent and nature of female criminality have taken place since the 1960s, and that the changes are related to the women's movement. In reality there is no empirical evidence to prove that patterns of criminal behavior of women have changed significantly since the late eighteenth century. Arrest, court, and prison records indicate that almost all women involved in crime continue to commit crimes traditionally associated with females, such as larceny/theft, prostitution, drunkenness, fraud, and homicide involving family members or male friends. These are primarily unsophisticated crimes that require little skill and education, and yield small rewards. The evidence does indicate that women who have been arrested, convicted, and incarcerated have been disproportionally from the lower socioeconomic class and members of ethnic or racial minority groups.

The persistence of these myths, despite evidence to the contrary, reflects societal attitudes regarding the acceptable role of women, and consequently influences the treatment of female offenders. Women who deviate from traditional norms become whores and must be punished to set an example, so that madonnas will not be tempted to fall from grace. A contradictory view of the treatment of female offenders holds that the criminal justice system is governed, to a degree, by chivalry to ensure that madonnas are protected and that potential madonnas are given another chance. Both viewpoints have had the effect of channeling attention away from examining how the daily realities of life may be influencing female criminality and how women criminals are treated by the criminal justice system.

EXTENT AND NATURE OF FEMALE CRIMINALITY

The myth that there has been an extraordinary change in the extent and nature of women's criminal behavior since 1960 can be dispelled by a reading and interpretation of the statistics presented in the standard source for gauging criminal activity in the United States, the *Uniform Crime Reports*, published since 1930 by the Federal Bureau of Investigation. According to the *Reports*, from 1960 to 1983 the number of arrests of women and men over 18 years old increased significantly. Actual numbers are more meaningful. Comparison of arrests of women and men over 18 years old from 1960 to 1983 follows:[1]

	Women	*Men*
1960	304,165	2,665,044
1975	515,673	2,847,612
1977	536,132	2,930,027
1980	1,093,363	6,405,633
1983	1,211,479	6,497,088

The number of arrests of women quadrupled and of men less than trebled. However, this significant increase took place from 1960 to 1980, whereas from 1980 to 1983, the increase was small for both men and women. Equally important, the ratio of arrests of women to those of men from 1975 to 1983 remained stable at one to five or six.

These data were referred to by those claiming that a major change had occurred in the extent of women's criminal behavior in the 1960s and 1970s. Therefore it is important to remember that there are sources of potential inaccuracy in the way the figures are derived, and that the numbers must be interpreted in the light of events taking place in the United States during those years. Data in the *Uniform Crime Reports*, for example, may be affected by lack of uniformity in number of agencies reporting, changes in numbers of men and women in the areas covered by a given agency, demographic shifts, and different ways in which each agency defines and records specific criminal behavior.

Events taking place in the United States from 1960 to 1983 affected the number of men and women arrested, and may provide some reasons for the disproportionate increase in the number of women arrested from 1960 to 1980 compared with that of men. For example, the baby boom of the 1940s and 1950s increased the number of men and women in the age of risk—15 to 30 years old—in the 1960s and 1970s. However, during the 1960s, many men of the age of risk were in the armed forces as a result of the Vietnam war. If those men had been in the community, perhaps the increase in the number of arrests of men would have been proportionally similar to that of women or perhaps even larger. Finally, if the armed forces' criminal arrests records were investigated and added to the civilian arrests records, a completely different trend might be indicated. A large number of men in the armed forces were arrested for crimes that led to their dishonorable discharge.

During the period 1960–83, the drug epidemic affected women as much as it did men. Supporting a drug habit required money, and crime provided the money for most addicts. In my study of women incarcerated in New York City, approximately 85 percent of the subjects were addicted to narcotics.[2] In her study, Anne Pottieger reported 29.6 percent of female heroin addicts relied on criminal activities—primarily prostitution, drug sales, and shoplifting—as their major source of income. The researcher noted that fewer women than men had steady employment and income, which might explain why more women than men relied on illegal means of getting money for narcotics.[3]

Another possible reason for the increase in the number of arrests of women from 1960 to 1980 may be found in the areas of law enforcement manpower and equipment, especially after the passage of the Omnibus Crime Control and Safe Streets Act of 1968. This act created the Law Enforcement Assistance Administration (LEAA) in the Department of Justice to serve as the department's funding arm, providing money to law enforcement agencies for the addition of personnel and for the purchase of equipment to improve detection and data collection. Apprehension and data-processing methods have been further improved with the use of computers and with the addition of mobile patrol and communication units. These have had an undoubted influence on the number of arrests and the manner in which arrests have been recorded. These funds and technological improvements have also provided many agencies with the resources and ability to record arrests of women separately from those of men for the first time. In agencies that had no separate listings for women, any data starting with a base figure of zero showed a marked increase, whereas the actual number of women arrested by those agencies may not have increased much, if at all.

Federal, state, and local legislation and policies establish reasons for arrests that especially affect women, both by creating new crimes and by determining which criminal codes to enforce. For example, welfare programs have provided a new means for women to commit fraud, and welfare fraud may account for one-third to one-half of arrests of women for fraud. And because of the serious crime rate in New York City, arrests for prostitution gradually ceased to be considered quality arrests in the 1960s and 1970s. However, in the summer of 1976, the Democratic National Convention was held at Madison Square Garden, and during that time prostitutes were told to stay away from the convention area or be arrested, convicted, and sent to jail; police were told to arrest women who ''hung around'' the convention area. After the Democrats went home, business returned to normal for both prostitutes and law enforcers.[4]

Finally, victims of crimes committed by women appear to be more willing than in the past to report these crimes to the authorities. This is epecially true of shoplifting and employee theft. Law enforcement agencies, responding to increased pressure from victims and to media publicity, may be taking a more aggressive role in arresting female offenders. In fact, the "get tough" policy directed at the apprehension and punishment of criminals that started in the late 1970s has affected both men and women offenders, and may account for the obvious increase in arrests for both from 1977 to 1980.

The rise in the incidence of arrests of women that has occurred since 1960 must be considered and interpreted within the context of the realities of events taking place. Clearly, a significant increase did take place, but so too for men, and for many reasons.

The claims that women have been committing more violent and more masculine types of crimes since 1960, and that women's crimes since 1960 have reflected expanded economic opportunities must be considered and interpreted.[5] Each *Uniform Crime Reports* is divided into two parts. Part I, "Crime Index," lists the crimes considered most representative of the trend of criminal activity across the country: violent crimes of murder, forcible rape, robbery, and aggravated assault, and property crimes of burglary, larceny/theft, motor vehicle theft, and arson. (Arson was added in October 1978.) Part II, which has no specific title, lists other crimes, such as simple assault, fraud, prostitution, vagrancy, drunkenness, drug abuse, disorderly conduct, and offenses relating to juveniles.

From 1960 to 1983, there was an increase in the number of women arrested for Part I crimes. Taken out of context, this seems to portend an ominous trend. But of all women arrested during that time, only one-third committed Part I crimes and, most important, the overwhelming number of women were arrested for larceny/theft. For example, in 1980, of a total of 1,093,363 arrests of women, larceny/theft accounted for 29 percent of all the arrests and 79 percent of arrests for Part I crimes; in 1983, of a total of 1,211,479 arrests of women, larceny/theft accounted for 20 percent of all the arrests and 80 percent of arrests for Part I crimes.[6] Again, the actual numbers are more meaningful. Table 2.1 lists, in rank order, the ten crimes for which women over 18 years of age were most frequently arrested in selected years from 1960 to 1983.

From 1960 to 1983, of the ten crimes for which women over 18 years old were most frequently arrested, only larceny/theft and aggravated assault are Part I crimes; the others are Part II crimes. The increase in arrests for Part I crimes is due primarily to larceny/theft, ranking first in 1975, 1977, and 1980, and second in 1983. It is a crime traditionally associated with women and one that is neither violent nor masculine in nature—and certainly is not a reflection of expanded economic opportunities. In fact, an overall view of the criminal pattern of women since 1960 shows that the reasons for arrest have

Table 2.1: Rank Order of Causes of Arrest, Women over 18: 1960, 1975, 1977, 1980, 1983[7]

1960

Total arrests	304,165
Drunkenness	102,698
Disorderly conduct	47,321
Larceny/theft	19,281
Prostitution/commercialized vice	17,943
Other assaults	11,125
Liquor law violations	10,574
Gambling	9,948
Vagrancy	9,858
Driving under the influence	8,963
Aggravated assault	7,176

1975

Total arrests	505,673
Larceny/theft	109,856
Disorderly conduct	70,506
Drunkenness	45,984
Driving under the influence	34,129
Narcotic drug law violations	30,827
Prostitution/commercialized vice	30,274
Fraud	29,184
Other assaults	21,289
Aggravated assault	13,546
Forgery/counterfeiting	9,292

1977

Total arrests	536,132
Larceny/theft	121,448
Disorderly conduct	52,908
Drunkenness	42,604
Driving under the influence	42,063
Prostitution/commercialized vice	34,466
Drug abuse violations	34,173
Other assaults	22,269
Fraud	19,106
Liquor law violations	11,909
Aggravated assault	11,590

1980

Total arrests	1,093,363
Larceny/theft	211,979
All other offenses (except traffic)*	184,263
Driving under the influence	116,606
Fraud	105,437
Disorderly conduct	89,798
Drunkenness	73,903
Prostitution/commercialized vice	55,858
Drug abuse violations	53,784
Other assaults	45,439
Liquor law violations	31,554

1983

Total arrests	1,211,479
All other offenses (except traffic)*	227,683
Larceny/theft	220,809
Driving under the influence	155,376
Fraud	92,297
Disorderly conduct	83,350
Prostitution/commercialized vice	77,477
Drunkenness	75,839
Drug abuse violations	68,462
Other assaults	49,062
Liquor law violations	33,020

*All other offenses (except traffic) includes state and local ordinances and laws other than those listed.

remained relatively stable, with only fraud and drug offenses new to the list (starting in 1975) and "all other offenses (except traffic)" (in 1980). In 1980 and 1983, the only Part I crime listed was larceny/theft.

An examination of Table 2.1 leads to several conclusions about women's criminal behavior since 1960. Traditional "women's crimes" were the major reasons for the increase in both the overall arrest rate for women and their arrests for Part I crimes. Arrests of women for violent crimes remained stable or declined. Most women continued to be arrested for victimless crimes: for being drug addicts, for being intoxicated, for being sexually loose, and for not conforming to culturally expected roles. Equally important, alcohol-related offenses and drug-abuse violations accounted for four of the ten reasons for arrest in 1960 and 1975, and five of the ten in 1977, 1980, and 1983. These crimes are often committed by women addicted to alcohol and narcotics. In reality, then, a very large number of women are being arrested for commiting crimes related to substance addiction; they are sick women.

Although not specifically listed in the *Uniform Crime Reports*, terrorists and revolutionaries, particularly the women, have received much attention since the 1960s; therefore they warrant some mention. Studies of women terrorists and revolutionaries clearly indicate that they have been neither feminists nor members of women's movements. Rather, they have acted on political or nationalistic beliefs and not to further women's rights. Vera Broido, writing about Russian women revolutionaries, stated, "To assign to revolutionary women the narrow partisan role of feminists is to distort their position in the revolutionary movement and to diminish their contribution to Russian history."[8] Women members of the Baader-Meinhof gang, according to Jillian Becker, "were in fact out for no cause but the gratification of their own egotism."[9]

It is important not to equate women terrorists and revolutionaries with the women's movement or feminism. This serves only to confuse the issues and goals of feminists, and to discredit the women's movement. The link between terrorism and the women's movement is another example of attempts to deny reality and, in so doing, perpetuate myths about women and their role in society.

FEMALE CRIMINALITY AND THE WOMEN'S MOVEMENT

Since a change in the extent and nature of women's criminality is not borne out by statistics or empirical studies, it may therefore seem strange that some have argued that a causal link to these changes is the women's movement. Although unfounded, myths concerning women criminals persist while realities of female criminality are often ignored. This is due, in part, to traditional views about the proper role of women in society and, in part, to some preconceived ideas about the impact of the women's movement on society.

The culturally valued role for women is that of wife and mother, and any deviation is believed to result in a disruption of the social order. The madonna/ whore duality rests on this concept. Therefore, when some women question their roles and ask for the opportunity to choose their place in society, they are perceived as threats to social stability. These attitudes have been particularly evident in times of social unrest. In such periods, traditional woman becomes a source of stability in an otherwise chaotic world. Two examples illustrate this point.

In the 1920's, Americans faced the challenge and stress of the postwar years, the start of gang warfare and bootlegging, and the poverty and unemployment that preceded the great depression. It was also the time when women had won the right to vote as a result of a vigorous campaign waged by members of the women's movement. The heightened anxiety of the period may explain why the New York City commissioner of correction, when asked to comment on the increase in the number of incarcerated women in the city, answered. "It is possible of course that the comparative emancipation of woman, her greater participation in commercial and political affairs and the tendency towards greater sexual freedom may be playing their part in bringing about this situation."[10] And in the 1960's and 1970's, Americans witnessed civil rights demonstrations, an active women's rights movement, antiwar protests, riots in cities and prisons, student demonstrations, terrorist activities, and a reported increase in crime. These conditions created an atmosphere of tension and anxiety. During that period, an increased concern about women's criminality appeared in the media and in the statements and writings of several academics.

Ironically, arrest records during the two world wars disprove the link between women's emancipation and their criminality. During the wars, especially World War II, when few women had difficulty finding employment, arrests of women decreased significantly.[11] To this degree it is valid to say that women who do not follow traditional roles and who work outside the home are less likely to commit antisocial acts.

However, many are still convinced that giving women equal opportunities in the economic and political life of communities will lead to their entry into the criminal life. The public rarely hears opinions on this issue from the men and women whose careers bring them into daily contact with female offenders or from the offenders themselves. Essie O. Murph, former superintendent of the New York City Correctional Institution for Women, considered the women incarcerated in the jail as "losers," the "bottom of the barrel" in our society.[12] A study I conducted while director of a rehabilitation program during Murph's tenure revealed that women incarcerated in New York City from 1930 to 1975 were poor, uneducated, unskilled, and, if employed, were waitresses or factory and domestic workers. They were unmarried mothers, most of whom had committed crimes involving petty larceny, prostitution, or drugs. This study found no evidence that they were involved with the women's movement. In fact, two women stated that they were taking the "rap" for their men; they held the weapons, knowing they would receive a shorter sentence then a man would.[13]

From her own experience, Farris Lawrence, an ex-offender, believed that women criminals were dependent on men and had a poor self-image. Recognizing that many women got into trouble with the law because of their relationships with men, Lawrence wrote:

> Women in American society have been taught to define themselves in terms of men and therefore depend upon a male system. Women are by nature dependent. Our society teaches us that to be smart, we should depend upon men for whatever we need. But I believe independence is the answer. Social and coping skills, including family life, education, and consumer training, are necessary to prepare women to deal with society without reliance on a public welfare system or on a temporary male guardian (a new boyfriend, until he gets broke). Women in prison need focus on self-definition, self-realization, self-appreciation, and self-sufficiency.[14]

Another ex-offender, Judy Glass, a counselor for women offenders at the Fortune Society (an organization in New York City dedicated to improving conditions in jails and prison and to helping ex-offenders), did not think more women were committing crimes, but that more were being arrested:

> . . . 75 percent of the women who come here from state prison were there for drug busts. Before the Rockefeller drug law, they would have gotten probation or a lesser charge. Also there is a great increase in women being prosecuted for welfare fraud. We are being prosecuted now for things that used to be dealt with by restitution or probation. Now there's jail.[15]

She also did not see any relationship between women criminals and the women's movement:

> From my experience, street women don't even relate to the women's movement that much. We think of it as a housewives' thing. We've always been liberated and we've always been considered aggressive. I doubt that more women are becoming aggressive because of the women's movement. I think poverty, poor education, or the lack of skills is more responsible.[16]

Those who work with female offenders are aware of the realities associated with these women. According to Margery Velimesis, who was the executive director of the Pennsylvania Program for Women and Girl Offenders in Philadelphia at the time:

> There is absolutely no evidence thus far that the increasing status of women or their expanding number of roles has led them to commit more

crime since this expansion mostly affects middle-class women. The jail and prison populations are psychologically about as far removed from the predominantly middle-class "women's movement" as one could imagine. The previously identified characteristics, poverty, main source of family income, few skills, mostly mothers—and the property crimes most women commit are evidence of the increasing strain that a technological, impersonal society is creating in the lives of poor and primarily minority group, inner-city women. As the quality of life deteriorates in the poverty sections of our big cities and as that life becomes more violent, women will also become more violent in their traditional roles of school girl, mother, lover, and unemployed or meagerly paid worker.[17]

When Judy Hansen was director of community relations for Pittsburgh Services for Women Offenders, she wrote:

> As the drug culture grows, as the country's economic situation deteriorates, and as the lot of the poor worsens, crime rates in general will continue to spiral. Until we deal with these root problems honestly and intellectually—instead of superciliously blaming such scapegoats as the women's rights movement for crime—we cannot hope to solve them.[18]

Two recent studies corroborate observations made in the 1970s: poverty and drugs are major determinants of female criminality. Rosemary Sarri studied 3,162 women processed in the prison for women in Michigan from 1968 to 1979. She reported an increase in drug-related crimes from 10 percent in 1968 to 15 percent in 1978. Furthermore, the women during that period were primarily poor and educationally disadvantaged, and 90 percent had children though only 15 percent were married. From 1968 to 1978 the proportion of nonwhite women increased from 57 percent to 73 percent.[19] Jody Grossman reported that 44 percent of 345 women incarcerated in the New York state prison for women were under the influence of drugs, alcohol, or both when they committed the crime for which they were incarcerated; 36 percent had committed the crime to obtain drugs for their own use.[20]

Those who have conducted recent empirical studies on female criminality and have worked with female offenders reach similar conclusions: that there is no evidence that could possibly link the women's movement either to the increase in crimes committed by women or to the nature of women's criminal behavior. They continue to act in traditional ways both in the crimes they commit and in the manner in which they commit those crimes. One study of men and women arrested for committing crimes such as burglary or robbery together noted that women were invariably the accessories; the men made the plans. In addition, women acting alone, even if they had some prior experience participating with men in burglaries or robberies, committed the traditional women's crimes of larceny and prostitution.[21]

In a 1984 study, Grossman reported that 40 percent of the 345 women imprisoned in New York State were accessories to a crime.[22] She concluded that major changes in commitments of women were related to revisions in the criminal and sentencing codes and a different approach taken by the courts, and not caused by changes in the criminality of women or the women's movement:

> The women's movement and the changing attitude in the home and workplace have affected predominantly the white, middle-class women in terms of expanded rights and opportunities in the workplace. The push for equal opportunity in employment has not affected the group of poor, minority women equally. Demographic data on the inmate population shows the woman offender to fall into this group: poor; uneducated; from minority backgrounds; typically unemployed; and in support of a family.[23]

The women's movement has neither involved nor benefited the majority of women in the United States. It has not even brought true equal opportunities for the minority of white middle- and upper-class women who have been most directly involved with the movement. Therefore, any discussion of the link between women's criminality and the women's movement is unrealistic. It only serves to perpetuate myths; it hinders efforts to learn the real causes of women's criminal behavior and to try to eliminate them.

CHIVALRY IN THE CRIMINAL JUSTICE SYSTEM

The realities of life that have helped shape the nature and extent of women's criminality are often overshadowed by concern with extraneous factors. Allusions to a drastic rise in the incidence of crimes committed by females and in women's violent and aggressive nature, as well as an assumed relationship between women's criminality and the women's movement, represent mere suppositions and conjecture, and are not borne out by evidence. Another extraneous factor is represented by the view that women benefit from a form of chivalry practiced by male members of the criminal justice system. This latter view is at odds with the realities of societal attitudes and values in relation to women and to racial and ethnic minorities. Women from these groups have been disproportionately present as offenders in the criminal justice system, and few, if any, experience chivalrous treatment. Chivalry is reserved for white middle- and upper-class women, except those who flout culturally expected behavior for ladies.

Despite these realities, the belief that chivalry exists is accepted by some criminal justice researchers and personnel; they point to the small number of arrested and incarcerated women in the United States to justify their beliefs. For example, in 1983, women accounted for 17 percent of all arrests and 3.81 percent of a combined total of state and federal prisoners.[24] Those who support the chivalry theory argue that the criminal justice system treats women differently—to their advantage—from men.

Studies done in the 1960s and 1970s to gauge the importance of chivalry are divided in their findings, and suggest that arrests and sentencing of women are influenced by many factors. Some studies, for example, have concluded that if women conform to stereotypical behavior by crying, or showing deference to police or concern for their children, they are less likely to be arrested.[25] Other studies, however, have found that police respond in a similar manner to the demeanor of both men and women. They are less likely to arrest men or women who are polite and respectful, do not resist, and, most important, have not committed a violent crime. A study by Moyer and White of police in a southeastern city confirmed that demeanor and type of offense, not the sex of the offender, influence the decision of the police. Police officers admitted that if the offense is not serious, the main factor influencing their behavior is the attitude of the person arrested, whether male or female. Persons who "bad mouth" officers are more likely to be arrested. Thus the officers admitted to exercising considerable discretion when making arrests.[26]

Often, however, police discretion is affected by formal or informal public policy. An example is arrests for smoking marijuana. Increased use by middle- and upper-class persons, and pressure for decriminalization, led to decisions not to arrest. This was particularly true in areas where the penalty was severe—as in New York, under the 1973 Rockefeller drug law.[27]

In the case of shoplifting, the low arrest rate of women before 1960 may have been the result of decisions by shop owners not to prosecute, on the rationale that it did not pay to go through the trouble of a court trial if the stolen merchandise was recovered when the woman was apprehended. In addition, the value of the item stolen probably determines whether the woman is arrested. Studies indicate that store administrators are more likely to call for the arrest of a person, man or women, if the item is expensive. Men are more likely than women to be involved with high-value thefts, which probably explains why fewer women were arrested for shoplifting in the past.[28]

On the other hand, there is evidence for a "get tough" policy by store managers and owners in recent years. Since 1960 arrests for shoplifting have increased so much that this crime has become a major cause of arrests of women. Perhaps the image presented in the news media of more aggressive, "masculinized" women criminals has prompted store-owners to treat crimes committed by women in the same manner as crimes committed by men; whereas in previous years women caught shoplifting were released without arrest if the merchandise was returned immediately, now there is a greater willingness to call the police. Only in dealing with shoplifters of financial means, and usually of the Caucasian race, do store owners still exhibit some of the old reluctance to involve the authorities.[29]

In another area of crime, employee thefts from businesses and corporations, there is also little clear evidence to support the chivalry theory. Some researchers have argued that chivalry is selectively applied to white women in high-status positions. On the whole, however, it seems that arrests of employees for theft tend to involve both men and women without discrimination, with lower-status employees much more likely to be arrested that higher-status ones. The highest officers of business companies are rarely arrested for theft.[30]

There is a widely held belief that a woman convicted of a crime is likely to receive probation if she is a mother. Since approximately 75 to 90 percent of incarcerated women are mothers, probation thus is not strongly influenced by motherhood, but probably by other factors, such as the nature of the offense, prior criminal history, family situation, and the social status of the offender.[31]

It is possible to cite still other reasons to explain why women may receive treatment different from that of male offenders. A less severe sentence may reflect the fact that women charged with Part I property crimes other than larceny/theft are usually accessories, committing the crimes upon the instructions of husbands or boyfriends. The same women, when acting alone, usually commit larceny/theft that is not violent. Women who commit Part I violent crimes—homicide or aggravated assault—usually do so spontaneously, in their homes, against people known to them, often in reaction to being beaten. Because the violent crimes are usually not premeditated or committed during another crime, the women may be more likely to receive probation or lesser sentences than men who commit similar offenses but under different circumstances.[32]

In another study, Stuart Nagel and Lenore Weitzman argued that sentencing depends on the type of crime committed. Those convicted of crimes traditionally associated with women received probation or a suspended sentence, whereas those convicted of nontraditional crimes were incarcerated. In other words, women who acted in expected criminal ways were treated with chivalry; nonconforming female offenders were punished.[33]

The various conclusions that chivalry exists and that women are treated differently from men have been challenged by researchers in the 1980s. Cynthia Kempiner studied 62,000 court cases in Philadelphia from 1970 to 1975. She found no evidence of more lenient treatment of women or sentencing disparity between the 5,000 women and 57,000 men defendants. She concluded that neither chivalry nor a change in women's criminal behavior influenced sentencing; rather, sentencing equity stemmed from civil rights legislation, revised sentencing codes, and a more aware and sensitive judiciary concerned with equality for all, regardless of sex or other distinguishing characteristics.[34] In her study of 543 felony cases in Dade County, Florida, from 1965 to 1976, Debra Curran also found no differential treatment of similarly situated male and female offenders. She concluded, as did Kempiner, that this was due to the civil rights movement, which made judges more likely to treat men and women equally.[35]

Other studies dispute the chivalry theory by pointing to the long recognized fact that a woman's socioeconomic class and racial or ethnic identity influence the sentence she receives. The few white middle- and upper-class women who are arrested usually are released on bail or on their own recognizance; if convicted they usually receive probation. The Manhattan Bail Project, conducted by the Vera Institute of Justice in New York City, disclosed that women released on bail while awaiting trial are less likely to be convicted than women detained in jail; and if they are convicted, are less likely to be incarcerated. Minority women tend to be poorer as a group than white women, and have little or no financial support from families or communities; consequently, judges are unlikely to release them on bail or on their own recognizance.[36]

Persistent values that result in different treatment for white women than for poor and minority women were reported by two researchers. Christy Visher evaluated the treatment of male and female offenders by officers in 24 police departments in 1977. She reported that chivalrous treatment was selectively given to white women who exhibited appropriate sex-role behavior. It appeared that white women had a "considerable advantage" over black women and black or white men because they were more passive and deferring to the officers.[37]

Candace Kruttschnitt found that a woman's social status influenced her sentence. Lower-status women, those who are ex-offenders, those who are economically disadvantaged, and especially those on welfare receive harsher sentences than women who are employed, who work toward a goal such as fulfilling their duties as wives and mothers, or students.[38] Differential treatment that could be called chivalry is traditionally reserved for white middle- and upper-class women by victims of crimes, by law enforcement officers, and by judges.

From this discussion it appears that the theory of chivalry has little support in the evidence, and that the reality of arrest, trial, and punishment involves many factors. In fact, some researchers have argued quite the reverse of chivalry: that minority, poor, dependent women are selectively discriminated against by the criminal justice system. If chivalry does in fact operate, it does so in ways that have been impossible to document conclusively, and without the consistency one would expect. Chivalry and the link between women's criminality and the women's movement seem to be mere impressions or hypotheses in search of evidence, not substantive issues in the understanding of the treatment of female offenders in the criminal justice system.

SUMMARY

Although the number of arrests of women increased between 1960 and 1983, that fact must be considered in the light of potential inaccuracies in *Uniform Crime Reports* data and of events taking place during that period that affected arrests of both men and women. The rank order of crimes for which women were arrested from 1960 to 1983 shows that women's criminal behavior continues to be in areas traditionally associated with them, such as larceny, prostitution, vagrancy, drunkenness, and fraud, with only drug-related crimes new to the list since 1960. These data, as well as conclusions reached in studies conducted since the 1970s and by professionals who work with female offenders and ex-offenders, have led to the rejection of suppositions raised in the early 1970s concerning changes in women's criminal behavior and a link between the assumed changes and the women's movement. Rather, available evidence shows that female offenders are, as in the past, uneducated, unskilled, and disproportionately from ethnic and racial minority groups; commit crimes yielding small rewards; and, more often than not, are arrested for behaving in a manner that is not socially acceptable for women. If chivalry does exist in the criminal justice system, it is reserved for white and conforming women.

NOTES

1. Federal Bureau of Investigation, *Uniform Crime Reports* (Washington, D.C.: U.S. Department of Justice, 1976), p. 183; ibid. (Washington, D.C.: U.S. Department of Justice, 1978), p. 175; ibid. (Washington D.C.: U.S. Department of Justice, 1981), p. 199; ibid. (Washington, D.C.: U.S. Department of Justice, 1984), p. 178.

2. Clarice Feinman, "Inmate Demographic Profile March 1975-December 1975," in *Women's Development Unit Project Annual Report January 1, 1975 to April 9, 1976* (City of New York: New York City Correctional Institution for Women, 1976), p. 18, Appendix H.

3. Anne Pottieger, "Crime Among Female vs. Male Heroin Users," paper presented at the 1984 annual meeting of the American Society of Criminology, pp. 19,23.

4. Interviews with Essie O. Murph, superintendent, New York City Correctional Institution for Women, January–June 1976.

5. Freda Adler, *Sisters in Crime: The Rise of the New Female Criminal* (New York: McGraw-Hill, 1975); Rita Simon, *The Contemporary Woman and Crime* (Washington, D.C.: National Institute of Mental Health, 1975).

6. *Uniform Crime Reports,* 1981, p. 190; ibid., 1984, p. 169.

7. Ibid., 1976, p. 183; ibid., 1978, p. 175; ibid., 1981, p. 199; ibid., 1984, p. 178.

8. Vera Briodo, *Apostles into Terrorists: Women and the Revolutionary Movement in Russia of Alexander II* (New York: Viking Press, 1977), p. vi.

9. Jillian Becker, *Hitler's Children* (New York: J.B. Lippincott, 1977), p. 283.

10. New York City Department of Correction, *Annual Report 1929,* pp. 13–14.

11. New York City Police Department, *Annual Report 1917,* p. 26; *1920,* p. 312; *1930,* p. 170; *1940,* p. 112; *1950,* p. 130.

12. Interviews with Murph, January–June 1976.

13. Feinman, op. cit., p. 18, Appendix H.

14. Farris Lawrence, "An Ex-Offender Evaluates Correctional Programming for Women, in *The Female Offender,* edited by Annette Brodsky (Beverly Hills, Calif.: Sage Publications, 1975), p. 99.

15. "Women, Prison and 'Getting Out,'" *Fortune News,* April 1979, p. 5.

16. Ibid.

17. Margery L. Velimesis, "The Female Offender," *Crime and Delinquency Literature,* March 1975, p. 108.

18. Judy P. Hansen, "Women's Rights, and Wrongs," *New York Times*, March 17, 1975, p. 29.

19. Rosemary Sarri, "Changes in Drug-Related Behavior of Incarcerated Female Offenders, 1968-1979," paper presented at the 1984 annual meeting of the American Society of Criminology, pp. 3-6, 11-12.

20. Jody Grossman, "Female Commitments 1982: The Offense," report prepared for the New York State Department of Correctional Services, March 1984, pp. 3-5.

21. Carol Lee Fenster, "Characteristics of Females Arrested with Males in Crime Partnerships," paper presented at the 1977 annual meeting of the Western Social Science Association, pp. 13-14.

22. Grossman, op. cit., p. 7.

23. Jody Grossman, An Examiniation of the Trends of Female New Commitments: 1960-1982," report prepared for the New York State Department of Correctional Services, March 1984, p. 6.

24. *Uniform Crime Reports,* 1984, p. 168: American Correctional Association, *Female Classification: An Examination of the Issues* (College Park, Md.: American Correctional Association, 1984), p. 34.

25. Meda Chesney-Lind, "Chivalry Reexamined: Women and the Criminal Justice System," in *Women, Crime, and the Criminal Justice System,* edited by Lee H. Bowker (Lexington, Mass.: Lexington Books, 1978), pp. 203, 207.

26. Imogene L. Moyer and Garland F. White, "Police Processing of Female Offenders," paper presented at the 1979 annual meeting of the Academy of Criminal Justice Sciences, pp. 19-22.

27. *New York Times,* July 8, 1979, p. 34; interviews with Murph, January–June 1976.

28. Chesney-Lind, op. cit., pp. 199-201.

29. Ibid., p. 201.

30. Ibid., pp. 199-201, 217.

31. Laura Crites, "Women in the Criminal Courts," in *Women in the Courts,* edited by Winifred L Hepperle and Laura Crites (Williamsburg, Va.: National Center for State Courts, 1978), p. 168.

32. Ibid., pp. 170-71.

33. Stuart Nagel and Lenore Weitzman, "Women as Litigants," *Hastings Law Review* 23 (1971): 171-81.

34. Cynthia Kempiner, "Changes in the Sentencing Patterns of Male and Female Criminal Defendants," *Prison Journal* 63 (Autumn-Winter 1983): 4-9.

35. Debra Curran, "Judicial Discretion and Defendant's Sex," *Criminology* 21 (February 1983): 41, 55-56.

36. Clarice Feinman, "An Afro-American Experience: The Women in New York City's Jail," *Afro-Americans in New York Life and History* 1 (July 1977): 204.

37. Christy Visher, "Gender, Police Arrest Decisions, and Notions of Chivalry," *Criminology* 21 (February 1983): 22-23.

38. Candace Kruttschnitt, "Social Status and Sentencing of Female Offenders," *Law and Society Review* 15 (1980-81): 256-59.

3

WOMEN IN
PRISONS AND JAILS

Major changes have taken place in the housing, supervision, and treatment of incarcerated women since the advent of the modern U.S. penal system in the 1780s. Women are no longer confined in attics or cells in male prisons, and guarded and abused by male staff, as was the case in state penitentiaries in the nineteenth century. Today, most states have separate penal institutions for women, staffed and administered predominantly by women. The federal government operates a separate facility for women convicted and sentenced for federal crimes. And, with some exceptions, women incarcerated in jails are supervised by female staffs in housing areas that are removed from male inmates and staffs.

However, despite improvements in the housing and supervision of incarcerated women, efforts to make them self-supporting members of the community have met with little success. This failure may be attributed, in part, to continuing adherence to practices in women's correctional institutions that are based on traditional attitudes toward the role of women in society and, perhaps, to a public preference for the punishment of nonconforming women. Furthermore, because the design and implementation of rehabilitation programs have been based on a traditional concept of the role of women, the programs have usually ignored the realities of the socioeconomic backgrounds of the women and the communities to which they return.

HISTORICAL BACKGROUND

The early years of the modern U.S. prison system coincided with the development of the "cult of true womanhood."[1] Expected to be pious, pure, and submissive, the ideal woman was one who became a wife and mother, and stayed home to care for her family. Women who did not adhere to the "cult" were considered a threat to the family and to social order.[2] It followed that women who did not conform faced rejection and punishment. Thus, the harsh treatment of incarcerated women in the early and mid nineteenth century reflected society's fears and hostility directed at nonconforming women.

At that time most Americans believed that female offenders, having fallen from their naturally pure state, were more depraved than their male counterparts. An unforgiving society rejected and stigmatized women while they were in prison and after they returned to the community. The popular belief that women criminals were more evil than men criminals stemmed from the conviction that men were naturally aggressive but women were naturally passive and domestic. Having gone against their innate tendencies, female offenders were considered to be "monsters," "the embodiment of the evil principle," and unable to distinguish right from wrong.[3] As such, women in prison were not deemed capable of reform and redemption. Rev. James B. Finley, a prison chaplain in Ohio, expressed the prevailing attitude when he wrote in 1846: "But no one, without experience, can tell the obduracy of the female heart when hardened and lost in sin. As woman falls from a higher point of perfection so she sinks to a profounder depth of misery than man."[4]

The treatment of incarcerated women prior to 1870 reflected society's unforgiving attitudes toward nonconforming women. They were crowded together in small, unsanitary, poorly ventilated quarters in men's institutions, where they were subjected to the demands and abuse of male guards. For example, in the New York Penitentiary at Auburn in the 1820s many were starved, beaten, and raped; several died, as did several of their babies born in the prison. One such woman, Rachel Welsh, having become pregnant while imprisoned, died in childbirth on January 12, 1826. The attending doctor diagnosed the cause of death as the severe flogging she had received during her pregnancy.[5] The horrible conditions at Auburn impelled its chaplain, B. C. Smith, to state that to be a woman in prison was "worse than death."[6]

So deep ran the disgust for such depraved women that even disclosures about the conditions at Auburn failed to arouse sympathy for women in prison. As a result, Governor DeWitt Clinton failed in his attempt to end the "policy of calculated neglect" of the women. The state legislature rejected his proposal to appropriate money to construct a separate prison for women because no community could be found that would agree to have such a prison built in its midst.[7]

The general public remained hostile toward criminal women and suspicious of any person or any organization involved in activities designed to help incarcerated women or ex-offenders in the community. One social commentator at the time wrote: "The habit of regarding and treating the convict as the irreclaimable enemy of society was too common even with good people, and a holy horror seemed to fill the minds of others that a society to benefit such creatures had been formed, as if humanity and sympathy for criminals were an endorsement of crime."[8]

Given these attitudes, reform-minded women in New York City who organized the Magdalen Society in 1830 and the Women's Prison Association (WPA) in 1845 had to endure society's anger because they worked to improve the conditions of women in prisons and jails, and assisted those who had been released and returned to the city. Both organizations established residences for female ex-offenders: the Magdalen Home in 1830 and the WPA's Hopper Home in 1846. These were the first halfway houses for women and the first attempts to apply philanthropy to the saving of fallen women. (Hopper Home, located in New York City, is the oldest existing halfway house for female ex-offenders.) The reformers, religious members of the white upper and middle classes, accepted the prevailing social values concerning the role of women. In keeping with their religious convictions, the reformers believed that delinquent women could be redeemed only if separated from men and supervised by virtuous women. They desired to inculcate a sense of morality and purity, based on their value system, in the erring women, in the hope that fallen women would be restored to the traditional role for women: wife, mother, and homemaker. The reward for women who gave evidence that true womanhood was returning was employment as domestic servants in good Christian homes.[9]

WOMEN'S CORRECTIONS: THEORY AND PRACTICE

The reformers were influenced by Elizabeth Gurney Fry, an English Quaker who established the theoretical and practical basis for women's corrections. In 1813 she volunteered to go to the women's section of Newgate Prison in London to teach and provide for the needs of children incarcerated with their mothers. She believed, as did most people, that the women were not redeemable, and she had not planned to help them. But she was horrified at the conditions in which the women and children lived, their treatment, and the hopelessness of their lives. Although it was considered extremely dangerous, Fry went into the prison to improve conditions for the women as well as for the children.[10]

She organized a group of women who conducted a school for the children; provided food, clothing, and work in prison for the inmates; and attempted to find jobs for them upon their release from Newgate. Their work demonstrated that even the most degraded women were redeemable. Fry's success in London brought about a significant change in attitudes toward female offenders among those interested in penal reform.

With the change in attitude, Fry proposed a program that became basic to women's corrections. Incarcerated females had to be separated from male inmates and male guards. Therefore, separate women's correctional facilities were required, to be supervised and staffed only by women. Since order, discipline, and structure were necessary to reform the women, Fry recommended that they be classified and placed into specific treatment groups and programs for personal hygiene, work, education, religious instruction, and preparation for employment following release. Using volunteers and community resources, she provided humane treatment rather than physical punishment.[11]

Reformers in the United States moved to implement Fry's program. The first experiment took place in New York City in 1825, when John Griscom organized the Society for the Reformation of Juvenile Delinquents and established the House of Refuge. A separate building for female delinquents was opened under the joint superintendency of Sophia Wychoff, wife of a city alderman, and Sarah Hewhurst, sister of the reform leader Isaac Collins. This was the first correctional institution to use the theory that delinquent females, separated from males and taught by moral women, could be uplifted and reformed.[12]

Soon many private and religious societies appeared in New York and other cities to help females. These societies established "homes," forerunners of modern halfway houses, where wayward and delinquent women could live and receive religious and vocational instruction, and medical care, from Christian women. Missionaries and volunteers went to the women's wards of almshouses, to jails and prisons, and to brothels and dance halls, to convince the women to reside in the homes and learn to mend their ways. Women who went to the homes and were reformed were placed in jobs with good Christians so that they would not relapse into sin.[13]

The value of this work was recognized. The courts sent women thought to be redeemable to these homes in lieu of sending them to jail or prison, and they assigned a matron to the Magdalen Home to assist in the supervision of the women and to report on their progress to the prison authorities. The work of these homes reinforced the concept that fallen women could be saved under the right circumstances, through the guidance of proper women.[14]

Except for these societies and homes, in which women supervised women, incarcerated women continued to be guarded by men. This served to increase the demands of women reformers to place women professionals in corrections, for the experiences of the reformers proved that Fry's program could work in the United States. The next step was to move the program into the prisons and jails on a permanent basis.

From 1825 to 1873, reformers achieved a few successes in acquiring matrons for women. One such success involved Eliza Farnham, head matron of the women's section of Sing Sing from 1844 to 1848, and a feminist, reformer, wife of a lawyer, and friend of members of the Brook Farm intellectual circle in Massachusetts. Farnham adopted Fry's program and added a component that made the program a model upon which U.S. women's corrections developed: to make the environment like a home and behavior between staff and inmates like that of a family. Farnham believed that environmental conditions caused criminal behavior; therefore, changing the environment would change behavior. She proceeded to break the rules in the prison by ending the silence system, by grouping the women together for purposes of educational instruction rather than religious instruction, and by establishing a library of secular rather than religious books. She and her staff taught the women to read and write, and instructed them in U.S. history, astronomy, geography, physiology, and personal hygiene. Literate women read books to those who could not read, even while the women worked. Farnham encouraged the women to become involved with handicrafts, and all worked. She decorated the women's wing with pictures, maps, flowers, and lamps, and she even brought in a piano. Women from outside were invited to speak to the inmates, including Margaret Fuller, a feminist writer and member of the Brook Farm circle. Alongside these innovative programs and services was a firm willingness to employ discipline if it was needed, for Farnham regarded self-control as necessary for true reformation. Solitary confinement was used when inmates did not respond to more gentle means.[15]

However, Farnham's approach appeared too radical to many people and met criticism. After a power struggle with the conservatives, led by the institution's Protestant chaplain, who did not approve of her secular program, she was dismissed in 1848. After she departed for Boston to work with the handicapped, all her improvements for the women at Sing Sing were eliminated, and the women returned to abuse, neglect, and ignorance.[16]

Setbacks such as the dismissal of Farnham did not stop the efforts of reformers, and their view of how women offenders should be treated gradually gained support. The next step was to convince a male legislature to establish a separate women's prison and to hire women superintendents and matrons on a permanent, full-time basis. They succeeded, and the first penal institution for women staffed by women opened in Indiana in 1873. By 1913 similar reformatories had opened in Framingham, Massachusetts, in Bedford Hills, New York, and in Clinton, New Jersey; the Federal Institution for Women opened in Alderson, West Virginia, in 1927. In 1932, the House of Detention for Women opened in New York City, one of the first separate jails for women. Whether reformatories or jails, the all-female penal institutions had one thing in common: traditional values, theories, and practices concerning women's role and place in society took root. The staffs, architectural designs, and programs reflected and perpetuated the culturally valued norms for women's behavior.

PROFILE OF INCARCERATED WOMEN

Most studies concerning incarcerated women have been conducted since 1960, the overwhelming number since 1970. National interest in the criminal justice system, and corrections in particular, awakened in the 1960s and reached its peak after the Attica Prison riot in September 1971. However, federal government reports failed to recognize the needs of women inmates and ex-offenders; indeed, *The Challenge of Crime in a Free Society* did not even mention women. It took the efforts of women's organizations to get government funding for research and programs for women inmates and ex-offenders.

One of the first comprehensive studies was conducted by Ruth Glick and Virginia Neto, and published in 1977. They studied selected prisons and jails in 14 states that held a total of 6,466 women prisoners. The researchers reported that two-thirds of the women were under 35 years of age, the largest number falling between 22 and 25. Over half were black. Only 20 percent were married, but 75 percent had at least one child. Over half the women were on welfare prior to incarceration. If the women worked, the jobs were clerical, domestic service, or other types of unskilled, low-paying work. Less than 60 percent had graduated from high school, and 15 percent had only an elementary school education. Most of the women had prior arrest histories, one-third having been in juvenile facilities.[17]

Subsequent studies corroborated Glick and Neto's findings. Whether in county jails or state or federal prisons, most of the women continued to be single heads of households responsible for children, in their mid-twenties, and possessors of less than a twelfth-grade education who had few, if any, skills and were underemployed or unemployed.[18] In 1980 a federal study reported that the typical female incarcerated in a federal or state prison was a young, poor, unmarried mother, and an unskilled member of a minority group who had committed a drug-related or economic crime.[19] Charlotte Ginsburg, executive director of the Program for Female Offenders in Pittsburgh wrote that there are "no feminists in county jails": instead, there are poor minority women with children to support, no job skills, and, more often than not a substance-abuse problem.[20] A 1983 study conducted by Jody Grossman, of the New York State Department of Correctional Services, reported that women accounted for 2.8 percent (830) of 29,543 state prisoners as of June 1, 1983. The typical incarcerated female was a resident of New York City (61 percent), from an ethnic or racial minority group (black, 58 percent; Puerto Rican, 16 percent), had not graduated from high school (49 percent), was between 21 and 34 years of age (19.7 percent were 21-24, 28.3 percent were 25-29, 19.6 percent were 30-34 years old), and had had prior commitments (41 percent).[21]

Just as the profile of incarcerated women has remained relatively constant since the early 1960s, so have their criminal acts and reasons for conviction. The kinds of offenses for which women are incarcerated, primarily drug-related and property crimes, differ little among the various types of institutions. Studies from the Federal Bureau of Prisons, Glick and Neto, the Women's Prison Association in New York City, CONtact, and the New York City Correctional Institution for Women report that in federal prisons, women were sentenced primarily for drug-related crimes, forgery, and larceny/theft;[22] in state prisons, 36 percent of the women were sentenced for violent crimes against persons, 39 percent for crimes against property, and 25 percent for either "victimless" or "other" crimes (a significant number of "other" crimes were drug-related offenses; 63 percent of the women were alcohol or drug abusers);[23] and in jails, women were sentenced primarily for petty larceny, drug-related crimes, and prostitution.[24] In her 1983 study on women incarcerated in the New York state prison, Jody Grossman reported that 20.3 percent of the women had committed robbery, 15 percent had committed drug-related crimes, 19.4 percent had committed homicide, and 10.5 percent had committed murder. Fully 51 percent of those sentenced for murder and 41 percent for homicide had no prior arrest record; almost all had killed a family member, close friend, or paramour.[25]

Although the number of incarcerated women increased between 1978 and 1983, the percentage remained relatively stable. The Bureau of Justice Statistics reported that by the end of 1983, women accounted for 4.3 percent (19,019) of the total state and federal prison population of 438,830, whereas in 1978 they numbered 4.2 percent (12,746) of a total state and federal prison population of 307,276.[26] At the end of 1983, three states (California, Texas, and Florida) held more than 1,000 women each and seven states (Ohio, New York, Georgia, Michigan, North Carolina, Illinois, and Louisiana) held from 500 to 1,000 women each in prisons.[27] The proportion of women in jail also had not changed since 1978. Women accounted for 6.5 percent (13,700) of a total population of 207,853 in 1982; of the 13,700 women, 8,111 awaited trial and 5,589 had been convicted.[28] As of September 1984, the federal system held 1,843 women of a total population of 32,143.[29]

The Federal Bureau of Prisons in 1984 had eight institutions that housed women: one all-female prison in Alderson, West Virginia; three cocorrectional prisons in Fort Worth, Texas, Pleasanton, California, and Lexington, Kentucky; and four cocorrectional metropolitan detention centers in New York City, Chicago, Miami, and San Diego.

In 1984, 43 states had prisons exclusively for women, 19 states provided cocorrectional institutions either as the sole facility for women or as an alternative, and seven states had only cocorrectional institutions. New Hampshire and West Virginia had no institution for women and sent women prisoners to federal prison or to prisons in other states: New Hampshire sent its women to the federal institution in Alderson, West Virginia, or to state prisons in Framingham, Massachusetts, and Niantic, Connecticut; West Virginia sent its women to the federal prison in Alderson.[30]

Although the number of women incarcerated in federal and state prisons and county jails has increased, the percentages of women making up the total prison and jail populations have remained relatively stable from 1978 to 1983. The typical female inmate, her profile, and the crimes for which she was convicted and imprisoned also remained similar between 1978 and 1983. Despite claims about the new female criminal, the evidence shows that female offenders and incarcerated women in the 1980s are not new types and are not significantly different from those in the past.

WOMEN ON DEATH ROW

Velma Barfield, white and aged 52, was executed by a lethal injection on November 2, 1984, in North Carolina. She was the first woman executed in the United States since 1962, when Elizabeth Ann Duncan, a 58-year-old white woman, died in a California gas chamber for hiring two men to kill her daughter-in-law. Barfield was convicted in 1978 of fatally poisoning her fiance with arsenic. She subsequently admitted to fatally poisoning three others, including her mother. Her family and friends, as well as groups opposed to the death penalty, petitioned Governor James Hunt, Jr., to use his power to stop the execution. Family and friends of the victim petitioned the governor to let the execution take place.[31] The pending execution of Barfield generated a great deal of interest in the media, particularly because of her sex but also because of a general continuing debate in the nation on the death penalty.

From 1608 to 1984, 12,264 persons have been executed in the United States, including 286 women. The first recorded executions of women were of Jane Champion in Virginia in 1632 and of Mary Dyer in Massachusetts in 1660.[32] The U.S. Department of Justice started to report death sentences and executions in 1930; they are published by the Bureau of Justice Statistics. From 1930 to 1962, 30 women were executed for murder in 13 states, and 2 were executed by the federal government in 1953—1 for kidnapping and the other, Anna Rosenberg, for espionage. Of the 32 women, 12 were black and 20 white, including the 2 executed for federal offenses.[33]

In 1972 the moratorium on the death penalty ended when the U.S. Supreme Court, in its landmark decision in *Furman* v. *Georgia*, declared that the death penalty, as a punishment, was not unconstitutional. Since then, 38 states and the federal government have provided for the death penalty, using the guidelines established by the Court. Four women awaited execution in 1972, 3 in California and 1 in Georgia. At the end of 1984, 19 women were sentenced to be executed in 12 states; 2 women were in the process of appealing their sentences. Of the 19 women, 5 were black, 13 were white, and 1 was a Native American.[34] They had all been convicted of first-degree murder. Except for the fact that they were sentenced to death, they were typical of most other female offenders.

Inmates on death row are required by law to be separated from each other and from the general prison population at all times. This isolation, plus the restrictions on work and other activities, results in little contact with people other than the correctional staff. Because there are so few women on death row, makeshift accommodations often have to be made because there are no death row housing areas in women's prisons. Consequently Sonia Lee Jacobs, sentenced to die in Florida, was in solitary confinement for security and financial reasons. In 1977 she filed a civil rights suit in U.S. District Court that charged discrimination based on sex, pointing out that men on death row were given opportunities to exercise outside of their cells. She won her case, the court ruling that solitary confinement, imposed solely because she was a woman sentenced to death, constituted cruel and unusual punishment. In March 1981 Jacobs' sentence was commuted to life in prison as a result of her appeal, and she was placed in the general prison population with other inmates.[35]

It is unlikely that the death penalty will be abolished in the near future. Given the fact that so few women—19 of a total of 1,464 persons at the end of 1984—had been sentenced to death, and that women's prisons do not have special areas for inmates awaiting execution, makeshift solitary confinement cells may continue to be the method of housing such women. However, as the number of women on death row continues to increase and more states become involved, departments of correction may follow the lead of the department in New Jersey. In November 1984 the New Jersey Department of Corrections created a special separate two-cell unit on death row in Trenton State Prison to house Marie Moore, the first woman sentenced to die in the state in this century. Two cells were set aside so that a female inmate can be locked in one while the other is searched, a routine security measure on death row. Marie Moore, a 38-year-old white woman, convicted in November 1984 of the torture slaying of her 13-year-old goddaughter, and of 29 other counts, including kidnapping and sexual assault against four juveniles and a 50-year-old woman, could be the first woman executed in New Jersey in this century. She shares death row with nine men, though a wall separates the male and female units.[36]

BLACK AND HISPANIC WOMEN

Whereas black women accounted for 37.7 percent (12) of the 32 women executed from 1930 to 1962, and 25 percent (5) of the 19 women housed on death row in 1984, they and other minority women account for over 50 percent of the incarcerated women in the United States.[37] On June 30, 1982, of a total of 13,700 women in jail, there were 6,011 whites, 5,934 blacks, 1,480 Hispanics, and 275 American Indians, Native Alaskans, Asians, and Pacific Islanders.[38] The Federal Bureau of Prisons (FBP) reported that as of September 1984, of a total of 1,843 women in its custody there were 1,016 whites, 783 blacks, 23 Asians, and 21 American Indians. However since 313 of the "whites" were Hispanic, 1,140 of the total of 1,843 women belonged to minority groups.[39] (The FBP identifies its inmates by both race and ethnicity.) In large urban states, over 50 percent of the women in state prisons are black—for example, 58 percent in New York in 1983.[40]

Women offenders have become subjects of extensive research only since the 1960s, so it is not surprising that little information is available on minority women. Several situations involving black women received the attention of the media in the 1970s. Angela Davis was arrested on October 13, 1970, on charges of kidnapping, murder, and conspiracy, and was held in the women's jail in New York City until extradited to California to stand trial. In 1969 she had become a professor of philosophy at the University of California in Los Angeles; in that same year, the Federal Bureau of Investigation (FBI) accused her of being a Communist and an associate of the Black Panthers and Soledad Brothers. Subsequently acquitted and freed, she returned to her teaching position.[41]

The Joan Little case followed in 1974. Little was accused of killing her jailer in Beaufort County, North Carolina. While she was in jail appealing a larceny conviction, her 62-year-old white jailer attempted to force her to perform oral sex, threatening her with an ice pick. She resisted, and during the struggle, he fell on the ice pick and died. Little escaped and the jailer was later found, naked from the waist down. When Little was captured, she argued that as a black woman accused of killing a white male law officer, she could not receive a fair trial if returned to Beaufort County. National publicity and support from civil rights and women's rights groups resulted in a change of venue and a successful claim of self-defense.[42]

A third black woman to gain national notoriety for her involvement with the criminal justice system is Joanne Chesimard. A member of the Black Liberation Army and involved in the 1973 shooting of two state troopers in New Jersey, which resulted in the death of one of the troopers, she is on the FBI's "most wanted list." Chesimard escaped from the women's prison in New Jersey in 1979 and has yet to be found.[43]

Despite the publicity about these women, the general public remains ignorant about minority female offenders, and scholars have paid scant attention to them. Although several studies since the 1960s have dealt indirectly or directly with minority women, most of them involve only statistical information. Glick and Neto reported that over 50 percent of the incarcerated women in the 14 states in their survey were black, although blacks comprised only 10 percent of the states' adult populations. In addition, more black women than whites were undereducated, underemployed, and single-parent heads of households below the poverty level. They were convicted and incarcerated primarily for drug-related offenses, murder, and larceny.[44]

Compared with white women in prisons and jails, minority women face more serious problems. They are more likely to be single, poor, and responsible for dependent children. They are less likely to have money for bail or legal counsel. Minority women also have problems similar to those of white female offenders: poor health, drug or alcohol addiction, inability to find and keep jobs (because they are unskilled and poorly educated), family concerns, and the fact that few support or rehabilitation programs exist for female offenders.[45]

Efforts to help minority women have been made, especially in urban areas where there are women's rights and civil rights groups, and large numbers of minorities. The efforts made in the New York City Correctional Institution for Women in the 1970s were particularly vigorous because the superintendent, and approximately 85 percent of the custodial and 50 percent of the treatment staffs, including the school principal, were black women.[46] My study of the staffs and inmates in this jail from 1932 to 1976 revealed that a large number of black women began working in the jail after de facto racial discrimination and segregation in employment and in the jail ended as a result of the 1954 U.S. Supreme Court decision in *Brown* v. *Board of Education*, which declared segregation based on race to be unconstitutional.[47]

At the same time, the inmate population in the jail also changed. Before 1955, a typical inmate was a married, 22-year-old white Protestant New Yorker, with an elementary school education, most likely working as a domestic. She was sentenced for prostitution, vagrancy, or disorderly conduct. By 1955 she was a single, 27-year-old black Protestant non-New Yorker, sentenced for prostitution, disorderly conduct, or a drug-related crime. The picture had changed again by 1975, when the typical inmate was a single, 22-year-old black Protestant New Yorker, with a tenth-grade education, who worked as a clerk, in a factory, or in a restaurant to support her child. Sentencing statistics changed considerably at that time because of the concept of "quality arrest," with petit larceny and assault replacing prostitution and disorderly conduct. Another obvious change involved drug addicts. During the 1930s and 1940s, whites comprised nearly 90 percent of the narcotics abusers, although few women were addicts. However, starting in the 1950s, when most of the women in the jail were black, most of them entered the jail addicted to narcotics although charged with other offenses.[48]

By the 1970s, Hispanic women had become a visible group in the prison population, reaching approximately 18 percent in 1975. Interestingly, observers noted that overt problems occurred between black and Hispanic (predominantly Puerto Rican) women rather than between white and black women. Fearful of being categorized as black, the Hispanic women spoke only Spanish and kept to themselves. The language issue and their attitude created tensions and hostilities between the two groups of women that resulted in verbal and, at times, physical confrontations. Hispanic women also complained that their cultural needs were being neglected. The administration acceded to their demands that the piped-in radio and tape recording include Spanish music and programs. However, tensions in the housing areas persisted, sometimes resulting in overt hostilities over such issues as television program selection. Those tensions, based on racial and cultural differences, were exacerbated by the fact that the Hispanic inmates continued to speak Spanish to each other and to form cliques.[49]

Women sentenced to the New York City women's jail after 1954 entered under the administration of Anna M. Kross, commissioner of correction from 1954 to 1965. Significant and lasting reforms were made by Kross in services for and treatment of inmates. Those programs benefited black, white, and Hispanic women. A new institution, the New York City Correctional Institution for Women, opened on Rikers Island in 1971, replacing the old House of Detention for Women. It was designed and equipped to provide improved medical care, social and mental health services, and educational, vocational, and recreational programs, all of which helped to make life in the jail more bearable.[50]

Unfortunately, three major problems precluded the ultimate success of the rehabilitation programs, including those specifically designed for minority women. First, planning for the programs failed to take into consideration the specific background problems and needs of minority women. Second, training programs prepared the inmate for typical female low-salaried employment: cook, waitress, hairdresser, or typist. Third, hostile societal attitudes toward female offenders resulted in a lack of committed funds, long-range planning, after-care services, and job placement on the part of government, labor unions, and the private sector. The school principal, Fannie Rogers, said: "We prepare them, but we can find no one to take them."[51]

In order to change the defeatist attitudes held by most of the women, and to provide a rehabilitation program that might help these women survive when they returned to their communities, Superintendent Murph proposed a pre-release project for sentenced women that would include counseling, vocational training, and work/study release opportunities. Her plan came to fruition in January 1975 when LEAA funded the Women's Development Unit Project (WDUP). By the end of 15 months of operation, working with approximately 250 women for an average of 2 months, WDUP had placed 27 women in academic and vocational training programs or jobs, and 6 women in community residences after their release from jail. During that same period, 16 women who had been through the WDUP program returned to jail.[52] It is unrealistic to believe that any program can change the values and life-styles of adult women in two months.

The problems of reintegration into the community for the Hispanic or black ex-offender were many—she was almost programmed for defeat. As a minority woman and an ex-offender, she faced obstacles in achieving economic self-sufficiency, education and employment skills notwithstanding. Certainly, as an unskilled, poorly educated, demoralized woman, her problems were extraordinary. Although less than half of those women were married, approximately 67 percent had children and remained the sole support of their families. In order for them to go out to work, someone had to be available to take care of the children. In addition, many of the women suffered from the poor health and scars of the drug addict.

A principal deterrant to "making it" after leaving jail is the lack of after-care support so vitally needed to assist women in their transition from jail to a self-supporting life in the community. Most of the women have no money, and few have families to support them emotionally or financially. After release, most women go on welfare, returning to their former manner of earning money. Murph estimated that 75 percent of the women would eventually find their way back to jail.[53]

On the other hand, a recent study argues that black women do have family ties that provide them with emotional support while incarcerated and when they return to their communities. In their 1979 study of women in the San Francisco County Jail, Laura Bresler and Diane Lewis found that there were obvious differences between the family relationships of black and white women. The typical white woman was a convicted prostitute in her late twenties, a high school graduate, separated or divorced, and her children, even prior to arrest, lived with her parents or former husband. As a child, she had lived in a home with both parents, and they had not been on welfare. The typical black woman was a convicted prostitute or thief in her early twenties, a single mother who lived with her children prior to her arrest. Her children were in the care of her mother or another relative. As a child, she had lived with one parent, usually the mother, and they had been on welfare. Two-thirds of the black women came from families headed by single women, whereas almost all the white women grew up in two-parent households. However, black women, much more than white women, had more contact and stronger ties with their families and children, and received more visits, phone calls, and mail; they expected to be welcomed and aided by their families, and to be with their children upon release from jail. Consquently, black women were less bitter and more hopeful than white women. Bresler and Lewis stressed that pre-release and post-release counseling and services needed to be responsive to the fact that ethnic and racial differences exist in areas of family and child care both while the mother is incarcerated and when she is released.[54]

Minority women have three strikes against them: sexism, racism, and the label "female offender." It is obvious that we need to know more about black and Hispanic women in order to intelligently plan pre-release and post-release programs that directly meet their individual ethnic and racial needs and problems.

PROBLEMS STEMMING FROM THE
LOCATION OF WOMEN'S PRISONS

Whereas most minority women live in urban centers, women's prisons are usually in rural areas. This situation is a result of ideas current in the nineteenth century, when the theoretical basis for women's corrections was developed. Women reformers believed that women criminals could be saved only if they were removed from the corrupting influences of cities and men. Prisons were therefore built in the countryside and staffed with women only.

Since women criminals were perceived as being potential madonnas—proper housewives—if only they could be rehabilitated, their prison regimen was designed to instill a sense of decency and home life. This was established from the very beginning by the various reform groups that arose in the nineteenth century; the prisons were run by upper-middle class women who, because of their social background, perpetuated the concept of the traditional woman. In the early twentieth century, lawyer and prison reformer Madeleine Doty wrote: "Someday the thing I have dreamed must come true. Prisons will be transformed, changed from a prison to a home. At its head will be a wise, intelligent mother, able to distinguish between the daughter who would be a militant and the one who would be a Jane Austen, treating each according to her need."[55]

Following this ideal, women's prisons were, and usually are, small, with an average capacity of under 250 inmates, and arranged with many cottages or other housing units within walking distance of the dining room and other common facilities. Often the inmates have their own rooms. When Sarah Smith, superintendent of the first women's prison, greeted the first inmate, Sallie Hubbard, in 1873, she "embraced her fallen sister" and, after praying for her salvation, took her to a room decorated with a bedspread, curtains, a table with a vase of flowers, and a Bible; it was a room, not a cell.[56] In the 1970s a superintendent of a women's jail said of the atmosphere, "We're a lot like a family here . . . this is home for most of them."[57]

Usually there are no signs of external security—concrete walls, fences, or gun turrets—since 95 percent of women's prisons are medium- or minimum-security facilities. Except for those women classified as maximum-security, the inmates are free to walk to and from their housing and other buildings. The purpose of this type of design is to create, as much as possible, a homelike atmosphere, with individual rooms, decorated by the women, in cottages or small buildings that simulate a home where they can be taught to be homemakers by the officers.

The openness of such prisons and the relative freedom given to most inmates are understandable, considering the type of women sent to them when they first opened at the end of the nineteenth century and early in the twentieth. Most of the women had convictions for prostitution, adultery, disorderly conduct, drunkenness, or stubbornness; few had convictions for property or violent crimes. For example, of the 640 women incarcerated from 1877 to 1913 whose records were studied at the prison in Framingham, Massachusetts, 56.8 percent had convictions for offenses against public order, 26.8 percent for chastity offenses, 12.5 percent for property offenses, and only 3.9 percent for violent offenses. They all served at least one year.[58] These were not dangerous or violent women who posed a threat to either the staff or community. All they needed for their rehabilitation, according to the reformers, was the model of pious, moral women in a domestic setting out in the country.

Although there is no evidence that women in prisons in the 1980s are more violent and pose more of a danger than inmates in previous decades, public perceptions of women criminals have been altered by unfounded claims in the media that depict a new, more dangerous type of female offender. As a result, several departments of correction have yielded to public pressure and have had fences, some with razor ribbon on the top, erected around the institutions' campuses. This has occurred at Jessup, Maryland, and Muncie, Pennsylvania. In New Jersey maximum security buildings were constructed on the women's prison campus at Clinton, and women with maximum-security status are securely confined and supervised in them. Only those women with minimum-security status are free to walk unsupervised on the open campus.

No matter how idyllic the location, however, many problems were, and continue to be, posed for the women inmates. Most of them come from cities, and since there is generally only one women's facility in a state, or none at all, it is usually impossible to place them in a facility near their homes. Because of the distance, and often the lack of public transportation, visits from friends and families are infrequent; furthermore, frequent phone calls are impossible because of the expense. As a result, it is difficult for the inmate to keep close ties with her family, her community, and even her lawyer. This problem is most severe for women in federal institutions, for the only such prisons are in West Virginia, California, Texas, and Kentucky; but it also poses a serious problem for women boarded out in prisons in neighboring states.

The rural locations, meant to remove women from corruption, have also removed them from schools, training programs, and jobs, usually found in cities, that could be taken advantage of in a work/study release program. If women do have the opportunity to study or work in the community where the prison is located, they cannot continue with either upon discharge from the prison because their homes are too far to allow daily commuting; they must start anew.

Location in a rural area also leads to staffing problems. Women living in the area, usually white, take jobs as correction officers because there are few jobs available in the community. Staff turnover is high and staff shortages common. (Often the institution, whether male or female, is the major source of employment and is necessary to the economy of the community.) Women incarcerated in these institutions, especially in the large industrial and urban states tend to be city women and members of minority groups. The differences in life-styles, race, and values create additional tensions among the women, both the prisoners and the staff.

Most states and the Federal Bureau of Prisons have only one all-female prison, and women of all security statuses are therefore housed in the same institution. As a result, minimum-security women have to live with restraints or fences that restrict their freedom of movement within the institution and on the grounds. In addition, women cannot be transferred to less secure, unfenced facilities when their security status is reduced. This is a particular problem for women in jails. Jails have to be maximum-security facilities because all types of offenders are detained in them. Therefore, women sentenced to short terms for misdemeanors must be held under maximum-security conditions because there are few, if any, community-based correctional facilities, work release residences, or prison camps for women.

The fact that women's prisons are usually small, with a number of cottages or small buildings on a campus in a country setting, often makes observers believe that the women have it easy and are fortunate. However, the remote locations of women's prisons create many problems for women inmates and for staffs.

INCARCERATED MOTHERS AND PREGNANT INMATES

Although mothering is in keeping with a woman's traditional role, incarcerated women are often denied that relationship, whether they have children prior to imprisonment or while institutionalized. This denial may result from long distances between the location of the prison and the women's homes and families, lack of money or personnel to properly supervise family visits, state law declaring incarcerated women unfit mothers, or a general attitude that female offenders should be punished for not fulfilling their role of womanhood.

When the prison reform movement directed attention to the problems faced by male and female inmates in the 1960s, serious concern developed about pregnant inmates, incarcerated mothers and their children, and the disruption of families. Efforts by women's groups, prison reformers, and female correctional personnel led to court decisions and legislation that resulted in slow but significant changes in policy affecting incarcerated pregnant women and mothers. Studies conducted since the 1970s provide both statistical data and information about the emotional and legal problems of these women.

Glick and Neto reported that 56.3 percent of the 6,466 women in their study covering 14 states had one or more children.[59] My study of 250 women in the New York City Correctional Institution for Women revealed that 75 percent of the women were mothers, but only one-fourth were married; more than 80 percent of the children were in the care of a relative.[60] In her study of inmate mothers, Phyllis Jo Baunach stated that of 196 women in three prisons, 70.4 percent were mothers, with an average of 2.2 children under the age of 18 years; 62 percent of the women had been living with their children prior to incarceration; 26.8 percent were married; and 81.7 percent of the children were being cared for by family members.[61] When interviewed, these mothers stated that their children suffered from physical, emotional, and academic problems. The mothers suffered primarily from separation anxiety and concern for their children. Because of the distance, and often a lack of transportation, between institution and the family home, visits were infrequent, with 55.2 percent of the women receiving one visit a month or none at all.[62]

Women who gave birth to children while incarcerated and those who have children in the community have to make several decisions about their relationships with their children: whether to tell them the truth about being in prison, whether to maintain contact through visits or only through letters and phone calls, and whether to give up custody of their children. The pregnant woman has a decision to make concerning whether to have an abortion, if medically possible. Baunach states that the children of 68 percent of the mothers knew that their mothers were in prison and that 51 percent of the mothers had told their children. Attempts were made by 89 percent of the mothers to keep in contact with their children; they planned to live with their children when released. Almost all the mothers expressed concern about the adjustment they and their children would have to make; would the children accept their mothers? would the mothers be able to be adequate parents? would the mothers be able to support their children?[63]

McGowan and Blumenthal wrote that on any given day, approximately 70 percent of the women in prisons and jails are mothers. Their children suffer from insecurity, lack of trust, confusion, and loneliness; they manifest these problems in emotional and physical illnesses and poor academic performance. Most children lived with their mothers prior to the latter's imprisonment; after that, 12.5 percent lived in foster homes and the others lived with relatives. Almost all of the mothers kept in contact with their children, and 75 percent wanted to reestablish their families upon release. McGowan and Blumenthal believed that it is "unrealistic" to expect the criminal justice system to strengthen family ties where none existed. However, the system has a "responsibility to prevent destruction of family life through ignorance or indifference and to help each woman who comes in the system to make the best plans for her children."[64]

McGowan and Blumenthal found a serious lack of pre-release and post-release family-oriented counseling, services, or legal advice for women who feared losing custody of their children. They worried that the children would lose respect for them or forget them. This latter concern was particularly strong among women who did not receive visits because of the location of the prison and the expense of transportation. Most of the women also feared that they would be unable to support and provide a home for their children, since most lacked money and job skills, and few were married. In some cases, the women had their furniture confiscated by landlords when rent payments were no longer made. That women's concerns may be well founded is suggested by studies indicating that the longer a women is incarcerated, the more likely it is that her family ties will disintegrate and that her children will not live with her when she is released.[65]

A study of mothers incarcerated in New York's prison for women at Bedford Hills in 1982 corroborated the findings of previous studies: 72.5 percent (250) of 345 women were mothers, with an average of 2.3 children; 45 percent of the women were single, 21 percent were widowed, divorced, or separated, 34 percent were married or in a common-law relationship; 61 percent had custody of their children prior to incarceration; and 77.1 percent of the children were cared for by relatives during their mother's incarceration. Almost all the mothers expected to live with their children upon release, but few were prepared to support their families; only 20 percent had been employed prior to incarceration.[66] According to Jody Grossman, who conducted the study, these findings have "significant policy and programmatic implications . . . ."[67]

The New York State Correctional Institution for Women at Bedford Hills has a nursery program that permits women who give birth while in custody to keep their babies until the children are one year old. The women and babies are housed in a wing of the hospital that holds an average of ten mothers and ten babies. All services and supplies are provided for the babies' care, and the mothers are involved in their upbringing. When the children are one year old, they are placed with their mothers' families or friends, or through the Department of Social Services. A follow-up study was conducted of 28 mothers and their babies who participated in the nursery program.[68]

Of the 28 mothers, 5 had committed robbery, 3 each had committed manslaughter, grand larceny, and burglary, 4 were youthful offenders who had committed weapon, robbery, or arson offenses, and 10 committed less serious offenses such as forgery and perjury. All were between 20 and 34 years old. Sixteen were single, nine had a common-law relationship and two were married (all information concerning one of the women was not indicated). They had a total of 64 children; for 8, the baby born while they were incarcerated was their first child. All the women were released by 1984. Eighteen babies left before their mothers were released, and 13 of those went to live with family members. Nine of the babies left with their mothers and remained with them. The follow-up study indicates that 21 of the 28 babies were with their mothers in 1984. Only five of the mothers were employed, the others receiving welfare benefits. Three of the 28 women returned as parole violators, but none of them had new offenses.[69] Those involved with the program agreed that it benefited both the inmates and the children by helping to keep families intact.

Another serious problem is that many women need counseling and training in skills that will prepare them for motherhood and parenting. A large number have a history of beatings and sexual abuse as children and as adult women, and therefore have no positive mother-child or parent-child experiences or role models. The problem is exacerbated, in part, by a lack of national family policy and little or no coordination among social service agencies. In addition, women constitute the largest and fastest-growing poverty group in the United States as single heads of households with dependent children and as aged women.

Perhaps an even more serious problem involves the legal issue of a woman's fitness to maintain custody of her children. Several states have laws reserving the right to declare an incarcerated woman an unfit mother and to remove her children from her custody. These children may be placed in foster care or put up for adoption. The rationale for this legal action developed in the late nineteenth and early twentieth centuries when reformers believed it was in the best interest of the children, who were often incarcerated with their mothers, to separate them from their mothers both physically and legally. The reformers felt that prisons and jails provided a poor environment for raising children, that criminal mothers would have an adverse and dangerous influence over their children, and that the children would learn to become criminals. Moreover, incarceration would not be punishment if women had their children with them or had control over them. Therefore, laws were passed to permit the state to remove children from such dangerous influences and circumstances.

Since the 1970s, efforts by women's and prisoners' civil rights groups have been made on behalf of incarcerated mothers and pregnant women, and changes have been made. Pregnant women now deliver their babies in hospitals, and the child's birth certificate no longer indicates the legal status of the mother or the name of the prison or jail. The need for prenatal and postnatal care has been recognized but is not always offered to pregnant women. This lack of important care continues to be a concern for inmates and reformers. However, several states such as New York and Pennsylvania, have been persuaded to provide special diets, exercise, and counseling programs, as well as medical specialists and obstetrical care.

Legal issues have also been addressed in some states. In August 1983, New York Governor Mario Cuomo signed a bill that "eliminates the automatic deprivation of an incarcerated parent's right to object to the adoption of his or her child and establishes a procedure for determining whether the incarcerated parent has permanently neglected his or her child." Furthermore, the bill stated that the Department of Correctional Services should "encourage family visits" and "assist inmates in fulfilling their family responsibilities."[70] However, states continue to reserve the right to remove a child from the mother's custody if there is a clear and convincing reason that the mother is unfit. The question of whether a woman is a fit or unfit mother, or what is in the best interest of the children, is usually determined by white, middle-class people, whereas most of the mothers are lower-class minority women.

Other reforms have been proposed and implemented to protect mothers, children, and family relationships. New York, North Carolina, and Florida have laws permitting women to keep their children with them in prison. However, either because some women do not believe prison is a place for children or because administrators have not been committed to this policy, few women appear to have taken advantage of this opportunity. Programs that permit weekend visits may be more acceptable to prison administrators and to mothers; several have been in existence for ten years or more.

The Purdy Treatment Center in the state of Washington opened in 1970 and probably has one of the most extensive parenting programs in the United States. Women on work release may have their children for weekend visits in apartments, located outside the institution, that are set aside for work release women. All women are encouraged to have visits with their children, in order to help prepare the women for family life and mothering, and to maintain family relationships. To assist the women, family counseling and a child development course are available. This course deals with parental rights and responsibilities, as well as child care and child development. Another program is the foster care program. The Department of Social and Health Services agreed to place the children of inmates in foster homes in the neighborhood of the prison. Foster parents and the inmate mothers jointly make decisions and plans concerning the children, and foster parents agree to bring the children to visit the mothers frequently and to allow the mothers to visit the children in the home. This program encourages the continuation and strengthening of mother-child relationships, provides the mothers with a sense of responsibility and control over their families, and provides the basis for a sound family re-union process when the mothers and children reestablish a home together. A third parenting program is extremely innovative. In 1975 a preschool nursery opened on prison grounds; children from three to five years old from the community attend four mornings a week, and the inmates' children attend the fifth morning. The inmates who work in the nursery as aides to certified teachers are carefully screened by the director, and must first complete the child development course. Inmates with child-related offenses are prohibited from working in the nursery. The nursery program trains the mothers to deal with disciplinary problems and to understand child behavior and development.[71]

Two parenting programs started in 1978 at the women's prison in Clinton, New Jersey. Title XX, a federally funded program, provides for child visits. Clinton is in a rural area in the center of the state, whereas most of the women inmates come from cities long distances from the prison. This program provides transportation from major population centers, to give children under

18 years old at least one visit a month with their mothers. During the day-long visit, mothers and children eat together and spend time in meeting rooms or nursery areas specially prepared with furniture and toys. Counselors and social service personnel provide guidance and assistance to help the mothers develop and maintain relationships with their children. In the other program, several women with minimum-security status, and within a few months of being released, are permitted to go to Camp Retreat with their children for a series of weekends from September to June. The camp is owned by the Salvation Army, which supplies the funding and personnel to provide family counseling. The purpose of this program is to prepare the mothers for return to their families by giving them and the children an opportunity be together for short periods of time so they can become reacquainted and learn to live together. Program staff reported that morale improved among the women who participated in the programs. However, a major problem, as with many of these programs, is that support services end once the women return home.[72]

The New York City Correctional Institution for Women provides several programs for inmate mothers and pregnant women. Contact visits are scheduled on a routine basis, and special contact visits are planned for Mother's Day, Christmas, and other holidays. These visits take place either in a room equipped with toys, books, and television or, weather permitting, in an outdoor recreation area. Parenting programs, family planning, and self-awareness programs are also provided. Approximately 35 pregnant women are in the jail at any given time. The women are taken to the hospital to have their babies. After a few days, they return to the jail and the babies are placed with relatives (a few go to foster homes). As of February 1985, however, women were able to keep their newborn babies with them in a nursery, an area of the jail designed and equipped for that purpose. The New York City Department of Correction agreed to provide this live-in program as a result of a lawsuit brought in federal court by the New York Legal Aid Society in June 1984. The lawsuit argued that the separation of mother and baby constituted cruel and unusual punishment under the Eighth Amendment. It also cited a New York State law that permits mothers to keep their babies in the state prison for women at Bedford Hills until the child is one year old. The court decided in favor of mothers and children, and the department is complying wth its mandate.[73]

Correctional agencies in other countries have had to decide whether to allow babies to live in prisons with their mothers. Israel, Finland, England, and West Germany are among those that have such programs. Each provides a nursery where mothers and babies live, a play area for the children, and food and medical care for both mothers and babies. During my tour of Holloway Prison in London, the staff told me that tensions were reduced, and both staff and inmates enjoyed having children to play with. A similar report was given to me at the women's prison in Lod, Israel. The women's prison in

West Germany goes further than most, in that provisions are made for children to live with their mothers, space permitting, until they are six years of age. Pregnant women many choose to have their babies live with them in a special compound, and newly committed women may also have their children, to the age of six, live with them in the compound. The prison also has counseling services and health care for mothers and children. From 1974 to 1978 only 1 of the 91 women in the program had returned to prison.[74]

During a 1984 visit to the New South Wales women's prison in Sydney, Australia, I learned that, as in the United States, live-in mother-child programs are not popular with prison administrators and policy makers. Judy Page, psychologist with the New South Wales Correction Services Department, argued for such a policy, claiming that it would benefit the entire correctional system because "female prisoners were easier to handle if they had their babies with them."[75] New South Wales had a mother-child cottage at Mulawa Prison for Women, but discontinued the program when several women threatened to use the children as hostages during a confrontation. Despite that experience, Page and other women involved in prison reform and women's rights continue to press for the restoration of the program, but with safeguards for the children. They have been partly successful; the Northern Territory, in a 1978 law, permits mothers to have children up to the age of five live with them in prison.[76]

Advocates on behalf of female prisoners continue to lobby and pressure for a wide range of programs for incarcerated mothers and their children. One obvious reason for this continued pressure is the fact that pregnant women are being sent to serve time in prisons and jails, but most facilities are not prepared or equipped to handle the medical and emotional needs of pregnant women. These women require prenatal and postnatal care by obstetricians and gynecologists, special diets and exercise, and counseling services to assist them in planning for the placement of the child. Equally important, pregnant women require counseling to decide, if medically possible, whether to have an abortion.

Another problem faced by pregnant women is forced abortions. Often because women criminals are considered unworthy of being mothers, or because of the expense and trouble of caring for pregnant inmates and their dependent children, correctional authorities have forced women to abort. In several cases, women or their advocates have taken the correctional authorities to court, declaring that their rights of protection against cruel and unusual punishment under the Eighth Amendment had been violated. In the 1974 lawsuit, *Morales* v. *Turman*, two female prisoners testified that when they had arrived, pregnant, at the (Texas) Gainesville School for Delinquent Girls, they were threatened with solitary confinement if they did not take the ten pills given to them. Both girls aborted, and were denied medical care during the process. Other such cases have been reported, which led the National Prison Project of the American Civil Liberties Union to cite forced abortions as a serious problem facing incarcerated pregnant women.[77]

However, there are women who want abortions, and many departments of correction, such as the Federal Bureau of Prisons and the New York City Department of Correction, permit and fund them. Some states will not permit abortions or will not fund them for incarcerated women. Anne Vitale argued that as a result of the 1973 U.S. Supreme Court decision in *Roe* v. *Wade*, women have the right to choose to have abortions and the state cannot deny them that right. Furthermore, under the Eighth Amendment, states are required to provide medical care for all inmates; abortions are medical concerns. And under the Fourteenth Amendment, inmates are guaranteed equal protection under the law; consequently, pregnant women inmates have a right to state-funded abortions if funds are available to free women.[78]

Other problems confront incarcerated pregnant women: hostility from staff members, who may mistreat them and assign them to dangerous jobs; poor medical care, with few medical specialists and unsanitary conditions in delivery rooms; and vaginal searches, for security reasons, when they return from the hospital after giving birth. In *Newman* v. *Alabama*, *Morales* v. *Turman*, and *Todaro* v. *Ward*, the courts found Alabama, Texas, and New York, respectively, guilty of violating the Eighth Amendment rights of pregnant women by denying them adequate medical care and access to medical specialists for specific women's needs. In addition, drug-addicted pregnant women face two other problems: drug withdrawal treatments may cause them to abort; and their babies may be born addicted.[79] Few departments of correction have established policy and implemented health care to deal with all of the above.

All correctional facilities that house females are faced with possibly having to deal with incarcerated mothers and pregnant women. Yet many have no programs, personnel, or policy to handle the medical and emotional needs of the women. The innovative mother-child programs and policies discussed above are significant because they are the exceptions, not the rules.

PHYSICAL AND MENTAL HEALTH CARE

All incarcerated women are entitled to adequate health care, according to decisions in *Newman* v. *Alabama*, *Morales* v. *Turman*, and *Todaro* v. *Ward*. In addition, in the 1974 Texas case *Estelle* v. *Gamble*, the court stated that "deliberate indifference" to the medical needs of prisoners constitutes an Eighth Amendment violation; it represents cruel and unusual punishment. However, because of the cost of providing medical care for a relatively small number of women in an institution, and because the institutions are located in rural areas, adequate health care and medical specialists to meet the needs of incarcerated women may not be available despite court decisions. That women have unique health needs requiring the attention of gynecologists and obstetricians, and the performance of special laboratory tests, is pointed out by a study on health care in correctional facilities that lists women's unique problems: Pap smears to detect cervical cancer; breast examinations; contraception and abortion information and procedures; prenatal and postnatal care; and treatment for menstrual problems and anemia.[80]

To compound the problem, incarcerated women are predominantly poor and from minority groups, and therefore often come to prison with health problems such as malnutrition, diabetes, high blood pressure, dental disease, and addiction to alcohol and/or drugs. These illnesses have often been diagnosed and treated poorly, if at all, since the women have usually had to rely on public health clinics. Many women have gone for medical care only when an emergency existed. In addition, inherited diseases are associated with specific racial and ethnic groups, often the groups overrepresented in the prison and jail populations. Black women may inherit sickle cell anemia, and need to be tested for that disease. Hypertension is more prevalent among black women than white women. And minority women are more likely than white women to have a higher rate of infant mortality. In addition, a large number of women in jails are held for prostitution, drunkenness, drug-related offenses, and vagrancy. Studies of these women indicate that they are prone to suffer from hepatitis, addiction, endocarditis, respiratory illnesses, venereal diseases, poor nutrition, and physical abuse.[81]

Once in prison or jail, women tend to gain weight, both from eating the starchy prison food and the snack food bought in the commissary, and from lack of exercise. Although addicted women are underweight and malnourished, the weight gain they and the other women experience tends to be an unhealthy one, placing many in the obese range.

A serious mental health problem stems from the overuse of psychotropic medication. Studies in the United States and several other countries indicate that incarcerated women are more heavily medicated than are men. In 1978, in the New York City jail system, 11.9 percent to 17.7 percent of the women received prescriptions for psychotropic drugs, compared with 1 percent to 6 percent of the men. In that same year, the Federal Bureau of Prisons reported that 10.5 percent of female inmates, but only 3.7 percent of male inmates, received such prescriptions.[82] In 1982, CONtact reported that 63 percent of the women in 39 correctional institutions surveyed had a serious alcohol or drug problem.[83] This suggests that providing psychotropic medication to incarcerated women may be exacerbating their substance dependency. Furthermore, some of these drugs pose a particular danger to pregnant inmates, causing them to abort or causing their babies to be born with nervous or brain disorders, or to be addicted.

Most of the lawsuits directing attention to prison conditions have been initiated by men, few by women. However, one important class-action lawsuit on behalf of women, *Todaro* v. *Ward*, charged that the health care services at the women's prison in New York State violated the Eighth Amendment because they constituted cruel and unusual punishment. The court declared that New York State failed to provide women inmates at Bedford Hills with access to adequate treatment by medical specialists or to provide them with basic medical care. The complaints in *Todaro* were filed in October 1974. By 1977 the court had decided in favor of the claimants, and the judgment went into effect that December. It was not until mid 1978, however, that improvements were made and a doctor was on call at all times for the female population of approximately 400.[84]

This is an example of the delays in reform in women's prisons even after courts order change. Implementation of the order often takes time, and many orders may not be enforced if women or concerned groups do not continue to be vigilant and persevere in seeking the prompt institution of needed reforms.

Reforms in mental health care also take a long time to be implemented after courts order changes. Women at Jessup have filed charges against the Maryland Department of Corrections, claiming that women do not receive the same mental health treatment as do male inmates; the only forensic mental health institution, Patuxent, is for men only. This class-action lawsuit asks that women be treated on an equal basis with men and have access to Patuxent. Dr. Henry Musk, psychologist and director of program services for the Maryland Department of Corrections, stated that in Maryland, as in all other states, the prisons and jails have a number of mentally ill and mentally retarded individuals who are committed to penal institutions where there is no treatment, although they should be sent to mental health institutions for proper care and treatment. He believes that there is an increased number of mentally ill persons in prisons and jails—the result, in part, of the movements of the 1960s and 1970s for the civil rights of institutionalized persons. Through these movements, many persons diagnosed as mentally ill, but able to function if properly medicated, were released into the community. Some have been caught in the criminal justice system and end up in prisons and jails. Once incarcerated, few, if any, receive any help, partly because of a lack of personnel and partly because the courts have upheld the right of inmates to refuse treatment. For example, in *McCray* v. *Maryland*, the court stated that the prison administration had the responsibility to determine whether the inmate was refusing treatment because of conscious rejection or because of emotional instability.[85]

In 1982 Dr. Musk conducted a study of mental illness in women's institutions. He reported that 85 percent of 49 state and four federal prisons, with a total population of 7,000, responded to his questionnaire; the largest held 600 women and the smallest, 20. Using a woman's history of hospitalization prior to incarceration as a criterion for mental illness, Musk ascertained that 13 percent (900 women) suffered from mental and/or emotional ills. In several institutions between 30 and 60 percent of the women fell into this category. About 4 percent (235 women) inmates were transferred to mental hospitals each year, for an average stay of two months. Treatment in these hospitals appeared to be ineffective, since only 21 percent of the institutions reported some improvement in the inmates when they returned.[86]

Musk reported that six prisons had no psychiatric services and that there are separate mental institutions for women in only ten states and in the Federal Bureau of Prisons system, whereas there are such facilities for men in 25 states and the federal system. Consequently, the prisons are usually responsible for treating women who manifest emotional or mental illnesses. Unfortunately, few can do so, because of lack of professional staff, lack of money, or lack of appropriate facilities within the prison. Approximately 10 hours a week of psychiatric consulting and 43 hours a week of psychological services are available in women's prisons, amounting to only 16 minutes per person per week. If the available time were devoted to the reported 13 percent who need it most, they would each receive two hours per week; no time would be left for the other 87 percent of the women, many of whom may have need for such services.[87]

In compliance with legislation to protect institutionalized persons against involuntary and arbitrary placement in a mental hospital (Civil Rights of Institutionalized Persons Act, Public Law 96–247, May 1980), prisons must prove that an inmate has a mental disorder before he/she is placed in a mental institution. Two doctors have to sign a statement to the effect that the inmate is a danger to her/himself or to others, and that the inmate needs treatment in a mental hospital; then a court order is required. Because of these strict criteria, and because most states do not have facilities for women, many women who need special treatment never receive it.[88]

Several prisons and jails have provided services to meet what is considered the unique physical and mental health needs of women. The new jail in Trenton, New Jersey, has a bathtub in the women's unit. And the New York City Correctional Institution for Women has arranged a schedule in the clinic for women who wish to have their legs shaved. On the other hand, because they are not considered a need of women or appropriate for women, gymnasiums and physical exercise are often unavailable to women inmates.

Despite efforts made in several prisons and jails, and by reform groups taking legal action against the prisons and jails, physical and mental health services and care for women remain inadequate at best in most prisons, and poor for most of the women in jails. Class-action suits, as shown by *Todaro* v. *Ward*, take a long time to win in court, and reforms may take even longer to implement. Because the prison and jail populations include a large proportion of women who have definite physical and mental health needs, particularly those who are pregnant, inadequate and poor care may literally be a matter of life and death.

REHABILITATION PROGRAMS

Rehabilitation programs for incarcerated women have been designed to conform to the social values of the dominant white, middle- and upper-class Protestant core culture, not the socioeconomic realities of either the backgrounds of the women in prison or the neighborhoods to which they return. Rehabilitation has meant the assumption of the role of wife, mother, and homemaker. The irony is that most are mothers, but few are wives or homemakers. The failure to reform the majority of female offenders stems, in part, from society's failure to recognize the historic fact that not all women have been given the socioeconomic opportunities that would enable them to conform to the idealized role of true womanhood. The reality has been that poor, uneducated, unskilled, marginally employed women, usually from immigrant and minority groups, have always been overrepresented in penal institutions. Described as "a dangerous class" by Dorothea Dix,[89] as "a serious eugenic danger to society" by Josephine Shaw Lowell,[90] and as "the bottom of the barrel" by Essie O. Murph,[91] imprisoned women have nevertheless been expected to return to true womanhood. When they did not, they alone were blamed.

Myths that women do not need to be self-supporting, or that they are not interested in nontraditional employment, are perpetuated by many correctional policy makers, and often prevent realistic and practical programs from being developed. We know that approximately two-thirds to three-quarters of the women are single heads of households with dependent children to support, and that only about one-quarter are married and have husbands to share in the support of the family. We also know that female heads of households constitute a large proportion of the group that lives below the poverty line. But although it is extremely important for incarcerated women to learn a skill and become self-supporting, they are not offered the academic or vocational training, work/study release, and job training programs that are offered to incarcerated men. Training for women continues to focus on traditional, low-paying female skills: food services, sewing, clerical work, and cosmetology. As it happens, these are the skills that are needed to maintain the prison or jail, and so the major concern is to train women to work in the kitchens, sewing rooms, and service areas of the institution.

Although these programs may reduce the cost of maintaining the institution, they rarely prepare the women for jobs in the outside world. In any case, many states have requirements for certain jobs: a licensed cosmetologist must have hundreds of hours of instruction and no felony convictions; and a licensed nurse's aide cannot have had a felony conviction or a history of drug use. A typist must be able to read and to spell correctly, but incarcerated women, 67 percent of whom never graduated from high school, are seldom skilled enough to do anything but copy typing. Many find that prostitution pays more than a low-level typing job. In addition, many incarcerated women are drug-dependent and/or addicted. Of the few addicts who are cured by imprisonment, most find their scars a hindrance to employment, especially in jobs such as waitressing, which often requires short-sleeved uniforms. In most cases, therefore, training women for traditional women's work is unrealistic if the goal is to make them self-supporting.

Equally important, women's institutions have few industries; therefore, women have few opportunities to learn a skill or to earn money while incarcerated, as men do. For example, in the federal prisons, women have an opportunity to work in 13 of 84 industrial operations, whereas men have access to 82 of the 84. Also, 11 of the 13 industrial opportunities for women are located in cocorrectional facilities and therefore are available to men. In Alderson, the only all-female prison in the federal system, only two industrial opportunities exist, and both are in traditional, low-paying skills: keypunching and sewing. State prisons provide the same type of industrial work for women, with most concentrating on sewing industries.[92]

In addition, because there is usually only one prison for women in a state (and two states have none at all), women cannot be transferred to other facilities in the state for academic, vocational, or work/study programs, whereas men are sometimes transferred so they can take advantage of these programs. And because of the rural location of most women's prisons, there are usually no work or study release opportunities in the surrounding communities, nor are community resources available to assist in the training and rehabilitation of the women.

Correctional policy makers often defend the status quo by maintaining that the comparatively small number of women does not justify the expense of providing all of these programs for them; that women will not have to work when released, since men will support them; that women are not interested in working; and that women are not interested in the type of training programs that are offered to men. In addition, it is argued that offering these additional programs to women would increase the number of supervisory and custodial personel needed. Also, additional money and time would be wasted on these particular women because they are "losers" and would not benefit from or use the skills when released.[93]

Because of these attitudes, little has been done to provide women inmates with skills needed to make them self-supporting. Government funding agencies are more likely to grant money for traditional training than for the nontraditional. In keeping with the attitudes toward women, typing is funded but not welding; and, as already pointed out, few incarcerated women are able to learn to type well enough to meet business standards, owing to their limited educational achievements. Private industry, too, has been reluctant to invest in women inmates because the cost per trainee is believed to be too high. Labor unions also play a role in determining whether inmates receive training and work release experience. When unemployment exists among their members, unions are very reluctant to support job programs for women (or men) inmates.

The difficulty for female ex-offenders to find employment is exacerbated by their lack of skills and by the reluctance of employers to hire women with criminal records. Many government-funded employment services were established after 1968 for the purpose of finding employment for ex-offenders. One such agency was the National Alliance of Businessmen. A representative of the Alliance reported that they did not even try to find jobs for women because it was impossible; men could be placed in jobs that required physical strength even if they had no specific skills, but women could not. Job placement staffs in other agencies said that they could find some clerical or typing jobs for women, but few were qualified for even these traditional jobs.[94]

The 1982 CONtact survey indicated that some improvements have been made, although they continue to be exceptions to the general situation. In addition to the basic educational, GED, and high school and college courses, an increased number of prisons provided traditional and nontraditional vocational training programs. Nontraditional training included electronics, appliance repair, metalwork, and animal grooming at Frontera, California; plumbing, electronics, wastewater treatment, and carpentry at Niantic, Connecticut; mechanical drafting and carpentry at Rockwell City, Iowa; and offset press operation, platemaking, silk screen printing, bindery operation, and optical technology at Jessup, Maryland. Similar programs existed at women's prisons in New York, Michigan, and Pennsylvania, and the federal cocorrectional prison at Lexington, Kentucky.[95] The CONtact survey was conducted through questionnaires. Consequently, we have no knowledge of the quality of the programs, how many women were involved, how many found employment using the skills, and how many of the programs still exist.

Another area of improved programming for women opened in 1979, when federal legislation permitted inmates to work for private industry for wages. In 1984, corporations in Kansas, Minnesota, Nevada, and Arizona hired incarcerated women. For example, the Best Western international hotel chain has a program with the Arizona Center for Women in which the company pays inmates regular wages, starting at $3,75 per hour, to work in the prison as reservation operators over toll-free telephone lines.[96] In addition, government and private funding has enabled organizations to establish community resources for inmates and ex-offenders. The Fortune Society in New York City, the Female Offender Program in Pittsburgh, and the Morrow Project in Trenton, New Jersey, provide housing, counseling, academic, and vocational training programs, and job placement opportunities. They also help women to get social security cards, drivers' licenses, birth certificates and other vital papers that are necessary for applying to academic institutions, and for jobs, welfare, and a number of other services that inmates and ex-offenders need.

Rehabilitation programs in the academic and vocational areas are being made available to women. More meaningful and realistic programs—designed to meet the needs of the women who are incarcerated, not to conform to the myth of womanhood—are being offered. But these are noticed, and notable, because there are so few. They are not found as program offerings in most prisons, and certainly not in women's jails. Consequently, only a small number of women benefit from these programs even though virtually all women need to be self-supporting when released. Until correctional authorities provide programming for women, at least on an equal basis with men, these significant disadvantages for women will continue.

WOMEN PRISONERS' LITIGATION

During the 1960s, the civil rights and women's rights movements led to legal action on behalf of prisoners' rights, but almost all the legal action came from men on behalf of men. This despite the fact that women are not treated on an equal basis with men and that both male and female inmates live under conditions that have been declared cruel and unusual punishment. Several reasons have been suggested to explain why women seldom go to court to improve the conditions under which they must exist. One is that women have been taught to be passive and accepting. Another is that women do not form support networks, and therefore few women have access to persons with the skills or resources upon which to build a legal case. And the commonly held idea that women are better off than men results in women being ignored by civil rights and prisoners' rights organizations that file class-action lawsuits on behalf of male inmates.[97]

There are even more compelling reasons why women file so few court cases on their own behalf or cannot find advocates to do it for them. Women's prisons are located far from the urban centers where the reform organizations are, and where legal aid and the courts are located. Therefore access to legal advice, law libraries, and legal advocates is not readily available. Women lack relevant legal knowledge, and few "jail-house" lawyers are found among them. If law libraries exist in the prison, often law librarians or assistance from other librarians is not provided. Prison adminstrators may place impediments in the way of inmates to prevent them from properly preparing legal briefs, and prison personnel may rely on the fact that women are less prone to be aggressive and hostile, and therefore can be coerced into not complaining to authorities outside the prison. In sum, incarcerated women have not been significantly affected by the women's movement and have not become aggressive, assertive, and litigious.[98]

Several court cases have, however, been filed by women inmates and as class-action suits on behalf of incarcerated women. These cases charge that women do not receive treatment equal to that of men in areas of physical and mental health care, and educational, vocational, and work/study release programs. In addition, women charge that institutions and departments of correction do not provide legal protection for incarcerated mothers and their children, and for pregnant women. These suits are primarily based on the Fourteenth, Eighth, and Fourth Amendments.

Several sex discrimination suits have been filed under the Fourteenth Amendment, charging that women are denied equal protection under the law and are denied due process guarantees. In *Glover* v. *Johnson* (no. 77-1229, E.D. Mich., October 16, 1979), the court found that women in the Michigan women's prison had "fewer" and "inferior" vocational and educational programs than men had. In addition, women were denied access to programs such as "work pass incentive and good time." The court ruled that incarcerated women had the right to programs substantially equal to those provided to men but "based on the needs and interests of female inmates."[99]

Citing cruel and unusual punishment, particularly in areas of health care and care for pregnant women, court cases have been filed under the Eighth Amendment. In *Todaro* v. *Ward* (431 F. Supp. 1129 [S.D.N.Y. 1977]) the medical system in the women's prison in New York was found to be "unconstitutionally defective," and improvements were ordered by the court.[100]

In *Forts* v. *Ward* (471 F. Supp. 1095 [S.D.N.Y. 1978]) inmates of the women's prison in New York filed a lawsuit under the Fourth Amendment, charging that their rights to privacy had been violated by having male officers in their housing area. The court ruled that male officers assigned to contact positions in a women's facility did violate the women's rights to privacy, and that except where "urgent necessity justified the exception," men should not be so assigned.[101]

Although women won these lawsuits, implementation of court-ordered change takes a long time and enforcement may not be enthusiastic. Compliance with court-ordered changes in *Glover* v. *Johnson* is still being carried out, years after the case was decided in favor of the women in Michigan's prison.

COCORRECTIONS

In the 1960s, the sex-segregated prison system came under scrutiny from groups of men and women activists espousing prisoners' rights and women's rights. They argued that a separate system could not be an equal one. After comparing the opportunities afforded male and female prison staffs and prisoners, the reformers concluded that female staff received limited and inferior employment opportunities, and that female prisoners received limited and inferior services and programs. Reformers sought to redress these wrongs, and proposed the integration of male and female prison staffs and prisoners as a solution to both problems.

The decision to integrate male and female prisoners in a cocorrectional prison is an extremely difficult one to make. It must take into consideration practical issues of security, the need for an integrated male and female staff, and the expense of redesigning prisons and providing services and programs to accommodate men and women in the same institution. The decision must also take into account the problems associated with emotional and sexual involvement between male and female prisoners.

A cocorrectional prison is one in which men and women prisoners live, supervised by a male and female staff, and participate in all activities together. However,in practice there have been so many variations on the way cocorrectional plans have been implemented in the United States since 1971, that it is virtually impossible to discuss them as a single entity. Conclusions regarding the comparative advantages or disadvantages of a cocorrectional prison, as against a single-sex prison, must therefore be based on assumption, theoretical considerations, and studies of a wide variety of noncomparable existing situations. For example, Denmark's state prison at Ringe is a totally integrated prison. Approximately 65 men and 25 women between the ages of 17 and 25 live in private rooms in the same housing units and participate in all activities together. A man and a woman are permitted to be alone together in one or the other's room until 10:30 each night, but they go to their own rooms to sleep. Those without a partner at Ringe may receive spouses or lovers in their rooms during visiting hours on the weekends.[102] This total integration of male and female prisoners may be possible only in a country such as Denmark, a small nation with a homogeneous population and a social value system that is accepting of sexual relations between unmarried people and of children born out of wedlock. The Chittender Community Correctional Center in Vermont represents almost the opposite end of the spectrum. There, men and women prisoners are permitted to work together but may not eat, or participate in educational, vocational, or recreational activities, together.[103]

The four major reasons for establishing cocorrectional institutions are quite different, and help to account for the vast variations in organization and policy. The most frequently cited reason for establishing a cocorrectional prison is economic; it is a way to make the operation of a prison and the provision of services and programs more cost-effective. Policies to establish cocorrectional prisons have often been determined by the need to find space for prisoners or to fill empty beds in order to reduce costs. When the federal cocorrectional prison in Fort Worth, Texas, opened in 1971, women were included because the women's prison was over-crowded. The women's prisons in Clinton, New Jersey, and in Framingham, Massachusetts, became cocorrectional to reduce the costs of running prisons that had empty beds. Since cocorrectional prisons are often linked to the prison census, the prison can be restored to a single-sex institution when the dominant population increases.[104]

A second reason for adopting a cocorrectional policy is to reduce the cost of providing services and programs for women. Because there are so few women in prisons, compared with men, the cost of providing equal or comparable services and programs can be prohibitively high. Prison systems have been under pressure to provide equal services and programs for women as a result of legal action taken by prison reformers and women prisoners. They base their claims on the fact that women prisoners do not have access to the same services and programs that men receive. In 1979, in *Glover v. Johnson,* the court declared the Department of Corrections in the state of Michigan in violation of constitutional guarantees by denying women prisoners treatment equal to that of men prisoners. To avoid litigation, other departments of correction are seeking ways to provide equal treatment for women prisoners at the lowest possible cost. One solution is to establish cocorrectional prisons.[105]

A third reason for accepting a cocorrectional policy is to provide for the needs of men. For example, the women's prison in New Jersey became cocorrectional to accommodate aged and infirm male prisoners who have full minimum-security status. In Illinois, the need for a minimum-security facility for men led to the conversion of the only women's prison into a cocorrectional one.[106]

The fourth reason for integrating male and female prisoners is to create a humane and more normal environment in which to rehabilitate the prisoners and provide the services and programs necessary for a more successful reintegration into the community upon their release.[107]

The supporters of the cocorrectional concept concur in this last reason for its adoption, and point out the benefits for men and women prisoners and staff. A cocorrectional prison, particularly one that permits male and female prisoners to share most activities, appears to have a less tense atmosphere, and the presence of men and women motivates staff and prisoners to be more interested in their dress, demeanor, and language. As a result, staff and prisoners have fewer concerns about violent or assaultive confrontations. Both male and female prisoners have a wide variety of services and programs intended to prepare them to work and function in the community. And male and female prisoners who have had poor relationships with members of the opposite sex have an opportunity to learn to relate to each other in a positive, nonexploitive manner.[108]

Those who support the cocorrectional concept also point out the benefits that apply specifically to either male or female prisoners. It is said that the more relaxed atmosphere and the presence of women reduces tension and violence among men; there appear to be fewer homosexual relationships, no reported sexual assaults, and few, if any, aggressive confrontations.[109] Women prisoners benefit from the availability of medical, psychological, legal, and social services, and educational and vocational programs that are not cost-effective for the small number of incarcerated women.[110] The respondents in a 1982 survey of cocorrectional prisons were "very emphatic about the benefits, noting that it is economically advantageous to share space, programming, and staff, and that it creates a more normal, positive atmosphere.[111]

Despite the apparent advantages of integrating male and female prisoners, even supporters of the concept admit that there are several serious disadvantages for female prisoners. One disadvantage results from the fact that most female and male prisoners come from the segment of society that maintains traditional views about the roles of men and women. When they are integrated in one prison, these sex roles come into play and many women appear to lose the motivation, ambition, and leadership qualities that are evident in an all-women's prison. Men, however, regardless of their share in the prison population, become the leaders, dominate traditional and nontraditional programs, and take over the best prison jobs.[112] Furthermore, many incarcerated women are mistreated, exploited, or abused by the men in their lives, and often get into trouble with the law because of the men. It has been observed that women in a cocorrectional facility continue their negative pattern with men and assume their traditional subordinate, dependent role; most do not share in or take advantage of the expanded services and programs, but spend their time and energy meeting the needs of their walk partners, the men they become connected with in prison.[113]

After conducting studies on male and female prisoners at Fort Worth, Texas, Heffernan and Krippel concluded that:

> . . . while to some extent the situation at Fort Worth is simply an extension of the larger question of the role of women in society, there are certain ways in which prison intensifies these issues. . . . As the women move into the walk partner relationship, they also tend to enter programs that reflect the interests of the men with whom they are involved.[114]

And Lambiotte observed that women:

> . . . focus their energies on their men and their relationships . . . male residents are able to define the female residents' relationship to them through labeling, verbal harassment, violation of women's physical space, the right to initiate relationships and their leadership in programs.[115]

A second disadvantage deals with services and programs. Although more are provided in a cocorrectional prison, especially nontraditional vocational training programs, women are not attracted to them because they do not want to appear unfeminine or to be competing with the men. Nor are the women encouraged to participate in these programs. It appears that men, but few women, benefit from the wide variety of services and programs. One study indicated that men attended programs usually found only in women's prisons, such as cosmetology, thus limiting opportunities for women even in traditional areas.[116] Janice Warner Cummings, the superintendent of the Albion cocorrectional facility in New York, observed that most women did not want nontraditional programs and that it was not as easy to meet the specific needs of women in a cocorrectional prison as in an all-women's facility.[117] Because there are so few women in prison, they tend to be a minority in a cocorrectional prison, and therefore programs designed to meet their special needs, such as family planning, parenting, and child care, are often neglected because they are not cost-effective. Ironically, one reason to adopt the cocorrectional concept was to increase service and program opportunities for women in the most cost-effective way. However, the financial problem continues to plague women even when the supposed solution is adopted.

A third disadvantage to women involves the problems associated with the opportunities for sexual contact with men. The burdens of pressure from the men for sexual favors, concern about birth control and pregnancy, and decisions about having an abortion or what to do with the baby fall on the women.[118] Most of the superintendents of cocorrectional prisons admit that sexual encounters occur, and that pregnancies have to be expected. Furthermore, they admit that much of the staff's time and energy are spent in supervision, reprimanding violators, writing up infractions, and dealing with the prisoners' emotional problems. In a 1982 survey of 21 "coed" institutions in the United States and Canada, the consensus was that the major problem created by the coed arrangement concerned violation of contact rules and pregnancies.[119] In an effort to avoid these problems, often more restrictions are placed on the mobility and activities of women prisoners, and they are supervised more closely than men. Because of the small number of women compared with men, it is easier to place limits and controls on them. The result is that women are under more strain and are more tense than the men.[120]

A fourth disadvantage has to do with the small number of women in the prison system, compared with men, and the fact that this results in the placing of women of all classifications in a single cocorrectional prison; however, men assigned to these institutions are classified, screened, and selected in an attempt to form a homogeneous group. Thus, supervision and planning programs for men are easier, whereas supervision and programming for a heterogeneous female population are more difficult and more expensive. This may result in the neglect of female needs in planning programs because it is too expensive to meet the needs of such a diverse but small female population. In addition, if adopted, the cocorrectional concept usually results in the loss of the only existing women's prison in the area. If men are sent to the women's prison, women tend to be more closely supervised and the relatively informal, relaxed atmosphere usually found in a women's prison is lost. If women are sent to the men's facility, the women's prison is closed and women become a minority in a male-dominated institution.

Equally important, when a male prison becomes cocorrectional, both male and female staffs and prisoners tend to suffer during the early stages of implementation. Women are viewed by male staff and prisoners as the disrupters of discipline, of the male social structure, and of the unspoken systems previously established between male staff and prisoners for running the prison. Women prisoners are oversupervised, and there is usually no female administrator to speak for them. Men prisoners are also more restricted, as efforts are made to keep the male and female prisoners separated. And both male and female staffs feel they have more work to do.[121]

The major disadvantage to male prisoners is the differential punishment process. Men who violate the rules are transferred to an all-male prison, which tends to be more punitive and more secure; the threat of transfer is used to control behavior. Women generally cannot be controlled with this type of threat, since there are usually no women's prisons to which to transfer them.[122]

Finally, the integration of male and female prisoners in one facility will obviously require an integrated male and female staff. It had been expected that an integrated prison system would prove to be a source of increased employment opportunities for females, and indeed more women have been hired and integrated into combined male and female staffs. However, the experience has been that positions for women administrators have actually been reduced; men become the superintendents of cocorrectional prisons, even those that were originally women's prisons and continue to have a majority of women prisoners.[123]

In essence, a cocorrectional prison system appears to be an attempt to adopt a male-type system to meet some of the needs of women in order to avoid litigation and the associated increased costs. "Going back to merely housing males and females together has little to offer either sex, and certainly not women, who are (and traditionally have been) the minority portion of the offender population."[124] We need research and data to evaluate the cocorrectional concept in order to come to any conclusions as to its value.

The real and potential disadvantages of integrating male and female prisoners may be difficult to mitigate or eliminate even if certain preventive steps are taken. To deal with the harmful effects of sex roles on women prisoners, it is important for staff and policy makers to understand the traditional roles assumed by men and women and how these roles surface in, and affect behavior in, a cocorrectional setting. Women will need to be counseled not to take a subordinate, dependent role in relation to men and to be encouraged to take advantage of services and programs. The neglect of women's special needs can be resolved by understanding those needs and establishing the services and programs to meet them. It is important to face the issue of and problems associated with sexual contact between men and women. A clearly stated policy dealing with physical contact, birth control, pregnancy, and plans for the birth and care of babies, as well as penalties for violations, has to be established and must be enforceable. This policy could provide the excuse for women who wish to withstand pressures from men for sexual favors to say "no." Furthermore, the staff must understand the policy and be able to enforce the rules, but not be preoccupied with preventing physical encounters between prisoners. Some feel that it is beneficial to have a community advisory board, in an effort to keep rumors and myths about cocorrectional activities from obscuring the positive aspects of such a prison.[125] The male-female ratio is the most difficult problem to resolve. The number of women prisoners in the system is so small compared with the number of men that equal numbers of each in one facility might be difficult to achieve, especially if men and women are classified and selected on an equal basis. Regardless of the male-female ratio, prisoners should have one set of rules to follow and should be subject to the same punishments.

Perhaps the above problems and suggestions for amelioration may be best handled by implementing a new proposal introduced by Dr. Esther Heffernan in 1979, the coordinate prison.[126] The coordinate prison has separately administered but contiguous male and female facilities with integrated staffs; they share services and programs while retaining their identities and autonomy. In the coordinate prison, both male and female special needs would be met, shared services and programs would be more cost-effective, male and female prisoners would have the opportunity to associate with one another yet have their own separate space and time, and women would have the opportunity to be administrators of the female institution and to be leaders and spokespersons for women prisoners. The coordinate prison would avoid the "separate but unequal" problem that has denied women staff and prisoners equal treatment with men in the prison system. It would also prevent women staff and prisoners from being overwhelmed in the predominantly male system.[127]

In September 1981, a coordinate prison opened in the state of Alaska. According to the report "Shared Resources" prepared by Charles F. Campbell, director of the Alaska Division of Corrections, it was inadvisable to develop a cocorrectional prison because of the small number of incarcerated women.[128] The coordinate system was adopted for two reasons. First, there would be a cost advantage, in that a wide range of services and programs could be available to women. This would eliminate the problem of disparity of services and programs that has led to legal action demanding equal treatment for women.[129] Second, the advantages of a cocorrectional prison would be gained without the disadvantages, particularly those faced by women:

. . . the women had typically experienced fairly unrelenting pressure, not as often for sexual involvement as for social attention and for conformity to a stringent and (for the woman) a thoroughly disadvantageous subcultural code.[130]

Whether these perceived advantages of the coordinate system will be realized remains to be seen.

The proposals to integrate male and female prison staffs and prisoners have elicited impassioned arguments from their supporters and opponents. This is due, in part, to the fact that there are many issues to be considered, and many benefits and problems associated with both proposals, but very little objective data for evaluating the proposals and basing conclusions regarding them. Any innovative proposal in the prison system requires long-range planning, a clear understanding of why the innovation is to be implemented, a well-trained support staff, and policies and practices that focus on the reasons for the innovation. It also requires an exploration of alternatives, such as the coordinate prison as an alternative to a cocorrectional one. In addition, whenever these proposals are implemented, research studies will be needed in order to evaluate their impact on the men and women prison staffs and prisoners. Finally, decisions to integrate male and female prison staffs and prisoners are difficult to make and, once made, require full commitment by the policy makers and adequate funding to ensure their success.

SUMMARY

Undoubtedly, improvements have been made in the lives of incarcerated women. However, innovative programs in job training, mothering and family life, and health care are conspicuous precisely because they are so few. Although changes have occurred since the first prison for women opened in 1873, the basic premises have remained the same. Both in and out of prisons, women tend to be treated according to traditional views; women criminals are disgraced and dishonored women who must be punished, but can be reformed by good women.

Given these entrenched values, it is understandable that programs change slowly and only after great effort. Legal action is painfully slow, and court-ordered changes meet resistance at the implementation stages. Even the much heralded innovation of cocorrections carries many problems, for women assume dependent, submissive roles when in contact with men.

Equally important are economic problems and societal attitudes toward prisoners, especially incarcerated women. Recession, inflation, unemployment, and the trend toward tax cuts make unlikely any increase in appropriations for programs deemed nonessential. Citizens who are unemployed or who feel the economic pinch in some other way resent tax money spent on prisoners for vocational training, job counseling, and work or study release programs. Tax cuts force budget cuts, and the corrections system, always the worst-funded part of the criminal justice system, has certainly been affected; there is money for custody but very little for other services or programs.

Although much publicity has been given to the woman criminal since the mid-1960s, the woman prisoner is largely ignored. She does not riot, escape, commit suicide, or do violence to staff and other inmates; she is out of sight and out of mind. Ironically, the publicity about women criminals has created an image of a more dangerous type of criminal who must be punished more harshly and confined more securely. Unfortunately, these images continue to mold perceptions and actions both of the public and of some professionals in corrections. In all this concern with theories, stereotypes, and images, the human being behind the criminal mask has been forgotten.

NOTES

1. Barbara Welter, "The Cult of True Womanhood: 1820-1860," in *Our American Sisters: Women in American Life and Thought* edited by Jean Friedman and William Shade (Boston: Allyn and Bacon, 1973), pp. 96-123.

2. Ibid., David B. Davis, *Homicide in American Fiction, 1789-1860: A Study in Social Values* (Ithaca, N.Y.: Cornell University Press, 1957), p. xiii.

3. Davis, op. cit., pp. 154-55; Cesare Lombroso and William Ferrero, *The Female Offender* (New York: D. Appleton, 1920), p. 152.

4. Cynthia Philips, *Imprisoned in America: Prison Communications 1776 to Attica* (New York: Harper & Row, 1973), pp. 53-54.

5. David Lewis, *From Newgate to Dannemora: The Rise of the Penitentiary in New York, 1796-1848* (Ithaca, N.Y.: Cornell University Press, 1965), pp. 94-95, 162-64.

6. Ibid., p. 164.

7. Ibid, pp. 164-65.

8. John Richmond, *New York and Its Institutions, 1609—1872* (New York: E. B. Treat, 1972), pp. 87, 458.

9. Ibid., pp. 82-85.

10. Lewis, op. cit., p. 160; Estelle Freedman, "Their Sisters' Keepers: An Historical Perspective on Female Correctional Institutions in the United States: 1870-1900," *Feminist Studies* 11 (1974): 79-80.

11. Lewis, op. cit.; Freedman, op. cit.

12. Freedman, op. cit., p. 80; Richmond, op. cit., pp. 317-20, 457-60; Philip Klein, *Prison Methods in New York State: Studies in History, Economics and Public Law* (New York: Longmans, Green, 1920), pp. 225-26.

13. Richmond, op. cit., pp. 317-476.

14. Klein, op. cit., p. 374.

15. Lewis, op. cit., pp. 237-41; Georgiana Kirby, *Years of Experience: An Autobiographical Narrative* (New York: AMS Press, 1971), pp. 190-211.

16. Lewis, op. cit., pp. 242-50.

17. Ruth Glick and Virginia Neto, *National Study of Women's Correctional Programs* (Washington, D.C.: National Institute of Law Enforcement and Criminal Justice, 1977), pp. xvii-xix, 102-56.

18. Clarice Feinman, "An Afro-American Experience: The Women in New York City's Jail," *Afro-Americans in Life and History* 1 (July 1977): 203–04; Charlotte Ginsburg, "Who Are the Women in Prison?" in *Women in Corrections*, edited by Barbara H. Olsson, (College Park, Md.: American Correctional Association, 1981), pp. 52–54; Jody Grossman, "Comparison of Male and Female Inmates Under the Department's Custody: As of June 1, 1983," report prepared for the State of New York Department of Correctional Services, November, 1983; U.S. Comptroller General, *Women in Prison: Inequitable Treatment Requires Action* (Washington, D.C.: U.S. General Accounting Office, 1980), pp. 3–4.

19. U.S. Comptroller General, op. cit., pp. 3–4.

20. Ginsburg, op. cit., pp. 52–54.

21. Grossman, op. cit., pp. 1–5.

22. U.S. Comptroller General, op. cit., p. 4.

23. "Woman Offender," *Corrections Compendium* (Lincoln, Nebr.: CONtact, Inc., July 1982), p. 6.

24. Glick and Neto, op. cit., pp. 141–56; Ginsburg, op. cit., pp. 53–54; Feinman, op. cit., pp. 203–04; Omar Hendrix, *A Study in Neglect: A Report on Women's Prisons* (New York: Women's Prison Association of New York City, 1972, pp. 16–18.

25. Grossman, op. cit., pp. 5–6.

26. Bureau of Justice Statistics, *Bulletin: Prisoners in 1983* (Washington, D.C.: U.S. Department of Justice, 1984), pp. 1, 5.

27. Ibid., p. 5.

28. Bureau of Justice Statistics, *Bulletin: Jail Inmates 1982* (Washington, D.C.: U.S. Department of Justice, 1983), pp. 1–2.

29. Information from Cathy Morse, public information officer, Federal Bureau of Prisons, February 20, 1985.

30. American Correctional Association, *Female Classification: An Examination of the Issues* (College Park, Md.: ACA, 1984), p. 30.

31. *New York Times*, September 19, 1984, p. A18; September 20, 1984, p. B15; September 28, 1984, pp. A1, A17; November 2, 1984, pp. A1, A20.

32. *Burlington County (N.J.) Times*, April 6, 1984, p. 9.

33. Bureau of Justice Statistics, *Bulletin: Capital Punishment 1981* (Washington, D.C.: U.S. Department of Justice, 1982), p. 17.

34. Bureau of Justice Statistics, *Bulletin: Capital Punishment 1983* (Washington, D.C.: U.S. Department of Justice, 1984), p. 13; "Death Row, U.S.A.," report from NAACP Legal Defense and Educational Fund, December 20, 1984, pp. 1–19.

35. Coramae Mann, *Female Crime and Delinquency* (University: University of Alabama Press, 1984), p. 259.

36. *New York Times*, November 25, 1984, p. 65.

37. Bureau of Justice Statistics, *Bulletin: Prisoners 1981 in State and Federal Institutions on December 31* (Washington, D.C.: U.S. Department of Justice, 1983), p. 20.

38. Bureau of Justice Statistics, *Bulletin: Jail Inmates 1982*, p. 1.

39. Information from Cathy Morse, February 20, 1985.

40. Grossman, op. cit., p. 2.

41. Angela Davis, *If They Come in the Morning* (New York: Signet Books, 1971), pp. 184–88.

42. Joan Little, "The People Set Me Free," *Poverty Law Report* 3 (1975): 1–3; Laurence French, "A Profile of the Incarcerated Black Female Offender," *Prison Journal* 63 (Autumn-Winter 1983): 84.

43. Information from the New Jersey State Police, Fugitive Unit, March 5, 1985.

44. Glick and Neto, op. cit., pp. 104, 123, 137.

45. Helen Green, "Black Women in the Criminal Justice System," *Urban League Review* 6 (Fall 1981): 59.

46. Feinman, op. cit., pp. 202–03.

47. Ibid., pp. 202; interview with Jessie Behegan, former superintendent, New York City Correctional Institution for Women, April 20, 1974; interview with Essie O. Murph, superintendent, New York City Correctional Institution for Women, January 16, 1976; interview with Florence Holland, former superintendent, New York City House of Detention for Women, April 8, 1974.

48. Feinman, op. cit., pp. 203–04.

49. Interview with Murph, January 16, 1976; interview with Holland, April 8, 1974.

50. Interview with Murph, January 16, 1976; Feinman, op. cit., p. 204; New York City Department of Corrections, *Annual Report 1955*, p. 7.

51. Interview with Fannie Rogers, principal Public School 233X, New York City Correctional Institution for Women, April 25, 1974.

52. Feinman, op. cit., pp. 205–07; Interview with Murph, January 16, 1976.

53. Interview with Murph, January 16, 1976.

54. Laura Bresler and Diane Lewis, "Black and White Women Prisoners: Differences in Family Ties and Their Programmatic Implication," *Prison Journal* 63 (Autumn-Winter 1983): 117–22.

55. Madeleine Doty, *Society's Misfits* (New York: The Century Co., 1916), p. 100.

56. Estelle Freedman, "Women's Prison Experience in Nineteenth Century America," paper presented at the 1978 National Archives Conference, p. 1.

57. Quoted in Kathryn Burkhart, *Women in Prison* (New York: Doubleday, 1973), p. 127.

58. Freedman, "Women's Prison Experience," fn. 4.

59. Glick and Neto, op. cit., p. 116.

60. Clarice Feinman, "Inmate Demographic Profile March 1975-December 1975," in *Women's Development Unit Project Annual Report January 1, 1975 to April 9, 1976* (New York: New York City Correctional Institution for Women, 1976), p. 18, Appendix H.

61. Phyllis Jo Baunach, "Mothering from Behind Prison Walls," paper presented at the 1979 annual meeting of the American Society of Criminology, pp. 1, 4–5.

62. Ibid., pp. 9, 11.

63. Ibid., pp. 16–17, 23–26.

64. Brenda McGowan and Karen Blumenthal, *Why Punish the Children: A Study of Children of Women Prisoners* (Hackensack, N.J.: National Council on Crime and Delinquency, 1978), pp. 3, 5–6.

65. Ibid., pp. 19–29, 57–58, 71, 119.

66. Jody Grossman, "Female Commitments 1982: The Family," report prepared for the State of New York Department of Correctional Services, February 1984, pp. 5–8.

67. Ibid., p. 10.

68. Jody Grossman, "Bedford Hills Mothers Follow-up," report prepared for the State of New York Department of Correctional Services, September 1984, p. 1.

69. Ibid., pp. 2–7.

70. Press release from the State of New York Executive Chamber, August 27, 1983, pp. 1–2.

71. McGowan and Blumenthal, op. cit., p. 28; *Female Offenders: Problems and Progress* (Washington, D.C.: ABA Female Offender Resource Center, 1976), pp. 26–27.

72. Interview with Sherry MacPhearson, Professional Services Department, Correctional Institution for Women, Clinton, N.J., May 3, 1979.

73. *New York Times,* December 4, 1984, p. B57; July 31, 1981, pp. B1, B7.

74. Beverly Greening, "A Prison for Moms and Kids," *Youth Authority Quarterly* 31 (Winter 1978), pp. 25–27.

75. John Davis, "Women in the Prison System: South Australia," paper presented at the Australian Institute of Criminology Seminar on Women in the Prison System, June 1984, p. 14.

76. Robert Donnally, "Infants and Aboriginal Women in Prison," paper presented at the Australian Institute of Criminology Seminar on Women in the Prison System, June 1984, p. 4.

77. Gerald McHugh, "Protection of the Rights of Pregnant Women in Prisons and Detention Facilities," *New England Journal of Prison Law* 6 (Summer 1980): 233–34.

78. Anne Vitale, "Inmate Abortions: The Right to Government Funding Behind the Prison Gates," *Fordham Law Review* 48 (March 1980): 567.

79. McHugh, op. cit., pp. 239, 242–45; Karen Holt, "Nine Months to Life: The Law and the Pregnant Inmate," *Journal of Family Law* 20 (1981–82): 523.

80. Edward Brecher and Richard Della Penna, *Health Care in Correctional Institutions* (Washington, D.C.: National Institute of Law Enforcement and Criminal Justice, 1975), pp. 33–35.

81. Judith Resnick and Nancy Shaw, "Prisoners of Their Sex: Health Problems of Incarcerated Women," in *Prisoners' Rights Sourcebook*, edited by Ira Robbins (New York: Clark Boardman, 1980), pp. 328–30.

82. Ibid., p. 337.

83. "Woman Offender," *Corrections Compendium*, July 1982, p. 6.

84. Resnik and Shaw, op. cit., pp. 340–43.

85. Henry Musk, "Violent and Nonviolent Mentally Ill Women Prisoners: Correctional Administrative Problems," paper presented at the annual meeting of the American Society of Criminology, pp. 1, 5–6.

86. Ibid., pp. 2–3.

87. Ibid., pp. 3–4.

88. Ibid., p. 4.

89. Dorothea Dix, *Remarks on Prisons and Prison Discipline* (Montclair, N.J.: Patterson Smith, 1967), pp. 6, 16–17.

90. Klein, op. cit., p. 45.

91. Interview with Murph, January 16, 1976.

92. U.S. Comptroller General, op. cit., p. 19.

93. Ibid., pp. 20–22.

94. Information from interviews conducted while I was project director of the Women's Development Unit Project, New York City Correctional Institution for Women, 1975–76: Essie O. Murph, superintendent; Fannie Rogers, school principal; and personnel with National Alliance of Businessmen, Women's Prison Association, and the Fortune Society.

95. "Women Offender," *Corrections Compendium*, July 1982, pp. 6–11.

96. *Burlington County (N.J.) Times*, April 5, 1984, p. 11.

97. Nan Aron, "Legal Issues Pertaining to Female Offenders," in *Representing Prisoners* (New York: Practicing Law Institute, 1981), pp. 191–94.

98. Ibid., p. 194.

99. U.S. Comptroller General, op. cit., pp. 8–9.

100. Ibid., pp. 9–10.

101. Ibid., p. 10.

102. Erik Andersen, "Ringe: A New Maximum Security Prison for Young Men and Women in Denmark," in *Confinement in Maximum Custody*, edited by David Ward and Kenneth Schoen (Lexington, Mass.: Lexington Books, 1981), pp. 159–73; "The State Prison at Ringe: Europe's Most Radical Corrections Experiment," *Corrections Magazine* 3 (March 1977): 30–33.

103. "Co-ed Institutions," *Corrections Compendium*, (Lincoln, Nebr.: CONtact, April 1983), p. 4.

104. David Anderson, "Co-Corrections," *Corrections Magazine* 4 (September 1978): 33–36.

105. Judith Resnik, "Should Prisoners Be Classified by Sex?" in *Criminal Corrections: Ideals and Realities*, edited by Jameson Doig (Lexington, Mass.: Lexington Books, 1982), pp. 110–12.

106. Anderson, op. cit., p. 34; "Co-ed Institutions," p. 1.

107. Anderson, op. cit., pp. 38–39; Resnik, op. cit., pp. 109–10, 118–20; Joan Potter, "Women's Work?" *Corrections Magazine* 5 (September 1979): 43–60.

108. Anderson, op. cit., pp. 36–40; Barry Rubak, "The Sexually Integrated Prison," in *Coed Prison*, edited by John Smykla (New York: Human Sciences Press, 1980), pp. 43–45.

109. Anderson, loc. cit.; Ruback, loc. cit.

110. Anderson, op. cit., pp. 38–39; Potter, op. cit., pp. 43–60; Resnik, op. cit., pp. 118–20.

111. "Co-ed Institutions," p. 1.

112. Joellen Lambiotte, "Sex-Role Differentiation in a Co-correctional Setting," in *Coed Prisons*, edited by John Smykla (New York: Human Sciences Press, 1980), pp. 224–26; James Ross and Esther Heffernan, "Women in a Coed Joint," in *Coed Prison*, edited by John Smykla (New York: Human Sciences Press, 1980), pp. 255, 260; Jacqueline Crawford, "Two Losers Don't Make a Winner: The Case Against the Co-Correctional Institution," in *Coed Prison*, edited by John Smykla (New York: Human Sciences Press, 1980), pp. 262–68.

113. Lambiotte, op. cit., pp. 225–26; Crawford, op. cit., pp. 262–68; Esther Heffernen and Elizabeth Krippel, "A Coed Prison," in *Coed Prison*, edited by John Smykla (New York: Human Sciences Press, 1980), pp. 118–19.

114. Heffernan and Krippel, loc. cit.

115. Lambiotte, op. cit., pp. 225, 227.

116. Ross and Heffernan, op. cit., pp. 254–55.

117. Letter from Janice W. Cummings, superintendent, Albion Correctional Facility, Albion, New York, November 21, 1983.

118. Lambiotte, op. cit., pp. 232–33.

119. "Co-ed Institutions," pp. 1–5.

120. Ross and Heffernan op. cit., pp. 253–54; Ruback, op. cit., pp. 48–49.

121. Interview with Dr. Esther Heffernan, chairperson, Social Science Department, Edgewood College, Madison, Wisconsin, March 30, 1984. Dr. Heffernan conducted research studies at the federal cocorrectional facility at Fort Worth, Texas, and at the Alaska Division of Corrections. She proposed the concept of a coordinate prison.

122. Ruback, op. cit., p. 49.

123. Ross and Heffernan, op. cit., p. 255.

124. Laurel Rans and Katherine Gabel-Strickland, "Evaluation of Co-Correctional Institutions for Adults," October 1976, p. 8.

125. Interview with Heffernan, March 30, 1984.

126. Ibid.; Esther Heffernan, "Women Offenders in the Alaska Criminal Justice System," report submitted to the Division of Corrections, State of Alaska, July 15, 1979.

127. Interview with Heffernan, March 30, 1984.

128. Charles F. Campbell, "Shared Resources," report on coordinate prisons in Alaska prepared for the Division of Adult Corrections, July 1982, p. 1. Charles Campbell was the first superintendent of the Federal Correctional Institution at Fort Worth, Texas, 1971–73.

129. Ibid., pp. 1–2.

130. Ibid., p. 2.

PART III

WOMEN PROFESSIONALS

Laws and customs which disable women from full participation in the political, business and economic arenas are often characterized as "protective" and "beneficial." These same laws and customs applied to racial and ethnic minorities would readily be recognized as invidious and impermissible. The pedestal upon which women have been placed has all too often, upon closer inspection, been revealed as a cage. We conclude that sexual classifications are properly treated as suspect, particularly when those classifications are made with respect to a fundamental interest such as employment.

(*Sail'er Inn, Inc.* v. *Kirby*, 5. Cal. 3d. 1, 485 p.2d 529 [1971].)

4

WOMEN IN
LAW ENFORCEMENT

On September 27, 1984, in New York City, more than 3,500 police officers attended the funeral of Irma Lozada, the first female police officer killed on duty in the city's history. On September 21, she had been shot in the head, with her own gun, by a male robbery suspect she was chasing. William McKechnie, head of the Transit Police union, commented:

> She was one of the guys when it came to working. She was out there to do the job and the fact that she was a woman was not in the forefront, because she did the job of a cop. . . . Some people are reluctant to work with females. Not with her . . . . She was respected as a police officer—and that's the highest compliment I can pay anybody.[1]

Despite McKechnie's statement about the professionalism of Lozada, the fact that a woman police officer had been killed while apprehending a suspect rekindled the ongoing debate over the proper role for women in law enforcement.

Women began to enter police work in the late nineteenth and early twentieth centuries, in response to the increase in social problems involving women and girls, problems that were beyond the interest or ability of men to deal with. Fundamental changes in urban life, especially the impact of immigration and industrialization, vastly increased the number of females among the homeless, the poor, and the unemployed. The nineteenth century saw a steady and marked rise in the arrest and incarceration rates of women and girls for prostitution, disorderly conduct, drunkenness, and vagrancy. As the incidence of crime by females increased, a need was felt for some sort of womanly presence in the police station to help these fallen females regain respectable places in their homes and communities. Eventually this presence was extended to the scene of the crime or arrest, and by the 1970s women had been integrated into police work, facing all the dangers inherent in the job, even death.

HISTORICAL BACKGROUND

As early as 1820, women had begun to replace clergymen as leaders in the crusade against sexual sin. By 1838 there were approximately 250 local groups of the Female Moral Reform Society in cities in the Northeast. By the end of the century, the Women's Prison Association, the Women's Christian Temperance Union, and other women's groups had entered the reform crusade. Although they were concerned with homeless and drunken women, their prime interest centered on eliminating prostitution.[2]

By the mid nineteenth century, prostitution had increased drastically, partly due to conditions resulting from the Civil War and partly from increased poverty, particularly among the urban immigrant and black populations. During the Civil War, women were attracted to the military zones for financial reasons. Many war widows were left homeless, without any means of support. Some became prostitutes, as did a growing number of poor women in the cities.[3]

In the 1860s there were 500 brothels in Chicago, filled with thousands of poor young women. In New York City there were an estimated 6,000 prostitutes; most of them were poor, young immigrants. There were guides to the brothels in New York City, Philadelphia, Baltimore, Washington, D.C., Boston, and Chicago. Since these guides listed only the upper-class brothels, the actual number of houses and prostitutes can never be known.[4]

By the early twentieth century, prostitution, as well as drunkenness and vagrancy, had become the major reasons for the arrest and incarceration of women. Reformers were eager both to convert sexual sinners to morality, and to protect arrested and incarcerated women from physical and sexual abuse. They were also concerned about the thousands of homeless women who were housed temporarily in police stationhouses each year. They urged local governments to hire police matrons to supervise women in the stationhouses and recommended separation of incarcerated persons by sex.[5]

In 1845, one year after the creation of the New York City Police Department, the Women's Prison Association and the American Female Moral Reform Society succeeded, against much opposition, in persuading the city to hire six matrons to supervise sentenced and detained girls and women in the jails. It was the first time a U.S. municipality had hired matrons, and it set a precedent. In Portland, Maine, for example, members of the Women's Christian Temperance Union had been accustomed to visit women in jails and detention centers, and accompanied them to court to protect them from abuse by men. They regarded this service so highly that they hired and paid women "visitors" to perform these functions. The Women's Christian Temperance Union and other women's organizations encouraged the city to provide the funds for the "visitors"; in 1878 Portland hired police matrons.[6]

However, there was much oppostion to having women as police matrons in the stationhouses. Police departments and men's reform groups argued that the women would be "contaminated and demoralized by contact with such depraved creatures" as prostitutes, vagrants, and alcoholics; certainly no "decent, sober, respectable women" would take the job.[7] The reformers, arguing that police matrons were necessary to prevent sexual abuse and attacks upon arrested and incarcerated women by policemen and male prisoners, and to protect young girls and first offenders from hardened women criminals, pressed for full-time positions for police matrons. The national, state, and local chapters of the Federation of Women's Clubs, the Young Women's Christian Association, the Women's Christian Temperance Union, and local Protective Leagues for Women and Girls addressed themselves to the need for women in law enforcement. Support for their position was given by President Rutherford B. Hayes at the 1886 National Conference of Charities and Corrections.[8]

By 1885 there were police matrons in 11 other cities; in 1888 New York and Massachusetts passed laws requiring cities with a population of over 20,000 to hire police matrons to supervise arrested and detained women. These were political appointees, and it was not uncommon for a woman to be hired upon the death of her policeman husband. Such was the case with Marie Owen. In 1893, after the death of her husband, the mayor of Chicago appointed her to the detective bureau. During her 30-year tenure her duties were those traditionally reserved for women; she worked with women and children, visiting courts and assisting men detectives in cases dealing with women and children.[9]

The police matron movement coincided with the professionalization of social work, and many women applied social work concepts and methods to their matron duties. They conducted interviews and wrote case histories; they went to court and made recommendations regarding sentences based on their case studies. In effect, they acted as probation officers to the court, and in reality many were so appointed. As probation officers to women released by the courts, they counseled them and assisted them in acquiring clothing, housing, and employment.[10]

By the end of the nineteenth century, many reformers, recognizing the need for women with full police powers to work outside the stationhouse, began pushing for appointment of women professionals who would work in the streets with prostitutes, runaways, and delinquents. The first steps were taken in Portland, Oregon, in 1905. During the Lewis and Clark Exposition, Lola Baldwin, secretary of the Travelers' Aid Society, was hired to protect women and girls from the miners, lumberjacks, and laborers attending the event, and to prevent the women and girls from approaching the men. Baldwin, called a "safety worker," was empowered to arrest men and women for illegal acts (although it was the women and girls who were arrested for prostitution, and the girls who were detained for being runaways).[11]

After the exposition, Portland's city government gave official approval to her work by organizing the Department of Public Safety for the Protection of

Young Girls and Women. Baldwin was appointed director. Neither she nor the police department wanted women to be called "policewomen," because neither wished to associate women with the concept or job of policemen. The women, called "operatives" or "safety workers," considered themselves social service workers. The fact that Baldwin held her post throughout the administrations of five mayors and six chiefs of police indicates that she was well thought of, did a good job, and did not go beyond her assigned task.[12]

Her career was typical for women who pioneered in law enforcement. She worked for a social reform organization that focused on protecting and caring for women and children; when she transferred from the organization to the police department, she kept the role of social worker for women and children. She did not see herself as a "cop."

POLICEWOMEN: THEORY AND PRACTICE

The title of policewoman first went to Alice Stebbins Wells in Los Angeles in 1910. Wells, a graduate of a theological seminary, was a social worker who dealt with women and children in trouble with the law. She believed that if a woman was invested with police powers, she could be of more help than if she worked through a private reform or charity agency. Accordingly, she acquired the signatures of 100 people in reform and social work, and asked the mayor to appoint her as a policewoman with full powers of policing. On September 13, 1910, she was appointed.[13]

Her appointment received wide publicity and elicited comments both favorable and hostile. She was caricatured in the press as an unfeminine, muscular woman wearing glasses, her hair in a bun, and carrying a gun. Policemen did not want her, nor did they know what to do with her. On the other hand, the idea of having someone in policing dedicated to helping women and children brought praise from many women's groups.[14]

Wells believed that a woman performed a special task in policing, she:

> . . . engages public interest in police crime prevention and commits police departments to it as a recognized and growing part of police duty. . . . As there existed inherently, though unfilled, a real place for women police officers, without whom a protective work for women, children and the home could not be developed, both the public and the Police Department accepted the innovation as right and needful.[15]

Her concept of the role of women in policing was the accepted one until the 1960s. Wells and subsequent policewomen espoused the prevention/protection theory. Their primary function was to prevent women and children from becoming victims of crime. They focused on women and children, and they operated in a separate women's bureau within the police department. They acquired their positions as policewomen and were accepted by police departments and communities because of their stated theory and focus, and because they carried out their duties effectively.

Their success was the start of a nationwide movement to hire policewomen in all police departments. Wells spoke to women's and civic groups in 75 cities throughout the country, urging the hiring of policewomen. Although not all police departments heeded her urgent request, by 1915 at least 25 cities had hired full-time paid policewomen. In 1912, Isabella Goodwin of the New York City Police Department became the first female detective. A reform mayor in Milford, Ohio, appointed Dolly Spencer chief of police in 1914, a position she held for two years, leading a crusade against gambling.[16]

World War I was a turning point for career policewomen. Mobilization resulted in the concentration of large groups of men—mostly young men away from home for the first time—and brought about an increase in the number of women and girls attracted to servicemen for patriotic, romantic, and financial reasons. The government created zones around military bases where houses of prostitution and sale of alcohol were forbidden and, along with private agencies, funded local reform committees that organized to protect servicemen, and to detain and supervise prostitutes and runaways. The women working on these protective committees were given police powers: they went out on patrol, supervising public places where women and girls could congregate and get into trouble, such as transportation depots, amusement areas, and rooming houses; they supervised detention centers for arrested women and girls; and they acted as probation officers. By the end of 1918, 198 women were involved in such protective work. One of them, Ellen O'Grady, became the first woman administrator in a police department when she was appointed deputy police commissioner in charge of the welfare bureau in the New York City Police Department in 1918. As a former probation officer with years of experience working with delinquent females, she implemented the protection and prevention theory in dealing with women and children.[17]

After World War I policewomen were at work in more than 220 cities, usually in separate women's bureaus. Their duties focused on specialized areas: juvenile delinquency, female victims of sex offenses, women criminal suspects, abandoned infants, missing persons, vice squads, matron duty, and clerical work. A few women were assigned to high-risk jobs in detective bureaus that involved investigating and apprehending persons suspected of being involved in vice, gambling, and organized crime. As a rule policewomen received lower salaries than men, had to meet stricter qualifying standards, got little or no training, and were seldom promoted except to detective and then only to do special undercover work that required a woman.[18]

The story of New York City's policewomen provides a good case study of the experiences women faced when they first entered the field of law enforcement. The New York City Police Department (NYPD) has had the largest number of policewomen and has kept annual reports that date from the end of the nineteenth century. In addition, many NYPD policewomen have written books and articles on their work.

When World War I ended, women reformers continued to believe in the importance of having women as official members of the NYPD in a position to help women and children. They therefore lobbied in the state legislature for a law that would permanently establish the position of policewoman in New York City. The legislature passed such a law in 1920. The first civil service examination for policewomen took place the following year, and on June 13, 1921, 25 women graduated from the new training school for policewomen at the Women's Precinct on 34th Street.[19]

A policewoman had to be a U.S. citizen between 21 and 35 years of age, have a high school diploma, and pass written, oral, and physical examinations. Experience in probation reform work with women and minors, teaching, or nursing was desirable. She would earn $1,769 a year, and her duties would involve the "moral protection of women and minors, the prevention of delinquency among women and minors, and the performance of such other duties as the Police Commissioner may assign."[20] In contrast, the civil service requirements for policemen mentioned neither education nor work experience, nor did they specify a job focus.

Opposition to policewomen had been based on the rationale that a self-respecting woman would not want to work with debauched women and criminals. However, the motivations and efforts of policewomen, appointed on a temporary war emergency basis, and the status of women who became police officers during the war and after the passage of the 1920 law, caused the opposition to ebb. Of the 25 women who graduated in 1921, all were white, middle-class high school or college graduates, and most were married; many had had careers in social work, probation, or education; and most of them participated as volunteers in social reform organizations. Several had been members of the war emergency group of policewomen in 1918. Adele Priess, one of the 1918 group, had graduated from Hunter College, had taught elementary school, and was a close friend of Theodore Roosevelt. The first director of NYPD Bureau of Women, Mary E. Hamilton, came from a wealthy family and had graduated from the New York School of Social Work.

Although these women were nontraditional in the careers they sought, they were traditional in background and in their reasons for becoming policewomen. They believed their roles in law enforcement to be that of social service, to protect women and children from becoming delinquents or victims of crimes. They became social welfare mothers to wayward and misguided women and children. In her book about her experiences in the NYPD, Mary

Hamilton wrote that "only a motherly policewoman" could offer help and advice to runaways, delinquents, and women in trouble.[21]

In 1921, the separate Bureau of Women was established so that policewomen could carry out their special tasks. At first the bureau was located in an abandoned stationhouse, physically separate from any police station. Called the Women's Precinct, it was in a poverty-stricken, high-crime area known as Hell's Kitchen. The women transformed the "dingy dirty rat hole" into a clean, decorated center that had a clubhouse atmosphere. They provided a hospitable place for troubled women and children to get help from other women, and a place to detain runaway girls. The precinct, wrote Hamilton, was the "very essence of the principles for which the modern policewomen should stand."[22]

Policewomen also went on patrol, usually in plain clothes rather than in uniform, watching women, girls, and children especially, in order to protect them from harm. Hamilton believed it was particularly important to save runaway girls, because "every girl whether good or bad is a potential mother and in her rests the hope of the next generation . . . ."[23]

The Women's Precinct closed after a short time in part for political reasons, but also because the legality of detaining women and girls in the Women's Precinct was questioned. The Bureau of Women was transferred to police headquarters and women were assigned to police precincts to act as matrons if women or children were being held, or for specific assignments.

The experiences of the policewomen in other municipalities were similar to those in the NYPD. However, federal law enforcement agencies did not hire women, nor did most state agencies. Women began to work for state police departments in 1930, when Massachusetts hired them; Connecticut followed in 1943. In both states they continued to work in special situations dealing with women and children. In federal law enforcement agencies and in states and cities with no policewomen of their own, such women were borrowed from the nearest jurisdiction or hired from private agencies, such as the Pinkerton Detective Agency.[24]

Meanwhile, there had appeared a nationally recognized professional organization to represent policewomen in their dealings with policemen, and to bring their case to the attention of government and the public. In 1915 Alice Stebbins Wells, the first policewoman, organized the International Association of Police Women (IAPW) and became its first president. The association quickly received the approval of the International Association of Chiefs of Police (IACP), whose president, Richard Sylvester, offered his assistance; in fact, the IACP constitution was used as a model for the women's organization.[25]

As the official voice of policewomen across the country, the IAPW pressed for giving women a separate status within police work, so that they could concentrate on the specialized tasks of social service and protection/prevention. It noted that women tended to perform certain types of police work, and gave as an example the activities of some Chicago policewomen: returning runaway girls to their homes, warning them of danger from men and loose women, suppressing petty gambling in stores frequented by children, eliminating "dance hall evils" and the sale of alcohol to minors, patrolling railroad depots for runaways and kidnapped children, and securing evidence or conducting investigations in crimes involving women or children.[26]

The IAPW also began to survey police departments to obtain information on the exact situation of policewomen across the country. The first survey was conducted in 1919–20 by the newly elected president, Lt. Mina van Winkle, director of the Women's Bureau of the Washington, D.C., Police Department. Since many departments did not cooperate in the survey, the results were incomplete; for example, New York City, with the largest number of police matrons, did not respond.[27] At least 146 cities had either police matrons or policewomen, and some had both; salaries ranged from $900 to $2,100 a year. A second survey, conducted in 1925, based on replies from 210 cities, revealed that there were at least 355 police matrons and 395 policewomen, and 22 women who did both jobs; the salaries ranged from $780 to $2,460 a year. The 1925 survey indicated that women were now firmly rooted in careers in policing. Later surveys by other organizations revealed gradual increases in the number of policewomen: there were approximately 1,534 in 1930, 1,775 in 1940, 2,610 in 1950, 5,617 in 1960, 11,234 in 1970, and 19,750 in 1980; almost all worked in large urban centers.[28]

By 1950, the special function of policewomen was recognized and accepted by men in law enforcement; their function was to work with women and children in a social service role. As Alice Wells wrote of the theory of police work:

> But we women, and men, who are interested in crime prevention, look more hopefully to the entrance of women into the police field . . . because it first centered and continuously engages public interest in police crime prevention and commits police departments to it as a recognized and growing part of police duty.[29]

Like Lola Baldwin in Portland, the women considered themselves social workers, not "cops," and believed they could influence police departments to alter their function from arrest and punishment to prevention and protection. They argued that women were by nature better suited to deal with women and children, that arrested women had the right to have women officers to talk to, and that only women should interview, search, and supervise women and children.

This social service role spilled over into working with juveniles. Many police departments set up separate juvenile divisions, and usually assigned women to work with young delinquents. Women used the tools of counseling and casework rather than punishment. Discussing this role, Mary Hamilton said that women would provide "the strong arm of the law as it is expressed in a woman's guiding hand."[30] She advised counseling rather than arrest, to avoid stigmatizing the young. However, policewomen must not be soft and easy with young girls and women. As mothers of the next generation, female offenders were considered a potential danger to society. Hamilton felt that these young girls and women had to be trained as moral homemakers, and that policewomen were obligated to perform that task.[31]

Equating police work with social work facilitated the acceptance of women as professionals; they neither competed with men nor claimed the same goals and duties. Rather, women articulated the idea that they were different from men, and thus could perform certain tasks better than men because those tasks fit their natural capacities and tendencies. Thus policewomen were accepted by men in police departments, by the public, and by social reformers. In 1919, for example, Richard Enright, commissioner of police in New York City, said he considered their work an "absolute necessity" in matters concerning women and children.[32] Louis Brownlow, a reformer, said that policewomen were social workers with a "devotion to mankind."[33] He believed that women would raise the morals and standards of police departments.

To be sure, policewomen also went on patrol upon occasion, but invariably in capacities that were consistent with their presumed natural abilities. They were used most frequently as decoys in investigations of rape, abortion, and prostitution. Until the 1960s, women's role in policing remained unchanged. Most of their work continued to be performed in the stationhouses and central headquarters, and continued to focus on women and children. Policewomen performed matron duties: searching, questioning, guarding, and escorting women and children to and from courts. They searched women who were dead on arrival at the stationhouses or in a hospital. When babies or children were lost or had to be taken to courts or shelters, policewomen cared for them and took them wherever necessary.[34]

But changes were taking place in the nation that would significantly transform the role of women in law enforcement. In 1938, in the midst of the depression, over 5,000 women applied to take the civil service examination to fill 29 vacancies for policewomen in New York City. These women wanted jobs and incomes. They were not typical of the middle- and upper-class reformers who originally became policewomen, although they were as well educated. The 29 positions were filled by 1942. In 1956, a newly formed organization, the International Association of Women Police (IAWP), replaced the International Association of Police Women (which had been disbanded during the depression). Along with the new name, many women in the IAWP espoused new goals for women in law enforcement.[35]

DISCRIMINATION

Traditional tasks were accepted by many policewomen, who perceived themselves as social workers more skilled and intelligent than policemen. They also enjoyed more regular hours and usually worked during the day. But there were severe restrictions on opportunities for those women. The number of women in police departments was kept low by quotas, usually 1 percent, and by job requirements that were higher for them than for men (a high school diploma and often college education, and work experience were required). In New York City, educational requirements for men were not stated in civil service announcements until 1955.[36]

Because policewomen did women's work, they were trained differently from policemen and did not follow the same course of promotions. In 1952 several New York City policewomen applied to take the competitive examination for the rank of sergeant, but were refused because, according to the civil service job description, the only rank and grade for women was that of policewoman. In 1961 policewoman Felicia Shpritzer applied to take the examination. She too was refused by the Civil Service Commission, but this time the matter went to court.[37]

Policewoman Shpritzer had made a career of law enforcement work. In 1938, when she found that her B.A. and M.A. degrees were no help in getting a job, an experience shared by many men and women during the depression, she along with some 240 other college graduates, took the examination for the police department. She entered in 1942 and, like most college-educated policewomen, was assigned to the Juvenile Aid Division. There she became friendly with Gertrude Schimmel, a Phi Beta Kappa from Hunter College who had entered the department in 1940 because she could not find a teaching job. She and Shpritzer served in the Juvenile Aid Division, where they waited more than 20 years for their first promotion. They watched many of the men who entered with them in the early 1940s receive promotions and move on to higher salaries and benefits, larger pensions, and jobs with greater status and responsibility. Schimmel later observed: "The veterans among us also knew that to have been deprived of the right to promotion through the years was a grievous, irreparable injury. There would be no restitution for the tremendous career losses that had been sustained."[38]

Their waiting was finally rewarded in 1961, when Shpritzer's suit against the commissioner of civil service (*Shpritzer* v. *Lang*) was decided in her favor. Nevertheless, the city and the police department denied her right to promotion while they appealed the case. In 1962 an appellate court voted in favor of Shpritzer, but the city and police still refused to budge. Finally, in 1963, another appellate court voted in favor of Shpritzer, and the police and city relented. It had taken 2 years, 3 court cases, and 13 judges to convince them that women deserved an equal right to promotion. In 1964 Shpritzer and Schimmel took the examination for sergeant and passed.[39]

As sergeants, Shpritzer and Schimmel were assigned to take turns supervising the women in the Bureau of Policewomen. They continued in this position even after passing the promotion examination for lieutenant, and Schimmel worked there even when, in 1971, she became the first woman captain in police history. Late in 1971 Schimmel made history again when she became the first woman to be named deputy inspector, the highest uniformed position in the department.[40]

Commissioner Patrick Murphy, who had entered the department in 1940, at the same time as Schimmel, ceased to talk to Shpritzer and Schimmel after they became sergeants, and never truly accepted women as equals in the department. In his book *Commissioner: A View from the Top of American Law Enforcement,* he wrote: "My pet wish is to pass over as quickly as possible the demonstration that women officers can do everything as well as men (et cetera, et cetera) and move to a more intelligent level of discussion and personnel deployment where women are used for the special capabilities they possess."[41] Their promotion was greeted more positively in 1967 by the new commissioner of police, Howard Leary, who considered the women extremely bright, capable, and tough.[42]

In large part, the victories of Shpritzer and Schimmel were possible because during the 1960s, Congress and the federal courts gave legal form to the great movements for civil rights. Title VII of the Civil Rights Act of 1964 prohibited sex-based discrimination in labor unions and nongovernment employment. In 1971, the U.S. Supreme Court, in *Reed* v. *Reed,* declared that any state law discriminating on the basis of sex violates the "equal protection clause" of the Fourteenth Amendment. This decision was reinforced in 1973, in *Frontiero* v. *Richardson,* when the U.S. Supreme Court decided that sex, like race, is a characteristic that must be justified if used as a classification of people for legislative purposes. In 1972, Title VII of the Civil Rights Act was amended to extend the regulatory powers of the Equal Employment Opportunity Commission to cover all government agencies; the commission is required to examine discriminatory practices in public as well as private employment. The commission is also empowered to enforce the Equal Pay Act of 1963, which prohibits discrimination on the basis of sex in payment for services.[43]

More legislation followed. The Crime Control Acts of 1973 and 1976 amended the Omnibus Crime Control and Safe Streets Act of 1968, which had created the Law Enforcement Assistance Administration (LEAA), the funding agency in the Department of Justice; LEAA provided financial assistance for improving law enforcement agencies in the nation. Approximately 40,000 police departments, courts, and correctional facilities received nearly $1 billion each year from LEAA. The Crime Control Act of 1973 prohibited discrimination against women in employment situations in any agency receiving LEAA aid. The Crime Control Act of 1976 prohibited LEAA from funding any agency on a local, state, or federal level that discriminated against women or other designated groups, and directed that if these practices were found, LEAA funds had to be terminated.[44]

Although LEAA and its enforcement powers came to an end in 1983, the power to terminate funds continues to be authorized under other legislation. The 1972 Revenue Sharing Act authorizes the Office of Revenue Sharing of the U.S. Department of the Treasury to stop the flow of revenue-sharing funds to any jurisdiction that engages in discriminatory practices. The Justice Systems Improvement Act of 1979 calls for the withholding of funds by the Office of Justice Assistance, Research and Statistics from any agency that uses the funds in a discriminatory manner. On October 31, 1978, the Pregnancy Discrimination Act amended Title VII, prohibiting discrimination on the basis of pregnancy, childbirth, or related medical conditions. Employers are to treat pregnancy like any other temporary disability in providing employment benefits.[45]

Women could now enter law enforcement agencies on all three levels of government. They could step beyond traditional roles for women in policing, and could apply for all positions and receive the same salaries, promotion opportunities, and benefits as men. Several hundred women received promotions to sergeant, lieutenant, captain, or deputy inspector, and were assigned to supervise men and women. Between 1968 and 1984, the number of women on patrol increased from approximately a dozen to thousands. Although several municipalities had assigned women to patrol in the 1960s, the Indianapolis Police Department became the first to do so formally in 1968. After nine years of pressure, Betty Blankenship and Elizabeth Coffal were assigned to "Car 47." At first male officers and dispatchers were reluctant to send them on field assignments. However, by 1972, they had proved that women could do the job as well as men. Furthermore, the public accepted them; women complainants preferred to talk to female police officers. Therefore, in 1972, eight more women officers were assigned to patrol duty; all ten were assigned on an equal basis with men.[46] In that same year, Washington, D.C., became the first municipality to deploy a significant number of women on patrol; 86 were so assigned.[47]

In 1972, New York City responded to the combination of legal, moral, and financial pressures by hiring and training women for patrol duty. The Civil Service Commission gave the first unisex examination for the position of police officer in 1983, and by 1984 there were over 700 women in the NYPD. Men and women now take the same examination; participate in the same training programs; are assigned from a single eligibility list, on an equal basis, to precincts and to patrol duty; and they are promoted according to the same standards. Women are now with special service bureaus that were once considered to be for men only, such as the homicide division, and in 1976 Captain Vittoria Renzullo became the first woman to be in charge of a police precinct. As of December 31, 1984, the NYPD had 1,798 female and 18,198 male officers, and 131 female and 2,586 male detectives—an increase from approximately 1 percent women in 1940, to 2 percent in 1979, to 10 percent at the end of 1984.[48]

Also in 1972, Pennsylvania became the first state to give men and women state troopers identical duties. Other states followed, and by 1984 all except South Dakota and Wyoming (only Hawaii did not appear on the *Uniform Crime Reports* list) had women as officers in their state police forces, approximately 1,113 (1.5 percent) of 68,357 state police officers.[49] On the federal level, once the Civil Service Commission ruled in 1971 that women could carry firearms, women became officers in the Executive Protective Service, the Secret Service, the Federal Bureau of Investigation, the Alcohol and Firearms Administration, the Drug Enforcement Administration, and other law enforcement agencies.

Since 1972 women have been integrated into law enforcement agencies throughout the nation. However, the degree of integration depends on whether departments voluntarily accepted women or were forced to accept them because of pressure from the legislature or the courts. Police Foundation studies of various cities in 1970 and 1974 showed that women could perform assigned tasks, including patrol, but that there remained "a significant amount of prejudice against women within police departments."[50]

Case studies in 1970 and 1974 indicated that although women were hired and assigned to patrol work, they were not really accepted by men in the departments. According to the 1970-71 Police Foundation survey of 60 of the largest police departments in the nation and in-depth analysis of 7 cities (Philadelphia, New York, Miami, Peoria, Dallas, Washington, D.C., and Indianapolis), most police departments had quotas of less than 1 percent for women, and the women had to meet higher educational standards than men. Women also had to meet weight, height, and physical examination standards based on those for men. Often there were separate examinations and separate hiring lists for women, and sometimes they could be hired only if a woman's slot was vacant. Once hired, they received little or no training. Special investigatory assignments usually involved vice, juveniles, or female victims of sex crimes, and the clerical work load was heavy. The 1974 Police Foundation report showed little change in the nature of these assignments. Often women were placed in separate bureaus.[51]

Information on the status of women in law enforcement since 1979 indicates that discrimination continues to exist, but it is more covert and subtle. The 1981 Police Foundation study updated the 1970 and 1974 studies of the progress of women in policing. The foundation reported that as of 1979, women composed 3.38 percent of sworn officers in municipal departments and

1.02 percent of sworn officers in state police departments. Discriminatory practices had diminished; the same eligibility requirements, selection process, and training programs applied to both men and women. However, problems continued to exist. Maximum age requirements, usually between 30 and 34 years old, negatively affected women, who as a group tended to be older than men when seeking careers in law enforcement. Women generally did better on written and physical examinations and on background investigations than did men, but minority women did less well in each area than white women. Even though women did better on average than men in examinations, the subjective oral interviews provided opportunities for discriminatory selection of officers, a practice that may account for the disproportionate number of rejections of women applicants. Also, not all jurisdictions assigned women to patrol duties on an equal basis with men.[52]

According to the study, the most serious problem involved promotions. Although the percentage of women in police work increased from 1.5 percent in 1972 to 3.38 percent in 1979, only a very small percentage of women were in supervisory positions and ranks; women accounted for 1.69 percent of municipal officers and 0.29 percent of state officers in a rank above police officer. Several factors may account for these percentages: the small number of women in law enforcement, compared with men; the fact that the majority of women have been hired since 1972 and few have seniority; and the continued practice of assigning women officers to secretarial duties, to juvenile divisions, and to special tasks such as guarding and searching female offenders, and dealing with rape victims. The study concluded that the "greatest challenge for women in policing in the eighties is to overcome barriers to promotion and obtain a significant proportion of supervisory and policy-making positions in police departments."[53]

The limited progress made by women in law enforcement is a result, in part, of continued covert and overt resistance by their male colleagues. One of the reasons most frequently cited by male officers for their reluctance to have women on patrol is the fear that women are simply not strong enough for the job. In such physical duty, men argue, women are vulnerable to being overpowered and injured, perhaps even raped; and the efforts of male officers to assist them would limit the effectiveness of the men. In a 1977 study of a class in the Michigan State Police Academy, it was found that although the women passed the course, which included physical training, and were respected by the men, they were considered by the men not to be strong enough physically to be desirable as duty partners.[54]

Aside from the degree to which the physical strength issue may affect confidence in women's ability, the strength and agility examinations required by all police departments have formed major barriers to the entrance of women recruits. Local and state training academies in New Jersey, for example, conducted physical agility courses that included running, jumping, shooting, boxing, judo, walking a balance beam, and dragging a 180-pound dummy for 50 feet against the stopwatch. Although the state police agreed in 1975 to hire women and minority members, by 1979 only two women had passed the physical agility course and become state troopers.[55]

It is not uncommon for local police departments either to introduce physical agility tests or, in the name of unisex policy, to revise their tests to make them more difficult for women to pass. For example, Toni Plantamura, who ran 70 miles a week and was in excellent physical condition, received a grade of 58 on the newly revised Paramus (New Jersey) Police Department physical agility test and a grade of 96 on the civil service written examination. Although she headed the civil service list, she was not hired by the department because she failed the physical agility test. The mayor explained that there was no law that you have to hire "No. 1."[56]

Many doubted that a woman would be hired by the Trenton (New Jersey) Police Department because of its revised physical agility test. The only woman on the force until the 1980s, Emily Bacovin, retired in 1979 after 37 years on the force, the last eight years as a detective in the Youth Division of the Criminal Investigations Unit. Actually, she had been doing the same work for years as a policewoman; her main assignment was to work with children. No woman replaced her for several years because the requirements established under the new policy made the physical agility test too difficult for women. However, three women succeeded by 1984, and were assigned to patrol duty on an equal basis with the 355 men in the department.[57]

Related to the issues of strength and agility have been the minimum limits on height and weight required by almost all departments. Early in 1979, Judge Shirley M. Hufstedler of the Ninth U.S. Circuit Court of Appeals wrote the decision that successfully ended a six-year suit brought against the Los Angeles Police Department (LAPD) by Sgt. Franchon Blake and other women to end certain practices that discriminated against women. The LAPD had to eliminate height and weight requirements and all gender-based job classifications.[58]

The situation in Los Angeles was repeated in most city and state law enforcement agencies. In 1978, Penelope Brace, a veteran of 15 years on the Philadelphia police force, won her lawsuit against the city and became the first woman detective in the city's history. The police department, with the support of Mayor Frank Rizzo, the former commissioner of police, had refused to promote her in 1976 after she passed the examination. The department attempted to intimidate her by trying to put her back on foot patrol, claiming that all detectives had to have that experience. Despite police claims that "big cops" are needed to deter crime, Brace won her case. One reason Philadelphia and Los Angeles complied with the Brace and Blake decisions was that, in both cases, the U.S. Department of Justice also sued for violation of the federal law prohibiting the allocation of federal funds through LEAA to any government agency that violated legislation prohibiting sex discrimination. In the Brace case, the Justice Department was withholding $4 million in LEAA grants from Philadelphia.[59]

Nevertheless, the Philadelphia Police Department (PPD) continued to discriminate against other women, and on July 15, 1980, the U.S. Department of Justice obtained a consent order that required the city to pay $700,000 to 96 women who had been denied either employment or promotions by the PPD. In addition, the PPD had to hire women for 30 percent of the next 2,670 police officer vacancies, and to promote women to the next 16 detective and the next 17 sergeant vacancies. One result of this consent order was that, in November 1980, Leslie Seymour became the first female line officer promoted to sergeant in the department. By January 1985, there were 437 female officers out of a total of 7,000 in the PPD; 3 were corporals, 13 were sergeants, 4 were lieutenants, none were captains, and 17 were detectives.[60]

Even if police departments hire women and have to promote some, they may discriminate in other, subtle ways. Women are not included in the "old boy" network, and are often ignorant of promotion and transfer opportunities, special assignments, and general gossip. In the New York City Police Department (NYPD), officers in the network who find out about the "plush" appointments and get them are called "Charley Gets." Women are excluded. In New York City, in fact, policemen fought vigorously to prevent the posting of all openings in the department. Word of mouth or locker-room posting had guaranteed that only men would hear of certain opportunities, and that women would be kept out of certain supervisory positions or special assignments. Ann Powers, president of the Policewomen's Endowment Association (PEA), spoke of the constant struggle of New York City policewomen for equal opportunity. Citing her own experiences, she related how she was sent alone on patrol in a high-crime area as punishment for demanding the right for women to go on patrol. When assigned to the polygraph division, she claimed she was given more work to do than men in order to keep her too busy to do her work as president of the PEA. However, she did persuade the department to assign a woman to the homicide division in the detective bureau, and in 1978 obtained a new contract giving policewomen the same rights and opportunities as men.[61]

Other harassments occur. When a woman is on patrol but is the only woman on the force or on duty at a given time, she is pulled off patrol duty to perform matron duties when a female is arrested. Policewomen are sent out as decoys to apprehend muggers, rapists, and soliciters of prostitutes. If the backup policemen do not like women officers and are not supportive of their role in policing, they are less likely to respond properly, and the women officers may experience physical harm before the policemen enter the action. At times, women are assigned to special duties in order to remove them from contact with other women in the department, or to punish them for demanding equal rights. Policewomen also experience sexual harassment from male officers. Each woman has to handle that situation on her own. In departments containing more than one precinct, women have to prove themselves in each precinct to which they are assigned. Sgt. Joan Pierson of the NYPD reported that it took the 12 women sergeants in the department as of January 1978, at least six months to be accepted in their precincts. Because there are so few women in each department, they tend to be transferred from one tour of duty, special assignment, or precinct to another more frequently than men. Each time a woman is transferred, she has to go through the lonely process of becoming familiar with new associates and responsibilities, and she must constantly prove her ability by working harder.[62]

Women who are trying to enter policing also have to contend with the severe budgetary restrictions that have gone into effect since 1975 in many municipalities. In New York City, funding cuts in 1975 reduced the number of women in the department from approximately 750 to 280, although by 1979 the number had increased to almost 500, and by 1984 to 1,798. The layoffs were handled on the principle of last one in, first one out. Over 500 of the 750 women, hired from the first unisex list in 1973, did not have seniority and many were still on probation; they were the first to go. The rehiring of women took a long time, more than five years. At the time of the layoffs, Deputy Chief Gertrude Schimmel reported that women in the NYPD had not made significant gains in the 38 years she had been on the force; women officers totaled a little over 2 percent in 1979, only a 1 percent increase since 1940.[63]

PERFORMANCE STUDIES

The difficulties placed in the way of women who seek to be police officers are mainly products of traditional ideas, not of objective, demonstrable shortcomings or weaknesses. Evaluations of policewomen's effectiveness on patrol have been made in five major studies: Washington, D.C., 1974; St. Louis, Missouri, 1975; California Highway Patrol, 1976; Denver, Colorado, 1977; and New York City, 1977. The reports show that women can perform the duties traditionally assigned to men and as effectively as the men. They also indicate that men are in no more danger with women as partners than with men as partners. In fact, the report on Washington, D.C., stated that the presence of women tended to prevent dangerous situations rather than to bring them on. The St. Louis study reported similar results: citizen reaction to policewomen was positive, and policewomen were perceived as being more polite and more sensitive than policemen.[64] In 1977, Glen Craig, commissioner of the California Highway Patrol, said results of a comprehensive study conducted by his department proved that men and women behaved equally well in the job: "Each male and female officer remaining on duty was performing acceptably."[65]

The most extensive report to date is one done in 1977 by the Vera Institute of Justice in New York City. It concluded that women performed as well as men: "women's 'style' of patrol was almost indistinguishable from the men's . . . citizens rated the female officers more competent, pleasant and respectful than their male counterparts. . . . there was no evidence of difference between male and female officers' behavior in the few incidents where civilians were agitated or where there were other indications of danger."[66] Perhaps equally important, the study revealed that policewomen received fewer patrol duties than men because thay had to guard women prisoners, and when they were on patrol, they were "less often assigned to ride with the same patrol partner; they therefore had less opportunity to gain knowledge of their precincts and of the ground rules for participating with a partner in patrol functions."[67] The constant shifting of policewomen from one precinct to another and from one assignment to another prevents them from becoming part of a team, and prevents policemen from understanding the strengths of their female partners.

One of these strengths is in dealing with victims of rape and battering. The victims of these assaults tend to view policemen as members of the "aggressor" group. Women officers are not viewed in this way, and are able to go into the examining room with the victim, observe firsthand the physical evidence of attack, and immediately receive from the doctor any specimens or statements about the injuries of the victim. Thus, the policewoman is able to act as a witness should the assailant be apprehended and go to trial. On the whole, women are likely to treat women victims and offenders more sympathetically; this is a matter of agreement among most researchers. Cynthia Sulton, project director of the Police Foundation's study on the role of policewomen, observes that women officers are usually willing to let prisoners with children make phone calls home.[68]

The final report on the study of women state troopers in New Jersey is being prepared. This study began in February 1980, when 104 women selected from the 1,631 applicants began 20 weeks at the New Jersey State Police Training Academy, in the first all-female state trooper training course in the nation. Of the 1,631 women, 670 passed the written examination, 116 passed the physical agility test and oral interviews, and 104 accepted the offer to participate in the training program. They ranged in age from 19 to 32 years, and 2 were black. There was a mix of single, married, and divorced women, and some were mothers. Thirty women graduated and went to work as part of the 32-female and 1,928-male state police force.[69]

The New Jersey State Police all-female class resulted from pressure by the Justice Department, starting in October 1975, to hire women and minorities by 1980. By 1979, the state police had only 2 women and 83 minority men. Of the 13 women in the class preceding the all-female class, 7 quit, 5 were injured and left, and 1 failed and was asked to leave. Finally, the state police agreed to establish the all-female class. The attrition rate of 70 percent was much higher than the 40 percent for men. During the exit interviews, several women admitted that their expectations of police work stemmed from unrealistic TV programs. Other reasons stated for dropping out included injuries; inability to cope with violence, blood, and guns; and a dislike of the military way of life. Only a few were asked to leave. A representative of the Justice Department also held exit interviews with the women, and found no discrepancies with what the state police interviewer reported.[70]

The instructors learned that several minor changes had to be made when they recognized that women had problems not experienced by the men. For example, women experienced foot injuries and falling during running-information exercises. When the instructors increased the distance between runners, the falling stopped; and when the women were authorized to wear low shoes and sneakers, foot injuries almost disappeared. The instructors and others were not able to give a reason for these differences between men and women recruits, nor a reason why the minor changes made such an obvious difference for the women. Instructors also learned that the women could handle stress, could use force, and could be trained physically to do the job. They found that menstruation proved no factor at all in training the women or in their performance. And, finally, they recognized that sexism existed, and that male state police officers and instructors had to be allowed to vent their feelings as well as to participate in classes to deal with sexist attitudes.[71]

Using the information learned from the all-female class, it was decided that subsequent classes would be coed. Women graduates have been assigned on an equal basis with the men, but many men are still skeptical about the ability of the women to do the job as well as men. At least one event gave them reason to think more realistically and less emotionally about the capacity of women troopers. Ten days after the first all-female class graduated, Trooper Cheri Kelcourse, five feet, one and a half inches, tall and weighing 105 pounds, stopped and grounded a fleeing sex offender with a flying tackle.[72]

The director of the state police, Col. Clinton Pagano, said of the women troopers: "We want to see, among other things, if they are willing to stop that suspicious car on a lonely road at night when they are all alone."[73] It would be interesting to know the proportion of male troopers who are willing to do the same thing.

THE NEW PROFESSIONALS

Obvious differences exist between the new professionals in law enforcement, the generalists, and the first generation of policewomen, the specialists. Women who entered law enforcement during the depression, such as Gertrude Schimmel and Felicia Shpritzer, and especially those who have chosen policing as careers since the 1960s, see themselves as law enforcement officers, not as social workers. They seek careers that will bring them the tangible rewards of job security, income, pensions, and other benefits, and that afford opportunities for advancement. They no longer adhere to the prevention/protection theory of Alice S. Wells, or to the mothering/nurturing role espoused by Mary Hamilton. The attitudes, career goals, and behavior of the new professionals closely resemble those of men in law enforcement.

The generalists' emphasis on integration of men and women in all aspects of law enforcement not only has changed the nature of much police work done by women but also has elicited hostile responses from many specialists and from most male officers and administrators. At the 1971 meeting of the International Association of Women Police, Sgt. Carolen Bailen of the St. Paul Police Department supported the position that specialization was too limiting and that women should participate in all aspects of law enforcement. Other officers took an opposing view and voiced regret over this change in role. Inspector Dorothy Gay of the Detroit Women's Bureau and Lois Higgins, a former Chicago juvenile officer and founder of the IAWP, saw patrol duty as a demotion from the kind of specialized work they were used to doing, and believed that women should continue to be specialists.[74]

The division between the generalists and specialists over roles and goals for women in law enforcement will soon cease to be a significant issue as more generalists join law enforcement agencies and as the specialists begin to retire. However, hostility from male colleagues will continue to exist and pose a major problem for women. They have to face overt and covert discrimination in various forms: subjective oral interviews that offer law enforcement agencies opportunities to reject female applicants for jobs and for promotions; physical agility training that may be developed to disqualify women; contested pregnancy and maternity leaves and benefits that may prevent women from keeping their jobs or may delay promotions; and sexual harassment in the form of verbal or physical abuse or rumors concerning their sexual preference or behavior.

Other problems also affect the new professionals. Increasingly tighter budgets work against women by decreasing the number of available positions. Fewer women will be hired, and the small numbers will affect their assignments. Some will be transferred from patrol duty to matron duty—that is, to search, guard, and assist in the transportation of female offenders. Only when tasks requiring the presence of female officers—such as working with juveniles, female offenders, rape victims, and decoy work in vice squads—are completed will women be assigned to patrol work. In addition, limiting the number of women hired will keep low the number of women being promoted to administrative positions. It will take years for them to accumulate the experience and seniority needed for promotions or appointments to top administrative positions.

Veterans' preference laws hinder women's opportunities for employment and promotions. However, this problem can be mitigated if law enforcement agencies wish to do so. For example, the Policewomen's Endowment Association exerted enormous pressure on the NYPD in the 1970s, and their efforts were rewarded with a union contract providing that all successful applicants for jobs or promotions who are ranked on lists that give preference to veterans must be offered positions before new examinations and new lists are prepared.

Ironically, attitudes concerning the special capacities of women operate to keep women in their traditional roles in police work, and women continue to contribute to this dilemma. Women's groups often argue that women officers should be on task forces for rape and battering victims. Police administrators may yield (with pleasure) to these pressures and assign female officers to specialized law enforcement tasks—that is, to traditional work. In other words, just as there is a call for minority men to deal with minority male offenders, there is a call for women to work with women victims and offenders. However, minority men become part of the "old boy" network, whereas women remain outsiders.

Despite these conditions, law enforcement work has an appeal for women: it offers job security, a good income and benefits, opportunities for advancement, and, for many, a challenge. Many college-educated women are attracted to state and federal law enforcement agencies, and in areas of high unemployment, they enter local police departments. These are the women, more likely than not, who seek careers leading to advancement. For women not so well educated and for educated minority women who find their racial or ethnic origins a hindrance to good employment in business and industry, police work has acquired growing attraction. In 1984, the starting salary for officers in New York City was $20,195, with benefits of pension, sick and maternity leave, and vacation time. Few jobs in the private sector offer that salary and those benefits to white or black women with only high school education and no special skills. When Marjorie L. Lewis, a veteran of 20 years in the NYPD, became the first black woman promoted to sergeant in 1971, she explained that although she had a college education, she was concerned with job security and a good salary; as a black woman she could best attain these goals in the civil service environment of police work.[75] Since 1971, many college-educated black woman have received supervisory or command positions in law enforcement agencies; in 1980, one became inspector in Washington, D.C., the highest ranking black female uniformed officer in the nation.[76] (Gertrude Schimmel of the NYPD was the first female police officer to hold that rank when she received her appointment as deputy inspector in 1971.)

Law enforcement offers women of all backgrounds opportunities for careers. Angeline (Angie) Deale, a Navajo, became an officer with the Navajo Police Department in Shiprock, New Mexico, in 1976. She became a juvenile officer in 1981 and runs the one-officer juvenile section of the department.

Because of her outstanding work with juveniles, the governor of New Mexico appointed her to the Juvenile Justice Advisory Committee in 1983. The committee is responsible for overseeing the state's juvenile justice system. In August 1984, the Navajo Police Department named Deale "officer of the year" in recognition of her important contributions to the department and to the Navajo community. She was the first Navajo police officer to receive this award. Deale, married and the mother of eight children, was pregnant with three of her children while carrying out her duties as an officer. She became a police officer because "she wanted a man's job."[77]

SUMMARY

The general picture that emerges from this examination of women in law enforcement is that after enormous effort, women have obtained significant changes in the law, many changes in practice, and little change in the outlook of most men in law enforcement. To avoid legal action by women charging sex discrimination, and the possible loss of revenue-sharing and other government funds, law enforcement agencies have been persuaded to allow women to become officers and, if necessary, to be promoted to supervisory positions.

In 1961 Felicia Shpritzer filed a lawsuit against the NYPD to gain the opportunity to take a promotion examination for sergeant, setting the example and precedent for others to follow. Since then a few women have been promoted or appointed to positions of authority and command; they have become precinct captains, deputy inspectors, detectives, and associate and deputy commissioners. In 1985 one became a chief of police.

Penny Eileen Harrington's career summarizes the recent history of women in law enforcement. In January 1985, Harrington became the first woman in the nation to head a large city's police department; the mayor appointed her chief of the 767-member Portland (Oregon) Police Bureau. She had filed numerous complaints in her ongoing struggle to end discrimination based on sex, and to end practices weighted in favor of men in the department. A college graduate, Harrington joined the bureau in 1964 and worked her way up through the ranks. She held the titles of officer, sergeant, lieutenant, precinct captain, and detective before becoming chief. Ron Smith, chief of staff for the International Association of Chiefs of Police, commented on her appointment: "It's long overdue . . . I think we'll see more of it."[78]

NOTES

1. *Star-Ledger* (Newark), September 23, 1984, p. 13; *New York Times*, September 27, 1984, p. 1.

2. David J. Pivar, *Purity Crusade: Sexual Morality and Social Control, 1868-1900* (Westport, Conn.: Greenwood Press, 1973), pp. 26-27.

3. Estelle B. Freedman, "Their Sisters' Keepers: An Historical Perspective on Female Correctional Institutions in the United States: 1870-1900," *Feminist Studies* 2 (1974): 82.

4. Pivar, op. cit., pp. 31-32.

5. Theresa M. Melchionne, "Policewomen: Their Introduction into the Police Department of the City of New York," (master's thesis, Bernard M. Baruch School of Business and Public Administration of CUNY, 1961), pp. 1-24.

6. Ibid, pp. 4-6; Chloe Owings, *Women Police: A Study of the Development and Status of the Women Police Movement* (repr. Montclair, N.J.: Patterson Smith, 1969), pp. 97-99.

7. Theresa M. Melchionne, "The Changing Role of Policewomen," in *The Ambivalent Force: Perspectives on the Police*, edited by Arthur Niederhoffer and Abraham S. Blumberg (Hinsdale, Ill.: Dryden Press, 1976), pp. 370-71.

8. Owings, op. cit., p. 97; Pivar, op. cit., p. 103.

9. Owings, op. cit., pp. 98-100.

10. Ibid., pp. 134-35.

11. Ibid., pp. 99-101; Melchionne, "Policewomen: Their Introduction," pp. 4-5.

12. Owings, op. cit., pp. 100-01.

13. Alice S. Wells, "Twenty and Two Years a Police Woman," *The Western Woman* 7 (July-September 1932): 15-16; Alice S. Wells, "Reminiscences of a Policewoman," *Police Reporter*, September 1929, pp. 23-28; George D. Wilson, "The World's First," *L.A. Police Beat* 27 (February 1972): 7; Owings, op. cit., pp. 101-04.

14. Wells, "Twenty and Two Years," p. 15; Wells, "Reminiscences of a Policewoman," pp. 23-28; Owings, op. cit., pp. 102-03.

15. Wells, "Twenty and Two Years," p. 15.

16. Ibid.; Wells, "Reminiscences of a Policewoman," pp. 25-28; Owings, op. cit., pp. 103-04, 106; Peter Horne, *Women in Law Enforcement*, 2nd ed. (Springfield, Ill.: Charles C. Thomas, 1980), pp. 28-29.

17. Owings, op. cit., pp. 107-17; New York City Police Department, *Annual Report 1918*, p. 85; and *1919*, p. 124.

18. Owings, op. cit., pp. 120-22, 223-46; Melchionne, "Policewomen: Their Introduction," pp. 96-98, 110-11; Wells, "Twenty and Two Years," p. 16; Mary E. Hamilton, *The Police Woman: Her Service and Ideals* (repr. New York: Arno Press New York Times, 1971), pp. 16-18; Horne, op. cit., p. 29.

19. Hamilton, op. cit., pp. 18-21; Melchionne, "Policewomen: Their Introduction," pp. 94, 110-13; New York City Police Department, *Annual Report 1920*, p. 240.

20. Hamilton, op. cit., pp. 18-21; Melchionne, "Policewomen: Their Introduction," pp. 110-13.

21. Hamilton, op. cit., p. 59.

22. Ibid., pp. 57-59.

23. Ibid., pp. 111-12.

24. Lois L. Higgins, *Policewoman's Manual* (Springfield, Ill.: Charles C. Thomas, 1961), p. xvi; Peter Horne, *Women in Law Enforcement*, 1st ed. (Springfield, Ill.: Charles C. Thomas, 1974), pp. 17, 22.

25. Owings, op. cit., pp. 104-05; Wells, "Twenty and Two Years," p. 15; Wells, "Reminiscences of a Policewoman," p. 28.

26. Owings, op. cit., pp. 191-200; William J. Bopp and Donald O. Schultz, *A History of American Law Enforcement* (Springfield, Ill.: Charles C. Thomas, 1972), p. 82.

27. Owings, op. cit., pp. 119-22.

28. Owings, loc. cit.; Catherine Milton, *Women in Policing* (Washington, D.C.: Police Foundation, 1972), pp. 7, 16; Cynthia Sulton and Roi Townsey, *A Progress Report on Women in Policing* (Washington, D.C.: Police Foundation, 1981), p. 11; Peter Horne, "Policewomen's Liberation—A Decade After," *Law and Order* 30 (July 1982): 60.

29. Wells, "Twenty and Two Years," op. cit., p. 15; Owings, op. cit., pp. 105, 261–63.

30. Hamilton, op. cit., p. 183; Felicia Shpritzer, "Major Administrative Problems of the Police Department in the Shelter and Detention of Minors" (master's thesis, Bernard M. Baruch School of Business and Public Administration at CUNY, 1961), pp. 1–123; Owings, op. cit., pp. 205–22.

31. Hamilton, op. cit., pp. 153–57.

32. New York City Police Department, *Annual Report 1919*, p. 167.

33. Higgins, op. cit., pp. xvii–xviii.

34. Ibid., pp. 3–7; Hamilton, op. cit., pp. 67–73, 89–102, 105–12; Shpritzer, op. cit., pp. 9–21; Milton, op. cit., pp. 8–9.

35. New York City Police Department, *Annual Report 1942*, p. 1.

36. Milton, op. cit., pp. 16–19; Municipal Reference Library. New York City, "Civil Service Announcement Folder, Civil Service Examination Announcement 1955."

37. Felicia Shpritzer, "A Case for the Promotion of Policewomen in the City of New York," *Journal of Criminal Law, Criminology and Police Science* 50 (December 1959): 417; Milton, op. cit., p. 73; interviews with Felicia Shpritzer, former lieutenant, New York City Police Department, June 27 and July 5, 1978.

38. Interviews with Shpritzer, June 27 and July 5, 1978; interview with Theresa M. Melchionne, former detective and deputy commissioner in charge of community relations, New York City Police Department, January 3, 1978; quoted in Catherine Milton, Ava Abramowitz, Laura Crites, Margaret Gates, Ellen Mintz, and Georgette Sandler, *Women in Policing: A Manual* (Washington, D.C.: Police Foundation, 1974), p. 27.

39. Interviews with Shpritzer, June 27 and July 5, 1978.

40. Ibid.; Milton, op. cit., p. 73.

41. Patrick V. Murphy and Thomas Plate, *Commissioner: A View from the Top of American Law Enforcement* (New York: Simon and Schuster, 1977), p. 249.

42. Interview with Howard Leary, former commissioner, New York City Police Department, March 6, 1979.

43. Milton et al., op. cit., pp. 49–51.

44. Ibid.

45. Sulton and Townsey, op. cit., pp. 16–17.

46. Horne, *Women in Law Enforcement*, 2nd ed., p. 34.

47. Sulton and Townsey, op. cit., p. 12.

48. Deidre Carmody, "The Police Divided over Assignment of Women to Street Patrol Here," *New York Times*, July 15, 1974, pp. 27, 38; Leonard Buder, "Police to Put Women on Homicide Squads," *New York Times*, November 16, 1977, p. B3; Murray Schumach, "First Woman Head of Precinct," *New York Times*, December 10, 1976, p. A1; interview with Ann Powers, president, Policewomen's Endowment Association, July 5, 1978; New York City Police Department Public Information Office, January 1985.

49. Sulton and Townsey, loc. cit.; Federal Bureau of Investigation, *Uniform Crime Reports* (Washington, D.C.: U.S. Department of Justice, 1984), p. 253.

50. Milton et al., op. cit., pp. v, 1–5.

51. Ibid., pp. 1–5, 36–45; Milton, op. cit., pp. 59–98.

52. Sulton and Townsey, op. cit., pp. 3–4.

53. Ibid., pp. 4–5.

54. Milton et al., op. cit., pp. 36–45; Michael T. Charles, "The Performance and Socialization of Female Recruits in the Michigan State Police Training Academy," paper presented at the 1979 annual meeting of the Academy of Criminal Justice Sciences, pp. 26–27.

55. "Jersey Considering Female-Trooper Test," *New York Times*, June 30, 1979, p. 22; *New York Times*, May 21, 1978, sec. 11, pp. 1, 23.

56. Alfonso A. Narvaez, "Woman Seeking a Police Job Sues Paramus, Accusing It of Sex Bias," *New York Times*, March 30, 1978, p. NJB3.

57. Cassandra Lawton, "No Woman Can Fill Her Spot on City Police Force," *Sunday Times Advertiser* (Trenton), April 22, 1979, pp. El, E8; Trenton Police Department Public Information Office, January 1985.

58. "Sex Bias Ruling Reversed Major Victory for Women of LAPD," *National NOW Times News*, June 1979, p. 3.

59. "Woman Officer Very Unhappy with Her Police Job," *Bucks County Courier Times*, April 20, 1978, p. C40; "Sex-Discrimination Trial Resumes After 2-Year Break for Police Study," *Philadelphia Inquirer*, August 15, 1978, sec. B, p. 1; "Penelope's Promoted," *The Trentonian*, September 16, 1978, p. 14.

60. *New York Times*, July 16, 1980, p. A19, *The Bulletin* (Philadelphia), November 19, 1980, p. C6; Philadelphia Police Department Public Information Office, January 1985.

61. Interview with Powers, July 5, 1978.

62. Ibid.; New York Women in Criminal Justice, Inc., "Minutes of Meeting, January 18, 1979."

63. New York Women in Criminal Justice, op. cit.

64. Peter Block and Deborah Anderson, *Policewomen on Patrol: Final Report* (Washington, D.C.: Police Foundation, 1974), pp. 5–7; Lawrence J. Sherman, "Evaluation of Policewomen on Patrol in a Suburban Police Department," *Journal of Police Science and Administration* 3 (December 1975): 434–38; *Women Traffic Officer Project: Final Report* (Sacramento: Department of California Highway Patrol, 1976); Harold Bartlett and Arthur Rosenblum, *Policewomen Effectiveness* (Denver: Civil Service Commission and Denver Police Department, 1977); Joyce L. Sichel, Lucy N. Friedman, Janet C. Quint, and Michael E. Smith, *Women on Patrol: A Pilot Study of Police Performance in New York City* (Washington, D.C.: National Institute of Law Enforcement and Criminal Justice, 1977).

65. Glen Craig, "California Highway Patrol: Women Officers," *The Police Chief*, January 1977, p. 61.

66. Sichel et al., op. cit., pp. xi–xii.

67. Ibid.

68. Interview with Cynthia Sulton, project director, The Police Foundation, June 4, 1979.

69. Mary Jo Patterson, "Training Tailored for Women," *Police Magazine*, September 1980, pp. 23, 25.

70. Ibid., pp. 25, 28.

71. Ibid., pp. 23, 26–28.

72. Ibid., p. 23.

73. Ibid., p. 28.

74. Milton, op. cit., p. 25.

75. "First Black Woman Promoted to Sergeant," *New York Times*, November 7, 1971, p. 58.

76. Roi Townsey, "Black Women in American Policing: An Advancement Display," *Journal of Criminal Justice* 10 (1982):456, 466.

77. *Farmington (N.M.) Daily Times*, August 18, 1984, p. A8.

78. *Navajo Times Today*, January 25, 1985, p. 2.

5

WOMEN IN THE LEGAL PROFESSION

Women have been members of the legal profession for over a century, and have used their expertise in courts and legislatures to gain the right to be admitted to law schools and state and federal bars, and to be permitted to plead cases before state and federal courts. The legal profession offers its members opportunities for status, wealth, and power, particularly as elected and appointed government officials. Consequently, resistance to allowing women to share in these advantages remains strong. Despite continuing opposition, women have entered the legal system in large numbers since the 1960s, and many have succeeded in breaking down formidable barriers; one, Sandra Day O'Connor, reached the top of the judicial hierarchy when she became a U.S. Supreme Court justice in 1981.

HISTORICAL BACKGROUND

The first woman in the United States to practice with the approval of the existing political and judicial leadership was Margaret Brent. The provincial court of colonial Maryland admitted her to practice before it in 1684. Among other business, she came before the court concerning the estates of Governor Leonard Calvert and his brother Cecilius. She was not really a lawyer, however, in the sense of one who was trained and officially admitted to the bar. The first woman to meet this criterion in a professional sense was Arabella A. Mansfield, who was admitted to the Iowa bar in 1869.[1]

The reasons that impelled women to enter law were somewhat different from those that drew women to the corrections and law enforcement professions emerging in the nineteenth century. At first, women in corrections and law enforcement began as unpaid reformers concerned with women and children, or as employees of community service agencies. Even when professionalization began, the reform aspect remained a major component in both fields, and women who entered them often came with a social service background. This altruistic element was not as important for women who entered law although they often contributed their time and support to worthy causes before and after they became lawyers. A common reason for going into law was interest spurred by early contact with judges and lawyers; this was true for women who came from families that had one or more lawyers. Several women entered law as a by-product of the need to handle large inheritances or to manage their own affairs. There also were some whose reform activities led them to realize that poor women needed legal assistance.[2]

Whatever their reasons, women entered law in growing numbers during the nineteenth century, and most of them already had a college education when they went to law school. Women's education was going through a revolution in the United States. Under the leadership of activists such as Hannah Crocker, Emma Willard, Frances Wright, and Catherine Beecher, educational seminaries for girls and teacher training schools for women opened. Many colleges and universities accepted women, the first and second being Oberlin in 1833 and Antioch in 1852. Iowa was the first state university to accept women; Michigan, Wisconsin, Boston, and Cornell universities also did so in the years from 1858 to 1874. Mount Holyoke, the first women's college, was founded in 1837 by Mary Lyon; Vassar opened in 1865, Smith and Wellesley in 1875, Radcliffe in 1879, and Bryn Mawr in 1885. The American Association of University Women was founded in 1882. Thus, by the end of the Civil War, a generation of college-educated women was ready for the next step. For some it was the law.[3]

The very full historical evidence of the nineteenth century makes it impossible to discuss all the women who entered law before 1900—which is unfortunate, since most of them were remarkable people. But it is possible to select a sample large enough to provide some flavor. Of 39 women lawyers, 27 were married, 16 to other lawyers. Nine became the law partners of their husbands. All had received encouragement in their quest to enter law from men who were lawyers or judges. Nine actively wrote or lobbied for reforms that assisted women. Only one woman retired from law after marriage. Except for Charlotte Ray, a black woman educated at Howard Law School and admitted to the Washington, D.C., bar in 1872, all the women were white. Fifteen were in their twenties when they became lawyers; 13 were in their thirties; 6 were in their forties; and 4 were in their fifties. Twenty-six lived and practiced in the West, where the first law schools to open to women were located. They were wives and mothers as well as reformers and activists. Using their education and their husbands' jobs as indicators, it appears that these women were middle and upper class.[4]

LAWYERS

Arabella A. Mansfield, the first woman lawyer in the United States, graduated from Iowa Wesleyan Seminary in 1866. She was married to a professor with whom she taught at Iowa Wesleyan; they both applied to be admitted to the bar and both planned to remain teachers. She prepared for the bar examination by reading in a private law office and was admitted to the Iowa bar in June 1869. She was admitted while others that year and afterward were denied the privilege. The Iowa court reinterpreted a statute providing that admission to the bar be restricted to ''white male citizens.'' The judge, basing his opinion on another section of the statute, said that the use of the word ''men'' might also be interpreted to include women. Restrictive words, he said, that unfairly treat persons might be fairly reinterpreted by the courts.[5]

Few other women were so positively received by the courts when they requested admission to the bar. Myra Bradwell, for example, studied law in her husband's law office in order to help him with his practice. In 1869, at the age of 38, she passed the bar examination and then applied to the Illinois Supreme Court for a license to practice. She proved that she was of good character and had met all the requirements for such a license, but the State Supreme Court cited four reasons to refuse her a license. First, under the common-law doctrine of coverture, a married woman did not have the legal right to enter into third-person contracts, and contracts were essential to the lawyer/client relationship. (Under the common-law doctrine of coverture, the husband and wife are to be treated as a single entity; in practice, the single person proved to be the husband.) Second, in the common-law tradition women had never been lawyers, and so the laws of the state of Illinois did not provide for such situations. Third, if women were permitted to practice law, they might also seek the right to hold public office. Fourth, admitting women to the bar would expose them to obscenities in court trials, thereby threatening their delicacy.[6]

That year Bradwell appealed her case before the U.S. Supreme Court, claiming that her rights were being violated under the equal protection clause of the Fourteenth Amendment. In 1872 the U.S. Supreme Court denied her appeal, declaring that the right to practice law was not protected under the Fourteenth Amendment, and that states could establish criteria for licensing. In a separate concurring opinion, Justice Joseph P. Bradley claimed that women's domestic role was essential to the preservation of the social order. Although he admitted that not all women married, he did not believe that they had a right to participate in the law. He concluded that the family was founded on ''divine ordinance'' and that ''The paramount mission of women is to fulfill the noble and benign offices of wife and mother. This is the law of the Creator.''[7]

Although Bradwell never reapplied for a license to practice law in Illinois, she received one in 1890 by a grant of the State Supreme Court and became the first women member of the Illinois Bar Association. She had not been idle during the 21 years between instituting her court case and receiving her license. She was actively involved in gaining the passage of laws to protect women in the state, specifically to prevent employment discrimination based on sex, to give married women the right to keep their earnings, to guarantee a widow a share in her husband's estate, and to provide that same right to widowers. She also founded and edited the *Chicago Legal News*. Her career demonstrated that there was no conflict between marriage and motherhood and a career. She had children—in fact, her daughter became a lawyer.[8]

Although Belva A. Lockwood did not have to wait as long as Bradwell to practice law, she had to overcome other obstacles. Born in 1830, she graduated from Genesee College, New York, in 1857 and received her masters degree from Syracuse University in 1870. Columbia College in Washington, D.C., refused to admit her because "her presence in the classes would distract the young men."[9] Lockwood was admitted to and graduated from National University Law School in Washington, D.C., and was admitted to the bar in Washington, D.C., in 1873, at the age of 43. Her practice involved litigation against the federal government that required her to plead before the U.S. Supreme Court. She applied in October 1876, and in November the Court denied her right to practice before it. The opinion was based on the common-law precedent that only men had been admitted to the practice of law before the Supreme Court, therefore women were excluded. Lockwood proceeded to draft a bill enabling women lawyers to practice before the U.S. Supreme Court. In 1879, after three years of lobbying, Congress passed such a law, and she became the first woman to practice before the U.S. Supreme Court. She was nevertheless refused admission to the Virginia bar in 1890.[10]

While denial of the right of married women to be members of the bar or to practice before a specific court was based on coverture or common law precedent, the denial of the right of single women was based on an additional rationale. The courts believed women must not be encouraged to remain single, to become educated professionals, or to have equal careers with men. Such women were "superfluous" and unnatural. When R. Lavinia Goodell applied to the Wisconsin Supreme Court in 1875 for admission, her request was denied by Chief Justice Edward G. Ryan, who spoke for the court when he declared that no state law had overturned the common-law precedent of refusing to grant women the right to practice law. Recognizing that not all women marry, Ryan declared: "It is public policy to provide for the sex, not for its superfluous members; and not to tempt women from the proper duties of their sex by opening to them duties peculiar to ours. There are many employments in life not unfit for female character. The profession of the law is surely not one of these."[11] He believed that women were naturally delicate, emotional, and sensitive, and destined by the laws of nature to be mothers and homemakers.

Because of these female characteristics, the client would suffer by not receiving full justice through the efforts of a woman lawyer. Women, lacking discretion, could not be trusted to keep a client's information a secret, as the profession demanded. In addition, exposure to verbal conflicts in the courtroom, he believed, would lessen a woman's purity and thus make her less desirable in the eyes of men.[12]

Belva Lockwood, the first woman to argue before the U.S. Supreme Court, advised women to fight back. Her own career set an example. As an active member of the Woman's National Equal Rights Party in California, she ran for president in 1884 and in 1888. She urged women not to be intimidated by public opinion and not to fear moving out of the conforming role of womanhood. She advised women to join forces and make the arduous effort to overcome discriminatory treatment of women seeking careers in law; women had to alter opinion so that the public would regard women lawyers as a natural part of the profession. They also had to overcome their own fears of being different and supposedly undesirable as women and as potential wives.[13]

Several women heeded Lockwood's advice and appealed to legislatures to have laws passed to admit women to the legal profession. R. Lavinia Goodell became a lawyer with permission to practice before the Wisconsin Supreme Court after the state legislature passed a law granting women the right in 1875. In 1884, Carrie B. Kilgore received the right to practice before the Supreme Court of Pennsylvania by a legislative act. Others went to court to gain entrance to law schools.

In 1888 the Women's International Bar Association was established, and in 1899 the National Association of Women Lawyers was organized in New York. These groups worked to gain admittance for women to all law schools and to all state bars and courts, and tried to improve the legal status of women in all areas of life. Finally, in 1918, the American Bar Association admitted its first women members.[14] But it was not until 1920, 51 years after women became lawyers for the first time, that all the states permitted women to practice law before the courts. In 1880 an estimated 75 women practiced law in the United States. In 1890 the estimated number of women was 135, and by the end of the century about 300. By 1920 the total number of women who had been admitted to the bar since 1869 was an estimated 1,600.[15]

LEGAL EDUCATION

In the nineteenth century, many attorneys, women as well as men, received their education and experience in a private law office. Women usually worked and studied with fathers or husbands. By the end of the nineteenth century, however, the professionalization of the law mandated that lawyers have a formal legal education. Phoebe W. Couzens was the first woman to enter a law school. In 1868 she matricualted at Washington University Law School in St. Louis, the first law school to admit women; she graduated in 1871. Subsequently she was admitted to practice in Missouri, Kansas, Utah, and the U.S. District Courts; she also became the first woman U.S. marshal (assigned to the Eastern District of Missouri). She was also actively involved in women's suffrage and prison reform. However, the first woman graduate of a law school was Ada Kepley, who graduated from Union College of Law in Chicago in 1869.[16]

Of the 39 women lawyers in the sample discussed earlier, 24 graduated from law schools: Boston University, Chicago Union College of Law (now Northwestern University Law School), University of Wisconsin, Hastings College of Law in California, Yale University, Washington University, National University, New York University, and the University of Pennsylvania. Some admitted women only under court order, and Yale reverted to an exclusionary policy after admitting Alice Jordan in 1885. Harvard Law School refused to admit Ellen A. Martin and M. Fredrika Perry, on the grounds that it was not proper for men and women to use the law library at the same time. Carrie Kilgore, denied admittance to the University of Pennsylvania Law School in 1871, went to court and won the right to enter that law school in 1881. The law schools of Yale, Harvard, and Columbia refused women until 1929, when Columbia broke ranks and the others eventually followed. The last law school to admit women was Washington and Lee, in 1972.[17]

Because of the time and energy involved in gaining admission to law schools, some women established their own law schools. The Woman's Legal Education Society, organized in New York City in 1890, set up the Woman's Law Class of New York University (NYU) in 1890. Its purpose was to educate women about their rights so that they could protect themselves and other women in need of legal advice. The idea came from Mrs. Leonard Weber, who in 1887 founded the Arbitration Society to aid poor women in need of legal protection. She soon learned that male lawyers did not want to work for poor people with no money to pay fees, nor did they want to contribute their time, free of charge, to the Arbitration Society. Weber asked Dr. Emily Kempec, a lawyer with a degree from the University of Zurich, to take charge of the legal services of the Arbitration Society. Kempec, as an alien, could not belong to the New York bar and could not, therefore, try cases in court.[18]

Weber and Kempec had the cooperation of Rev. Dr. Henry M. Mac-Cracken, vice-chancellor of NYU. The Woman's Law Class received permission to meet at the NYU Law School, and Kempec lectured to non-matriculated women. It is not surprising that MacCracken agreed to cooperate with the women, since they were members of the elite: leaders of the social, educational, and philanthropic communities in New York City. Many were married to politicians and lawyers.[19]

Although men attended Kempec's class on Roman law, they did not recognize her as an official teacher. In fact, the first Woman's Law Class did not pose a threat because most men and most members of the NYU faculty considered it a novelty. Of 15 women in the class, 4 paid and 11 received scholarships from the society. At the end of the year of classes, 13 women were tested on their knowledge of the law by MacCracken, Judge Noah Davis, and a partner in the law firm of Solomon, Dullon, and Sutro. (Sutro's wife was a member of the society.) They all passed and were awarded certificates of graduation, but they were not officially lawyers.[20]

Although newspaper articles about the graduation of the class described the women's appearance as sweet and lovable, not lawyerlike, the women took their studies seriously and proved to be qualified students. In 1892, 57 women enrolled in the Woman's Law Class and it became a permanent program for women at NYU. In the first four years of the class, all but one woman went on to law school, and two passed the New York bar examination. Three received their Bachelor of Law degrees from NYU in 1893: Katherine Hogan, who passed the bar in 1894; Cornelia Hood, who went on to lecture at the Brooklyn Institute; and Melle Stanleyetta Titus, who became the first woman member of the New York bar. In the class of 1893, Titus was first in her class of 105 men and 5 women. She was admitted to the U.S. Circuit Court of Appeals for the New York District.[21]

The second women's law school, Washington College of Law in Washington, D.C., was started by Emma Gillett and Ellen Spencer Mussey. Mussey taught in a business school in Washington, D.C. When her lawyer husband became ill, she worked in his law office. Rejected by the local law schools, she read for the law and passed the bar examination. She began practicing law in Washington, D.C., in 1893, at the age of 43, and in 1896 was admitted to practice before the U.S. Supreme Court. Then she joined with Gillett to start a law school that would not refuse women (it also admitted men). Gillett had received her degree from Howard University, a black university that admitted women regardless of race. She was admitted to the bar and to practice before the U.S. Supreme Court in 1890. The women became the deans of their new law school, which in 1949 merged with American University.[22]

Both women had political and legal connections in Washington, D.C., which contributed to their success with the law school. Mussey practiced probate, commercial, and international law, and for 25 years was counsel to the Norwegian and Swedish legations. She was also a member of the National American Women's Suffrage Association. Gillett was appointed by President James Garfield to be the first woman notary public in Washington, D.C. With a male partner she practiced probate, realty, and pension law. She also founded the Women's Bar Association of Washington, D.C.[23]

By 1920, 102 of the 129 law schools listed in the Educational Directory of the U.S. Bureau of Education admitted women. Until the 1970s women were admitted to law schools in limited numbers, but only after being questioned about their personal life plans, such as marriage, children, and career goals. They were asked if they planned to practice law or just to look for a husband. Often they were told they were taking places in the law school that should go to men who had families to support, or simply that women did not belong in law.[24]

In 1920 Beatrice Doerschuk reported on 297 women in law school and in practice. Women were at a disadvantage for several reasons. As youngsters they were not taught the simple legal and business procedures that boys were. Few women graduated from top law schools because they could not get into most of them and were limited by quotas in others. According to Doerschuk, most of the women who went to law school wanted to become lawyers because thay had respect for the law and confidence that they could succeed. However, she estimated that only half of the women who went to law school eventually practiced law. Many were discouraged by discrimination.[25]

Since the 1920s, opportunities for a legal education have improved considerably. Women have benefited from Title IX of the Higher Education Act of 1972. Title IX is similar to Title VII of the Civil Rights Act of 1964, in that if forbids discrimination on the basis of sex. It covers student enrollment and faculty hiring, and extends the provisions of the Equal Pay Act of 1963 to cover academic faculty. It provides that any school so discriminating shall be denied federal financial assistance.

The pressure of financial penalties has encouraged law schools to admit more women students and to allow them the opportunity to compete equally with men. The number of women enrolled tripled between 1969-70 and 1974-75, and increased tenfold from 1966 (2,600) to 1975 (26,000). The National Center for Education Statistics reported that women constituted 7.5 percent of the first-year class in 1969-70 and 23.4 percent of the first-year class in 1974-75. By 1984, women accounted for slightly more that one-third of all law students; in law schools in large urban centers, such as New York University in New York City and Rutgers in Newark, New Jersey, approximately half of the law students were women. Most law schools have women's groups that encourage women to enter the legal profession. The women at Rutgers publish the *Women's Rights Law Reporter Journal*, and women on other campuses have organized for mutual support and information, and as a lobby group for equal rights in the profession.[26]

From studies conducted in the 1970s and early 1980s, it appears that women students have been accepted on an equal basis with men. Women lawyers who went to law school during this period did not feel that they were discriminated against, although they were apprehensive when they entered. The growing number of women students, up to 50 percent in some law schools, helped to bring about changes in sexist tradition. For example, "ladies' days" when female students were intensely questioned on legal issues in rape and dower, have ended, and scholarships are given to women as well as to men. And, most important, women have become members of faculty and deans.[27]

In 1972 the Committee on Women in Legal Education of the American Association of Law Schools (AALS) conducted a study. Eighty-one of 124 AALS-accredited law schools responded to the questionnaire, which covered four areas: recruitment and admission, faculty, placement, and intraschool policy. The results of the study indicated that the status of women law students had improved in all areas. College undergraduate grade scores and LSAT scores for men and women applicants were about the same. However, several law schools admitted that they gave special consideration to athletes and to Ivy League applicants, most of whom were men. Forty percent of the schools reported active recruitment programs for women, supplemented by women's groups in many schools that carried on their own recruitment campaigns. For both men and women students the attrition rate was low and reasons for leaving were similar: financial problems, inability to keep up with the academic work, change in career goals, and family problems.[28]

Despite this generally favorable situation, some problems still exist. Only about half of the law programs include a course on women in the law. And whereas women accounted for approximately 36 percent of law students by 1984, they numbered less than 30 percent of students in six of the top ten law schools in the nation. Women therefore have disproportionally low representation in prestigious law firms and as law clerks because these positions are, for the most part, offered to the top students of prestigious law schools as a result of their being given summer positions in influential law firms after their second year of law school.[29]

In addition, there are few women members of law school faculties or administrators to provide role models or a support system for women students. According to a study by Donna Fossum, in 1950 women made up 3.5 percent of the legal profession and less than 0.5 percent of all full-time law school faculties, five women held tenure track positions of a total of 1,239 members of law school faculties. Of these five women, all were teaching in the school from which they had earned their J.D. degrees, and three of the five taught family law courses. By 1960, women still accounted for 3.5 percent of all lawyers and only 0.5 percent (11) of approximately 1,645 tenured track teachers. Of the 11, 3 taught courses in family law, 4 in trusts and estates, and 5 in legal research and writing. Some slight gains were made by the end of the 1960s; women made up 4 percent of all lawyers and 1.7 percent (39) of approximately 2,341 tenure track teachers, but they continued to teach the subjects considered women's specialties in law practice. Women law professors were underrepresented among those who taught courses related to business; these courses were considered by members of the legal profession to be the most "intellectually challenging and prestigious."[30]

At the start of the 1980s, virtually all of the nation's law schools had at least one tenure track female member of the faculty; women were represented in all academic ranks. (Ruth Ginsburg of Columbia Law School became the first woman full professor in 1972.) In addition, the number of women on law school faculties increased significantly. In 1980 they numbered 820 of a total of 5,535 full-time faculty in approved law schools; women accounted for approximately 15 percent of law school faculty and only 8.3 percent of all lawyers.[31] The American Bar Association (ABA) and the AALS collect data on the number of male and female faculty in law schools: each had different statistics for the start of the 1983 academic year, the differences resulting from the manner in which the data were collected. The ABA, which sends questionnaires to ABA-approved law schools, reported that in the fall of 1983 there were 7,484 full-time and part-time faculty, and deans and librarians who taught in law schools. Of these, approximately 15 percent (1,170) were women: 712 full-time women faculty of a total of 4,451, 337 part-time women faculty of a total of 2,530, and 121 women deans and librarians who teach of a total of 503.[32] The AALS, which sends questionnaires to all known law schools, reported that in September 1983, there were 1,697 women teaching at law schools, approximately 25 percent of a total of 6,073 faculty. The AALS does not categorize female faculty by academic rank.[33] By 1983 women lawyers accounted for approximately 15.3 percent of all lawyers, and therefore had equaled the percentage of women faculty according to ABA data.[34]

Despite these gains in numbers, women teaching in law schools remain concentrated in the so-called women's specialties, such as family law, legal research and writing, property law, and constitutional law; not surprisingly, constitutional law includes civil rights and discrimination law. Few teach business-related courses such as corporation, securities, and antitrust law.[35]

DISCRIMINATION: LAWYERS

The degrees and types of discrimination increase as women move from law school to active participation in the profession. Many firms are reluctant or unwilling to hire women. Students interviewing for their first job report that some firms, especially the largest and most prestigious ones, make it clear that they do not hire many women, do not make women partners, do not pay equal salaries for the same work, and do not give women the same work opportunities as men. A New York University Law School study done in 1970 found open discrimination. Women applying to private firms were told "We just hired a woman and can't hire another," or "We don't like to hire women," or were asked "Are you planning children?"[36] Around the same time women students at Columbia University sued the top 12 law firms in New York City to break their exclusionary policies against women; by 1976 several of the firms began to hire women.[37]

Being hired, however, is only the first step; many women find that even after they enter a firm, their paths are not easy. Generally they earn less than men for the same work. In 1970, Harvard Law School, a leading source of lawyers for prestigious law firms, reported that 99 percent of the male students, but only 44 percent of the female students, received two or more job offers. A 1970 study of the graduates in the classes of 1953 to 1959 showed that 70 percent of the women who worked full-time earned less than $20,000 a year, whereas only 16 percent of the men made less than that. In 1967, James J. White conducted a study of 1,300 men and 1,300 women, all of whom had graduated in the same year. He reported that men earned $1,500 more than women in the first year, and after ten years men's median income was $8,300 higher than women's. Women were not often promoted and were rarely made partners. They also had little contact with clients and seldom participated in policy-making meetings or social gatherings with clients and colleagues. Women were usually assigned to do the legal research, and the men went to court and tried the cases.[38]

White tried to determine the degree to which discrimination was based on objective factors. He found no scholastic difference between men and women in law schools; in fact, law schools reported that women usually worked harder than men, ranking in the top third of their class. He found no evidence that women are less motivated and dedicated than men, nor any proof that women either drop out or change careers after graduation any more than men do. If they do, it is for the same reasons, financial and personal.[39] (Bysiewicz in 1972 reported that there were no differences in these areas.)

The *American Bar Association Journal* published the results of a survey of only 605 male and female lawyers conducted to ascertain the status of women in the law; in 1983 there were 94,000 women lawyers (15.3 percent) of a total of 612,000. According to the survey, men accepted women as their colleagues and treated them as equals. However, 17 percent of the women and 7 percent of the men believed that discriminatory treatment of women existed. Women said that they were given less responsiblilty, fewer choice assignments, lower salaries, and less respect than men. The men pointed to the fact that women were treated more gently by not getting the dirty jobs; in other words, discriminatory treatment protected women.[40]

The survey found specific areas in which women were at a disadvantage compared with men. Only 35 percent of the men had female colleagues; about two-thirds of all male lawyers did not work with women. The median income for men was $53,000, and for women it was $33,000. The explanation for income disparity focused on the fact that a large number of women are relative newcomers to the profession; three-fifths of them were under age 35. Although women were more likely to have graduated with honors (25 percent of the women, compared with 18 percent of the men finished in the top 10 percent of their classes), men were more likely to have graduated from prestigious law schools and to have had a greater number of job opportunities than women. Furthermore, women were concentrated in the practice of family and criminal law and, in their present positions, were more likely than men to be writing briefs, preparing cases in litigation, and conducting research. On the other hand, men were concentrated in the practice of real estate and corporation law and, in their present positions, were more likely to be involved with litigation and pleading cases in court.[41]

The personal lives of male and female lawyers were also examined in the survey. A marked difference appeared between the men and women: 85 percent of men and 54 percent of women were married; 8 percent of men and 32 percent of the women had never been married; and 24 percent of the men and 59 percent of the women had no children. Women who did have children returned to the practice of law within a short time; the length of maternity leaves averaged from two months (33 percent) to four to six months (27 percent).[42]

Other studies have indicated that negative or discriminatory treatment of women in the legal profession continues to exist, to the detriment of women. The New Jersey task force study on sex discrimination in the state's courts reported that female lawyers experienced hostile remarks or demeaning jokes from male lawyers and judges. In addition, few women received court appointments for lucrative guardianships, receiverships, and condemnations.[43] Donna Fossum noted that male clients do not feel comfortable with women lawyers and state to male lawyers in law firms or businesses that they do not want a woman assigned to their cases. This affects the hiring, assignment, and promotion opportunities for women in law firms of all sizes.[44]

An article in the *Wall Street Journal*, "Men's Club Attitude in Naming New Partners," discussed discrimination against women in large law firms. For example, women who graduated from Harvard and Columbia Law Schools in the 1970s have had a difficult time getting jobs with influential law firms, and especially in becoming partners. Of 26 women in the 1972 class at Columbia Law School, 10 went to work in large law firms; 1 became a partner, 5 were passed over for partnerships, and the others gave up or were encouraged to leave before the decision was made. By comparison, 20 percent of the men in the 1972 class were partners in influential law firms; 50 percent were partners in law firms of all sizes and prestige, compared with only 11.5 percent of the women. And of the 1974 class at Harvard Law School, 22 percent of the 75 women were partners in law firms, compared with 45 percent of the 481 men. Reasons cited for this disparity include women do not belong to the right private clubs; women are not part of the collegiality of companies and do not play golf or associate with the men; women are not respected by male colleagues and are still called "honey" or "sugar," and assigned to menial tasks; and women have to work much harder than men to prove themselves and to be accepted.[45]

One way to avoid some of the discrimination is for women to open their own law offices. In theory this option has always been open to them, but in fact it is open only to those few who have the money and contacts to start a business from the ground up. A law office requires books, insurance, secretarial help, and all the other expenses of any commercial operation. There must be a constant search for clients, a difficult task for women, who are not part of the "old boy" network (as is evident when the men lawyers and judges meet informally in social situations from which women are excluded). There is still strong belief among many clients that they will not get competent legal advice and defense if a woman represents them.[46]

Certain areas are considered appropriate for women, such as family law, estate law, legal aid and criminal law, legal research and documentation, and library work. These have relatively low status and income.[47] Indeed, the low financial returns may be one reason why women faced little resistance from men when they began entering criminal practice at the turn of the century. As Clarence Darrow said, "You won't make a living at it, but it's worthwhile and you'll have no competition."[48] Clara Foltz was called the "Portia of the Pacific" because of her work as a criminal attorney in California. Marilla Ricker was the "Prisoners' Friend" because she defended poor prostitutes and criminals. Martha Strickland became assistant prosecuting attorney in Detroit. Laura DeForce Gordon achieved fame as a criminal attorney in California. Anna M. Kross graduated from New York University Law School in 1912 and joined other women lawyers in defending prostitutes in the New York City Women's Night Court. Elizabeth Blume-Silverstein, who specialized in criminal law in Newark, New Jersey, at the turn of the century, was considered a "kook" because of her specialty. Perhaps those who called her that were jealous of the fact that, unlike most who practiced criminal law, she received a fee of $100 to $200 a day when she started to practice in 1913.[49]

In the quest for equal opportunity for jobs and money, women have been encouraged to enter government jobs, because such employment is based on competitive examinations that objectively recognize ability. Government jobs also provide tenure, benefits, regular hours, and an opportunity for promotion. In 1960 more women lawyers than men started to enter government. By 1980, 17 percent of all women lawyers worked for government—local, state, and federal.[50] However, most of the women lawyers who enter government are hired for positions two grades lower than men and never catch up. A few women lawyers have held key policy-making positions in the federal government and have had different experiences. For example, while working as the army's general counsel, Jill Wine, assistant special prosecutor at the Watergate trials, commented that women are still asked, "What's a pretty girl like you doing in a place like this?"[51] On the other hand, Deanne Siemer, while working as the general counsel for the U.S. Defense Department (she graduated top of her Harvard Law School class in 1968 and had been a trial lawyer and partner in a Washington, D.C., law firm), stated that she had no difficulty as the highest-ranking woman in the Pentagon: "People know me, I have no problem at all being a woman here."[52] Other women have also found careers in government; many women lawyers work for the U.S. Department of Justice. As of September 1984, there were 542 women assistant U.S. attorneys of a total of 2,238 (there were 163 women of a total of 1,611 assistant U.S. attorneys in 1977), and as of September 1983, there were 1,080 women lawyers of a total of 4,422 in the U.S. Department of Justice.[53]

Despite problems faced by women in the legal profession, many have succeeded. A discussion including twelve such women appeared in the *American Bar Association Journal*. The women included judges, trial lawyers, a member of Congress (Geraldine Ferraro), a prosecutor, two law school professors and a dean, partners in large law firms, a public interest lawyer, and a head of a government legal office. They ranged in age from 35 to 51. Most of their fathers had been in the professions, and the mothers of all but one had worked full-time while raising their children. They were brought up in large cities in small families, and all were encouraged to succeed in nontraditional areas. Six of the women are mothers and all had their children after entering the legal profession. Two had not married, four had their first marriage end in divorce, and three of the latter had remarried. All had one thing in common: they entered the legal profession when women were still tokens and had to overcome many obstacles in order to succeed.[54]

JUDGES

Few women were judges until the 1970s. The first woman judge served in an appointed position as justice of the peace in South Pass Mining Camp, Territory of Wyoming. Esther Morris received that position in 1870. The second woman judge, Marilla Ricker, was appointed U.S. commissioner by the judges of the District of Columbia trial court in 1884, only two years after she was admitted to the Washington, D.C., bar. Carrie B. Kilgore, who sued the University of Pennsylvania Law School to force it to admit her and other women, became the first woman master in chancery in Philadelphia in 1886, three years after she graduated from the university law school. Catherine McCulloch was elected justice of the peace in Evanston, Illinois, in 1907. However, women had to wait until after the passage of the Nineteenth Amendment to be eligible for elective judgeships in most states.[55]

Florence Ellinwood Allen became the first woman elected to the judiciary as other than justice of the peace. She was elected judge of the Court of Common Pleas in Cleveland, Ohio, in 1921, and in 1922 became the first woman elected to a state supreme court, the Ohio Supreme Court. She left that position in 1934 when President Franklin D. Roosevelt appointed her to the U.S.

Court of Appeals for the Sixth Circuit; she was the first woman to serve on a U.S. Court of Appeals.[56]

By 1930, 12 states had women judges; the number was 21 in 1940 and 29 in 1950. Annette Adams became the first woman judge on a state appeals court in 1942, in Sacramento, California. The first woman to serve as chief justice of a state supreme court was Lorna Lockwood, who had been on the Arizona Supreme Court for four years before assuming its leadership in 1965. Despite these appointments, fewer than 200 women served on state courts in 1971 and only 240 served on state courts in 1973.[57]

In 1977, nine women sat on the state courts of last resort, 18 on intermediate appellate courts, 130 on general jurisdiction courts, and 317 on courts of limited jurisdiction; in that year women constituted approximately 4 percent of all state judges.[58] However, 10 states had only 1 woman member of their major trial courts and 20 states had no women judges. Finally, in 1979, when Montana selected a woman judge, all states had at least one woman on their courts.[59] By 1984 the number of women sitting on state courts increased: 22 on the courts of last resort; 46 on intermediate appellate courts; 356 on general jurisdiction courts; and 497 on courts of limited jurisdiction.[60] Women constituted approximately 6 percent of all state appellate judges and 4 percent of all state trial judges.[61] And between 1965 and 1984, four women held the position of chief justice of a state supreme court: in Arizona, Michigan, Connecticut, and California.[62]

Until 1979, only a few women had served on federal courts; there had been none on the U.S. Supreme Court and only two on the U.S. Court of Appeals (Florence Allen and Shirley Hufstedler, appointed in 1934 and 1968, respectively). Appointments of women to the federal bench moved very slowly until the late 1970s. In 1949, President Harry Truman appointed Burnita Shelton Matthews as the first woman to serve on a U.S. District Court. In the period between the presidencies of Truman and Carter, 19 women were appointed to the federal bench; during Carter's four-year term an additional 40 women were appointed. By the end of 1984, President Ronald Reagan had appointed six women to federal judgeships including Sandra Day O'Connor to the U.S. Supreme Court in 1981.[63]

The number of women federal judges has increased since the 1970s: 7 women served on the federal bench in 1977 and 45 in 1980, including 10 on the courts of appeals and 31 on district courts.[64] By 1984, approximately 8 percent of federal judgeships were held by women: 1 on the U.S. Supreme Court; 11 on the U.S. Court of Appeals; 43 on U.S. District Courts; three on U.S. Circuit Courts; and 43 U.S. magistrates.[65] In addition, women had served on U.S. Bankruptcy Courts, Tax Courts, the Court of Claims, and the Air Force Military Court of Review.

Up to 1970 the overall percentage of women judges matched the percentage of women lawyers: 1.5 percent in 1960 and 4 percent in 1970. However, by 1984 this had changed; women accounted for approximately 8 percent of all federal judges, 6 percent of all state appellate judges, 4 percent of all state trial judges, and 15.3 percent of all lawyers. It remains to be seen whether the percentage of women judges will once again match that of women lawyers.

DISCRIMINATION: JUDGES

Women judges are often assigned to jurisdictions that are traditionally considered the specialty of women, such as municipal or domestic courts, which have little status, are not arenas for important cases, and provide few contacts for persons seeking a political career. About 12.4 percent of the judges in family courts are women, twice the rate of women on any other limited jurisdiction courts.[66]

Some women have resisted such sexual stereotyping. Florence Allen, elected to the Common Pleas Court in Cleveland in 1920, was told by her fellow judges, all men, that she was to have a special division created for her: divorce judge. She informed them that the voters who elected her expected her to keep her campaign promises to improve the inefficient criminal court, and therefore she could not accept their offer. In the end they learned to treat her as an equal, but only when court was in session.[67]

Another case is that of Marie M. Lambert, who broke the male monopoly over Surrogate Court judgeships in New York City. The Surrogate Court judge appoints lawyers to handle estates and act as guardians of estates of individuals held incompetent to oversee their own affairs. The executor of the estate receives a fee. The judges are carefully selected by political and legal elites to ensure that the appointments go to the proper persons. Until 1977, men controlled that court. In 1977, Lambert won election to the Manhattan Surrogate Court, despite the fact that the male-dominated New York Bar Association rated her "not approved."[68]

The limited number of women on the bench before the 1980s did not stem from the lack of qualified women. A U.S. Department of Justice criterion that a person had to have 15 years' experience as a practicing attorney to be considered for a judgeship excluded most women and minority group members, who were relative newcomers to the law. Mildred Jeffrey, chairperson of the National Women's Political Caucus, said in 1977, "The process of selecting federal judges is a disaster for women. At every stage of the selection process we have found well-qualified women excluded or overlooked. The President must take charge immediately to get more women on the bench."[69]

In 1978 Congress enacted the Omnibus Judgeship Act which created 152 new judgeships, thereby increasing the number of federal judges by 25 percent. It was hoped that women and minority members would have an opportunity to gain entrance into the federal judicial system. However, the old obstacles remained. In addition, selection panels usually did not include women. Senator Jacob Javits' six-member panel had no women, President Carter's panels had no women as chairperson, and no women's bar association was asked to contribute.[70]

Appointments were finally made. In March 1979, the Senate confirmed the judgeship of Phyllis Kravitch, a Georgia Superior Court judge in Savannah, to the Court of Appeals for the Fifth Circuit. In May 1979, Amalya L. Kearse was confirmed for the Second Circuit U.S. Court of Appeals. Kearse had been the first woman and the first black to become a partner in one of the leading Wall Street law firms. Ann Thompson, prosecutor of Mercer County, New Jersey, a black woman and former municipal judge, became a U.S. district judge in New Jersey in November 1979.[71]

These general efforts, although important and effective in their own way, affect only a few women; most women lawyers with aspirations to a judgeship will have to find other avenues. In considering this problem, one researcher has developed a theoretical model of the kinds of things women must do. Beverly Blair Cook, a political scientist at the University of Wisconsin, Milwaukee, argues that women must achieve what she calls the "manifest offices," positions that have historically been sources of candidates for judgeships: U.S. district attorney, state district attorney, private practice trial work, and membership in a legislature. Until recently women have rarely been allowed access to another route, clerkship under prominent judges; but in 1975, 14.4 percent of such clerkships were held by women.[72]

Several studies have been conducted since 1980 to learn more about women judges. One dealt with women on the state bench. In 1980, questionnaires were mailed to all 549 women judges serving on state courts. Data gleaned from this study include the following: the average age was 48, with 30 percent under 40; the average woman obtained her first judicial position at age 42 and had been an attorney for 13 years; the typical judge was white, graduated from a private law school, and identified herself as a moderate-to-liberal Democrat. Equally important, most of the women had worked in law firms; 81 percent had at one time been in private practice. Many had experience with government as prosecutors or public defenders, or had been law professors: 31 percent had held bar association office. Finally, 46 percent decided on their own to become a judge.[73]

A study of women on the federal bench was conducted to see to what extent women judges resemble their male colleagues. Data were gathered from the questionnaires used by the Senate Judiciary Committee in confirmation hearings following the enactment of the 1978 Omnibus Judgeship Act. When the new women judges were compared with male federal judges, marked differences were noted. Women as a group were more likely to have been judges at the time of their appointment, and less likely to come from large law firms or to have been active in party politics. Furthermore, women, more so than men, were educated in public schools and came from low-status racial or religious groups. In addition, as a group, women were outstanding students, many having received awards and many continuing their intellectual interests with research, writing, and part-time teaching in law schools. Equally important, almost 90 percent showed a commitment to feminism, and an equal number showed an interest in the underprivileged by accepting pro bono cases. Given their background, experience, and commitment, it remains to be seen whether they will have an impact on judicial decisions, and if so, whether their impact will be felt on issues affecting women's and minority rights.[74]

One of the new federal judges appointed during the Carter administration, Amalya L. Kearse, has made such an impact. In a two-to-one decision, the Second Court of U.S. Court of Appeals decided that prosecutors could not systematically exclude people from juries solely because of their race. This was the first time a federal appeals court had invalidated the use of peremptory challenges to keep black and Hispanic people off juries. Speaking for the court, Kearse argued that such exclusion of jurors by race violated the right to a fair trial under the Sixth Amendment, and that it was "fallacious and pernicious" to assume that persons of the same skin color "will ipso facto view matters in the same way."[75]

Women constitute only 8 percent of all federal judges and only 4 percent of all state trial judges. Consequently, their feelings of isolation may be greater than those of women lawyers; women judges cannot form partnerships with other women. And because they are either elected or appointed, some of their time must be spent in the public or political arenas. Women lawyers who seek judgeships and women judges are at a distinct disadvantage compared with their male counterparts, for they cannot belong to the all-male club. As Beverly Cook put it, "The male club is the quasi-social linchpin of institutional sexism."[76] By keeping women out of their clubs, men keep women out of their business and political networks: "The institutions with the most financial, influential, and legal power have the smallest percentage of women . . . ."[77] As a result, women have to be smarter, work harder, and overcome enormous opposition to get judgeships and to gain recognition on the bench.

The "old boy" network also constitutes a barrier to women judges who seek appointments as members of faculty for judicial education programs. Women judges who become judicial educators are often designated to teach courses considered appropriate for women: family law. Because issues of divorce and alimony are emotional ones that transcend judicial objectivity and often become personal, women judicial educators frequently receive negative evaluations from a predominantly male judge class, and are not reinvited to teach. These evaluations may be used as an excuse not to keep women on the faculty, for men judges with low ratings are reinvited.[78]

During a symposium for women judges held in 1982, the women discussed the problems and discriminatory treatment they faced as women in a male-dominated judicial system. In particular, they felt pressure to remain on the bench despite burnout or vulnerability due to their high visibility: "Because they believed they were watched more closely and criticized more readily than their male colleagues, they felt they must prove their success by staying on the bench."[79] The women also had a commitment to stay on the bench to serve as role models for other women; they believed that if they left their judicial positions, men would replace them, and a foothold gained for women would be lost. They expressed feelings of isolation and told of sexual harassment. Male colleagues exhibited subtle or overt sexist attitudes and behavior; several women spoke of sexual advances by male colleagues. In addition, jealousy and hostility on the part of male lawyers and judges resulted in less cooperation with the women, refusal to recognize the women as judges or to discuss court business with them, exclusion of women from informal social meetings, and passing over of women when committee assignments were made. Most of the women believed that they had the respect of most of their male colleagues. However, they also believed that "it was imperative for women to earn and maintain even greater respect."[80] They would have to work harder to be more efficient, to be more competent, and to avoid any mistakes.

THE NEW PROFESSIONALS

Even as women have been fighting discrimination at the various levels and in the various branches of legal education and practice, they have been trying to define their own roles as lawyers and judges. This has become particularly urgent since 1960, as federal laws have helped break down many of the traditional barriers against women. In the 1960s women in the legal profession were broadly divided into two groups: the diplomats and the fighters. The diplomats, who preferred to work within the system and through channels, believed that discrimination is best dealt with by working harder to gain the respect of men. Separate women's professional organizations, they argued, segregate women and make them stand out. The fighters blamed the diplomats for the low salaries, low status, and limited opportunities women face in the profession. They accused the diplomats of accepting whatever was given to them by men in the profession, and even of joining with men in putting down women lawyers and judges.[81]

There was yet another divergence among women lawyers and judges, over the degree to which women should remain in the traditional areas of family and juvenile law. The diplomats' view was set forth in 1960 by Neva B. Talley, then president of the National Association of Women Lawyers

(NAWL). She said that as more women entered employment outside the home, they would seek out women lawyers, feeling "that a successful professional woman can better understand their feminine fears and hesitations . . . ."[82] Women's unique instincts made them especially suitable for certain areas of law, as well as for protecting society against the evils of subversion. "Just as the female of the animal species in the jungle is first to hear faint noise of an approaching enemy and be instantly alerted to protect her young, also the woman is more likely the first to hear the faint whimper from the baby's cradle when he has kicked loose his cover on a cold winter night. Should we not use these innate tendencies of alertness to support and strengthen our form of government?"[83] A woman lawyer should "cater to the demand and capitalize on the fact that she is a woman trained in the field of law, but not a 'feminist' in the general conception of extreme female tendencies."[84] In effect, Talley told women lawyers to know and keep their place in society and in the law.

In 1969, the NAWL met in Dallas to celebrate the centennial of women in the legal profession. According to Marjorie Childs, national chairperson of the Women Lawyers Centennial and referee of the juvenile court of the City and County of San Francisco, "The climax of women lawyers' achievements during the centennial year" was the election of the NAWL's past president, Neva B. Talley, as chairman of the Family Law Section of the American Bar Association (ABA). Childs believed that although Talley had worked for the section for many years, her election to the chair of an important ABA section was a major recognition of the work of women in the profession.[85] It is significant that Talley was appointed to the "family" law section.

At the same meeting, questions arose on the place of women in the legal profession. Are they women lawyers and judges or are they lawyers and judges? Judge Sarah T. Hughes questioned the need for a separate women's bar association: "Would it not be better to work with men? It would be harder to accomplish some of our goals, but wouldn't it be more worthwhile? When we did get somewhere, we would have gotten there together and not just be a group of women who did something."[86] She was answered by Marguerite Rawalt of the District of Columbia Bar, who strongly disagreed: "We've gotten to the place where women have to become militant to get anywhere."[87] She was supported by many, among them Representative Martha Griffiths, Democrat from Michigan, who believed that women have to unite to fight inequities in the legal system.

The majority of the women at the NAWL centennial meeting supported the concept and fact of separate women lawyers' and judges' associations. Speaking for the majority, NAWL President Jettie Pierce Silvig stated, "When we finally attain true equality in the law and under the law, then and only then will the need for our organization cease to exist."[88]

The diplomats have lost ground. As more women have entered law schools and have passed bar examinations, fewer have been willing to take a back seat in their chosen profession. Law schools have women's groups that work against discrimination in the academic end of lawyering. Women's divisions of local and national bar associations strive to end discrimination in the work place. The National Women's Political Caucus, National Organization for Women, and other women's groups have organized to support efforts made by NAWL and the National Association of Women Judges to remove barriers to equal access for women to law firms and to state and federal judgeships. Women in the law have been publishing the *Women Lawyers Journal* for almost a century, and the articles reflect the change in attitudes of the women; they have become fighters.

Despite the increase in the number of women lawyers and judges, progress cannot be measured solely in numbers, for this ignores the qualitative aspects of careers. This mistake was made, for example, in an article in the *Wall Street Journal*. The author suggested that "law may become the first traditionally male profession to achieve full sexual integration."[89] In sheer numbers this position has some support. Between 1975 and 1984 the number of women lawyers increased from approximately 16,000 to 94,000 (from 4 percent to 15.3 percent). The number of women judges in state courts increased from approximately 474 in 1977 to 921 in 1984. Only a few women had sat on federal courts up to 1979; in 1984 there were approximately 72. These figures are not nearly so impressive when compared with the proportion of women in the U.S. population—over 50 percent, and in the work force—over 40 percent. Moreover, in terms of income, women lawyers are likely to earn $33,000 a year, compared with $53,000 for men; women judges are likely to earn $22,500 a year, compared with $41,700 for men.[90]

In any case, the "old boy" network will continue to exert its incalculable influence, even when there is an "old girl" network alongside. Men will no doubt still get the first chance at the good jobs, the best referrals of clients, the legal positions most likely to increase status and open the way for political ambitions. Politicians will continue to offer rhetoric about equality during elections, then tread water once they enter office. Mayor Edward Koch of New York City promised to reduce discrimination in the courts. Although he did indeed appoint a woman to the Criminal Court in Queens (a low-status court in the judicial system), he also appointed two women to the Family Court, precisely the kind of work that has been stereotyped as women's domain.[91]

The real impetus for change therefore will come not from without but, continuing a century-long tradition, from women lawyers and judges themselves. The political climate has changed since President Carter appointed 40 women to the federal bench. President Reagan appointed only six during his first term in office, although one of them, Sandra Day O'Connor, made history by becoming the first woman justice on the U.S. Supreme

Court. In order to achieve equality in the law and under the law, women lawyers and judges will have to work harder to succeed.

The new professionals in the legal system, primarily fighters, are succeeding and are establishing themselves as role models for other women. They go to court to fight discrimination, they seek opportunities in all areas of the law as lawyers and judges, and they have made the necessary accommodations to combine family life and careers. Florence Allen, the first woman elected to a judicial position, remained single and, while on the Ohio Supreme Court, said, "I don't cook, or sew, or shop, for the simple reason that I haven't the time or energy for these things, any more than the men judges have."[92] Sandra O'Connor, however, combined family life and career. By the 1970s women assumed this dual role, some with difficulty and others quite successfully. In 1977, two-thirds of female trial judges had children and paid for child care. It helped, as in the case of O'Connor, to be married to a lawyer who gave her moral and practical support; he had influential political and legal connections. In fact, many women lawyers and about half of women judges are married to lawyers.[93]

The dual career however, can add to the strain felt by women, perhaps more so for women judges, who are more likely to be in the public eye than women lawyers. Many women judges expressed the feeling that their visibility made them more open to scrutiny and censure if they did not continue to have a traditional family life. Moreover, in cases of domestic discord, they were more likely to agree to any settlement in a divorce so as to avoid publicity. And regardless of the support given by husbands, women lawyers and judges carried the responsibility for running the home and for seeing that the children were well cared for.[94]

The new generation of professionals refuses to be treated as second-class citizens. In a survey of women judges conducted by Beverly Cook, 71 percent of the women said they would walk right up to the front door with men at male-exclusive clubs that had a separate, side entrance for women. Women who were 55 years and older took a more traditional view and said they would ask for a different meeting place; the younger, unmarried women were much more adamant about entering the front door with their male colleagues than were the married women with children.[95]

Other women have established their own codes for success. Patricia Wald, judge on the U.S. Court of Appeals for the District of Columbia Circuit since 1979, advises women to set their own standards and build their own career ladders. She had taken a ten-year leave of absence from the law to raise her five children. When she returned to law, she took jobs in the public sector that gave her more and more influence and power until she was appointed to the federal bench.[96] Other women refuse to take jobs or cases that are stereotyped as women's work, such as family law. Others develop skills and interests, and make themselves experts in specific areas; fluency in Spanish helped one woman gain a partnership in a Wall Street firm dealing with Latin America. There are women who find a common interest with men with whom they do business, such as fishing; the idea is to find a common ground and exploit it. The women believe it is important to find a style that is comfortable for them, to learn when to pass over a condescending remark with a humorous answer or to take a stand and fight. For example, one woman lawyer organized a protest against a private male club because women could not enter without a male escort before one in the afternoon; the club subsequently revised its bylaws so that women could eat lunch at any time, unescorted. Another woman, responding to a question as to whether her husband minded her being out late at night, said, "I stopped asking permission when I was 12."[97]

SUMMARY

Women in the legal profession have a tradition of relying on their legal expertise and professional organizations to remove barriers that have kept them from certain law schools, areas of specialization, and employment and advancement opportunities in private companies and in government. Full equality is still denied to them because sexist attitudes pervade the male-dominated profession as well as the nation. Although held in low esteem since the 1960s, when political scandals, such as Watergate, involved many lawyers, the legal profession continues to offer its members power and wealth, particularly insofar as so many elected and appointed members of government are lawyers. Consequently, lawyers are in a position as members of legislatures to make laws, as executives to implement laws, and as members of the judiciary to interpret laws. Their potential for power is enormous. Those who hold power and wealth are loathe to share them and men in the legal system are loath to share what they have with women.

By 1985, probably the only position in the legal profession not held by at least one woman was that of chief justice of the U.S. Supreme Court. In order to succeed as lawyers and judges, women have had to be smarter, work harder, and be better at what they do than their male colleagues. Describing what women have had to to and what they still must do, Justice Sandra O'Connor said:

> . . . you must work harder because you are pioneers. You are breaking a barrier that has stood in the way of women before you, and you are providing a platform for women after you to stand on. You are doing this not only for yourselves. The ability of women to acquire judicial positions in the future will depend on the reputations of you who precede them. You simply have to be better. That is a terrific burden.[98]

NOTES

1. Kathleen E. Lazarou, "Fettered Portias: Obstacles Facing Nineteenth-Century Women Lawyers," *Women Lawyers Journal* 64 (Winter 1978): 21–22; Julia C. Spruill, *Women's Life and Work in the Southern Colonies* (New York: Norton Library, 1972), pp. 236–41; Robert E. Riegel, *American Feminists* (Lawrence: University Press of Kansas, 1968), p. 135.

2. D. Kelly Wiesburg, "Barred from the Bar: Women and Legal Education in the United States 1870–1890," *Journal of Legal Education* 28 (1977): 494–99; Frances E. Willard and Mary A. Livermore, eds., *American Women: Fifteen Hundred Biographies* (repr. Detroit: Gale Research Book Tower, 1973): vol. I, pp. 10, 87–88, 94, 115, 117, 211, 283–84, 286, 293–94, 326–27, 339, 350–52; and vol. II, pp. 460, 468–69, 484, 487, 531, 557, 571, 609, 699, 718, 737, 759, 768, 789; *Notable American Women 1607–1950: A Biographical Dictionary* (Cambridge, Mass.: Belknap Press, 1971): vol. I, pp. 188–90, 651–52, vol. II, pp. 36–37, 329–30, 356–57, 492–93, 606–07, and vol. III, pp. 121, 540–41, 590–92; *For the Better Protection of their Rights: A History of the First Fifty Years of the Woman's Legal Education Society and the Woman's Law Class at New York University* (New York: New York University Press, 1940), pp. 3, 7, 9–11.

3. Eleanor Flexner, *Century of Struggle: The Woman's Rights Movement in the United States* (New York: Atheneum, 1971), pp. 29, 122–24.

4. Willard and Livermore, op. cit., vol. I, loc. cit., and vol. II, loc. cit., *Notable American Women*, vol. I, loc. cit., vol. II, loc. cit., and vol. III, loc. cit.

5. Lazarou, op. cit., p. 22; Riegel, loc. cit.; *Notable American Women*, vol. II, p. 492–93.

6. Lazarou, op. cit., pp. 23–24; Weisberg, op. cit., p. 489; Karen DeCrow, *Sexist Justice* (New York: Vintage Books, 1975), pp. 30–31.

7. DeCrow, op. cit., pp. 30–33; Leo Kanowitz, *Sex Roles in Law and Society: Cases and Materials* (Albuquerque: University of New Mexico Press, 1973), pp. 43–44.

8. Lazarou, op. cit., p. 25; DeCrow, op. cit., pp. 34–35; Weisberg, op. cit., p. 449.

9. Lazarou, loc. cit.

10. Lazarou, op. cit., pp. 25–26; Riegel, op. cit., p. 136; Willard and Livermore, op. cit., vol. II, pp. 468–69.

11. Lazarou, op. cit., p. 21.

12. Ibid., p. 27; Weisberg, op. cit., pp. 490–91.

13. Weisberg, op. cit., p. 499; Riegel, op. cit., p. 136.

14. Lazarou, op. cit., pp. 28–29; Juvenal L. Angel, *Careers for Women in the Legal Profession* (New York: World Trade Academy Press, 1961), pp. 6–7, 19; Beatrice Doerschuk, *Women in the Law: An Analysis of Training, Practice and Salaried Positions* (New York: Bureau of Vocational Information, 1920), p. 36.

15. Lazarou, op. cit., Angel, op. cit., Doerschuk, op. cit.; Weisberg, op. cit., p. 494.

16. Lazarou, op. cit., p. 22; Weisberg, op. cit.

17. Weisberg, op. cit., pp. 486, 494; Doerschuk, op. cit., pp. 19–27. See note 2, Willard and Livermore; *Notable American Women*.

18. *For the Better Protection of Their Rights*, loc. cit.

19. Ibid., pp. 16–17.

20. Ibid., pp. 18–20.

21. Ibid., pp. 21–31.

22. *Notable American Women*, vol. II, pp. 36–37, 606–07.

23. Ibid.

24. Doerschuk, op. cit., pp. 19–20; Doris L. Sassower, "Women in the Law: The Second Hundred Years," *American Bar Association Journal* 57 (April 1971): 332; Beatrice Dinerman, "Sex Discrimination in the Legal Profession," *American Bar Association Journal* 55 (October 1969): 951.

25. Doerschuk, op. cit., pp. 9–10, 22–25, 29, 58.

26. *Project on the Status and Education of Women* (repr. Washington, D.C.: Association of

American Colleges, 1977), p. 4; Albie Sachs and Joan Hoff Wilson, "Sexism and the Legal Profession: A Study of Male Beliefs and Legal Bias in Britain and the United States," *Women's Rights Law Reporter* 5 (Fall 1978): 64; Donna Fossum, "Women in the Law: A Reflection on Portia," *American Bar Association Journal* 69 (October 1983): 1389.

27. Fossum, op. cit.

28. Shirley R. Bysiewicz, "1972 AALS Questionnaire on Women in Legal Education," *Journal of Legal Education* 25 (1973): 503–07.

29. Ibid., pp. 507–12; Fossum, op. cit., p. 1393.

30. Donna Fossum, "Women Law Professors," repr. *American Bar Foundation Research Journal*, Fall 1980; pp. 904–12.

31. Ibid., pp. 912–13; Barbara A. Curran, "The Legal Profession in the 1980's," unpublished paper, American Bar Foundation, 1984, pp. 1, 8.

32. Information from Barbara Studerman, American Association of Law Schools, February 28, 1985.

33. Ibid.

34. Ibid., Fossum, "Women in the Law," op. cit., p. 1389.

35. Fossum, "Women Law Professors," pp. 912–13.

36. Sassower, op. cit., p. 332.

37. Jim Drinkhall, "Ladies of the Bar," *Wall Street Journal*, May 31, 1978, p. 46.

38. Barbara Deckard, *The Women's Movement: Political, Socioeconimic, and Psychological Issues* (New York: Harper & Row, 1979), pp. 133, 143; James J. White, "Women in the Law," *Michigan Law Review* 65 (April 1967): 1052–53, 1067, 1093; James J. White, "Women in the Law," in *The Professional Woman*, edited by Athena Theodore (Cambridge, Mass.: Schenkman, 1971), pp. 647–59.

39. White, "Women in the Law" (1967) and "Women in the Law" (1971).

40. Bill Winter, "Survey: Women Lawyers Work Harder, Are Paid Less, but They're Happy," *American Bar Association Journal* 69 (October 1983): 1386.

41. Ibid., pp. 1384–88.

42. Ibid., p. 1386.

43. *New York Times*, November 27, 1983, p. E6.

44. Fossum, "Women in the Law," p. 1391.

45. *Wall Street Journal*, December 20, 1983, pp. 1, 17.

46. Sachs and Wilson, op. cit., p. 67.

47. White, "Women in the Law," (1967), p. 1062; Cynthia F. Epstein, *Woman's Place: Options and Limits in Professional Careers* (Berkeley: University of California Press, 1970), pp. 153, 160–62.

48. Quoted in Weisberg, op. cit., p. 497.

49. Willard and Livermore, op. cit., vol. I, pp. 294, 327, and vol. II, pp. 609, 699; David Ward, "Women in the Law," *Star-Ledger* (Newark), February 26, 1979, p. 12; Clarice Feinman, "Imprisoned Women: A History of Women Incarcerated in New York City, 1932–1975," (Ph. D. diss., Department of History, New York University, 1976), pp. 192–94.

50. Curran, op. cit., p. 12.

51. Bernard Weinraub, "The Women Who Make Policy at the Pentagon," *New York Times*, December 4, 1977, p. 82.

52. Ibid.

53. Sylvia G. McCollum, "The Federal Government and Affirmative Action: A Default of Leadership," *Resolution* 1 (Summer 1975): 10–12; Drinkhall, op. cit., p. 46.

54. Vicki Quade, "Women in the Law: Twelve Success Stories," *American Bar Association Journal* 69 (October 1983): 1400.

55. Beverly B. Cook, "Women Judges: The End of Tokenism," in *Women in the Courts*, edited by Winifred L. Hepperle and Laura Crites (Williamsburg, VA.: National Center for State

Courts, 1978), pp. 85–86; Larry Berkson, "Women on the Bench: A Brief History," *Judicature* 65 (December 1981–January 1982): 291.

56. Berkson, op. cit., Cook, op. cit., p. 85.

57. Berkson, op. cit., pp. 292–93.

58. Cook, op. cit., p. 88.

59. Berkson, op. cit., p. 293.

60. Information from Daina Farthing-Capowich, National Center for State Courts, unpublished fact sheets, 1984.

61. Ibid.

62. Ibid.

63. Berkson, op. cit., p. 292.

64. Ibid., pp. 292–93.

65. Farthing-Capowich, op. cit.

66. Cook, op. cit., p. 89.

67. Ibid.

68. Ibid., p. 103, fn. 11.

69. Martin Tolchin, "U.S. Search for Women and Blacks to Serve as Judges Is Going Slowly," *New York Times*, April 12, 1977, pp. 1, 34.

70. Susan Ness, "A Sexist Selection Process Keeps Qualified Women off the Bench," repr. *Washington Post*, March 26, 1978.

71. *New York Times*, March 22, 1979, p. A7; Tom Goldstein, "City Lawyer and Connecticut Judge Joining Circuit Court: Amalya Lyle Kearse," *New York Times*, June 25, 1979, p. B2.

72. Cook, op. cit., pp. 92–93.

73. Susan Carbon, Pauline Houlden, and Larry Berkson, "Women on the State Bench: Their Characteristics and Attitudes About Judicial Selection," *Judicature* 65 (December 1981–January 1982): 295–98.

74. Elaine Martin, "Women on the Federal Bench: A Comparative Profile," *Judicature* 65 (December 1981–January 1982): 307–13.

75. *New York Times*, December 5, 1984, p. 1.

76. Beverly B. Cook, "Sex Discrimination in Politics and the All-Male Club," in *Women in the Judiciary: A Symposium for Women Judges*, edited by Marilyn Roberts and David Rhein (Williamsburg, Va.: National Center for State Courts, 1983), p. 17.

77. Ibid.

78. Norma Wikler, "Overcoming the Obstacles to Women in Judicial Education," in *Women in the Judiciary: A Symposium for Women Judges*, edited by Marilyn Roberts and David Rhein (Williamsburg, Va.: National Center for State Courts, 1983), pp. 24–25.

79. "Women Judges' Day-to-Day Professional Experiences," in *Women in the Judiciary: A Symposium for Women Judges*, edited by Marilyn Roberts and David Rhein (Williamsburg, Va.: National Center for State Courts, 1983), p. 29.

80. Ibid., p. 31.

81. Dinerman, op. cit., p. 954.

82. Neva B. Talley, "Women Lawyers of Yesterday, Today, and Tomorrow," *Women Lawyers Journal* 46 (Summer 1960): 22.

83. Ibid.

84. Ibid., p. 25.

85. Marjorie M. Childs, "The Women Lawyers Centennial," *American Bar Association Journal* 56 (January 1970): 70.

86. Quoted in ibid.

87. Ibid.

88. ibid.

89. Drinkhall, op. cit., p. 46.

90. Ibid,; Curran, op. cit., pp. 1, 8; Farthing-Capowich, op. cit.; Fossum, "Women in the Law," pp. 1389–93.

91. *New York Times*, March 29, 1979, p. B1.

92. Quoted in Beverly B. Cook, "Women as Supreme Court Candidates: From Florence Allen to Sandra O'Connor," *Judicature* 65 (December 1981–January 1982): 318.

93. Ibid.; Beverly B. Cook, "The Dual Role of Women Judges," in *Women in the Judiciary: A Symposium for Women Judges*, edited by Marilyn Roberts and David Rhein (Williamsburg, Va.: National Center for State Courts, 1983), pp. 7–8.

94. "Balancing Personal and Career Life with Career," in *Women in the Judiciary: A Symposium for Women Judges*, edited by Marilyn Roberts and David Rhein (Williamsburg, Va.: National Center for State Courts, 1983), p. 43.

95. Cook, "Sex Discrimination in Politics and the All-Male Club," p. 18.

96. Laurel Sorenson, "Women in the Law: A Woman's Unwritten Code for Success," *American Bar Association Journal* 69 (October 1983): 1414.

97. Ibid., pp. 1415–16.

98. Quoted in Barbara Babcock, "Comments and Observations," in *Women in the Judiciary: A Symposium for Women Judges* edited by Marilyn Roberts and David Rhein (Williamsburg, Va.: National Center for State Courts, 1983), p. 50.

6

WOMEN IN CORRECTIONS

Despite recent court decisions and legislation intended to eliminate sex-based discrimination in employment, the corrections system remains the most sex-segregated, male-dominated component of the criminal justice system. Many women in the system have been attempting to replace the sex-segregated structure with one that offers equal employment opportunities for women. Women's right to work in their chosen field should no longer be a debatable legal or constitutional issue, since the courts and legislatures have already determined that right. However, the experiences of many female officers and administrators reveal that impediments exist that prevent them from achieving their goal.

The history of the prison system in the United States shows that the public has had little regard for those who guard inmates. Cinema and television have created a stereotype of cruel and brutal male guards and sexually suspect female guards. Given the degree of general ignorance about correction officers, it is not surprising that women officers are the least known and least understood of all women in the criminal justice system. Even social scientists have tended to concentrate on men, who make up most of the inmates and officers, to the detriment of the women.

In the 1970s, however, ignorance and neglect began to diminish as women moved out of all-women institutions; in doing so, they competed directly with men for positions in the system and asked for equality of pay and opportunity. Predictably, all the traditional stereotypes about women have surfaced in the ensuing debate.

HISTORICAL BACKGROUND

Women entered corrections as reformers in the nineteenth century, an age of growing social problems, rapid changes in the status and role of women, and enormous zeal for reform. The Women's Christian Temperance Union, the Moral Reform Society, and the Women's Prison Association were among the organizations that tried to improve the lot of women and of society. The reformers were ladies of the middle and upper classes who felt an obligation to be useful in society. They were part of a remarkable development in the roles of women. On the one hand, the idea had arisen, and was to become especially strong in the Victorian era, that proper women were housewives and mothers who had no employment outside the home, not even as part of their husbands' businesses. These women were devoted to the "cult of true womanhood," with its emphasis on feminine subordination and passivity, except in a few areas such as community service. But from the mid nineteenth century on, there were increasing numbers of women from the propertied classes who had acquired college educations, even advanced and professional degrees. Many of these educated women entered employment as teachers, lawyers, social workers, settlement house workers, and the like, instead of becoming traditional housewives. Women of this sort managed as best they could in an often hostile male world.[1]

Both homemakers and professionals, however, agreed on the need for certain kinds of reform affecting "fallen" women. One of the first goals was the eradication of prostitution, an offense that carried strong moral overtones. Prostitution was one obvious result of urbanization, industrialization, and immigration. Vast numbers of poor, uneducated women, especially immigrants, provided the cheap labor that powered U.S. business in the nineteenth century. Their lives were hard, and many discovered the quick and tangible rewards of selling their bodies. In doing so, they violated all of the womanly ideals held sacred by the wealthier classes, and in general were regarded as destructive temptresses. Here was a field ripe for reform.[2]

In 1834 a group of ladies formed the New York Female Moral Reform Society. From the very beginning they took the then novel view that the true blame for prostitution rested on men, whom they accused of destroying innocent women in order to satisfy base desires. Society could be cleansed of prostitution mainly by controlling men's sexual behavior (which would also eliminate adultery) and by converting the prostitutes into good Protestants. The reformers, fired by the religious zeal of the Second Great Awakening, expressed "a strident hostility to the licentious and predatory male."[3]

Despite the strong moralistic tone of their program, the reformers also attacked some of the economic conditions that encouraged prostitution. They proposed that women be given more economic opportunities, especially in areas then considered men's work, and they encouraged the organization of unions to protect the rights of working women. Nevertheless, there was no attempt to make basic changes in either economy or society.[4]

This conservatism was typical of most women's reform movements of the nineteenth century. The wealth and position of the reformers made the movements traditional rather than militant. The reform programs were usually phrased in religious terms, and the prostitutes were "fallen" women whom the good and pious must "uplift." There were also other elements of a more self-interested nature. Curbing prostitution, it was argued, would reduce the number of illegitimate births; and since most prostitutes were immigrants, a reduction in illegitimacy would lessen the increase of elements that threatened to "bastardize American civilization." Josephine Shaw Lowell, a patrician active in the development of women's corrections, considered prostitutes "a serious eugenic danger to society" that had to be removed.[5] Thus the efforts against prostitution also carried class connotations.

It quickly became apparent that one part of the reform program, the reining in of male sexual desires, was not feasible. Reformers therefore concentrated on the other part, the rehabilitation of fallen women. Since men were corrupters, they must be kept away from susceptible women, which meant that facilities for the raising up of prostitutes and other fallen women had to be strictly segregated from the male world. This view was soon established as a basic element of the reform movement, where it fit easily with another belief of proper women: that, on the whole, women were the moral and spiritual superiors of men. The segregation of women in corrections was therefore justified on both practical and theoretical grounds. The natural result was the creation of a prison system for women only, staffed by women; many reformers became professionals in corrections for women.

The U.S. penal system had, by the late eighteenth century, undergone a major change. Under the impetus of fervent religious belief, it was decided that the usual punishments for crimes—flogging, mutilation, death—should be replaced by rehabilitation. Through religious instruction, meditation on past wrongs, and hard work, criminals could be made to see the evil of their ways and to recant their antisocial views. Criminals thus reformed would be saved for both God and society.

Women were not at first considered worthy or capable of benefiting from this new approach. Female offenders seemed especially depraved because they had deserted the proper womanly place and done those things that only evil men were supposed to do. Since these women were obviously beyond redemption, little effort was made to help them, and conditions in prisons became atrocious. The lack of institutions specifically for women meant that females were incarcerated in wings, rooms, and attics of men's penitentiaries, separated from the male inmates but supervised by male guards. All women, regardless of age, offense, background, health, or maternal status, lived in one limited space amid constant turmoil. Some prison officials even feared that the overcrowding, sickness, deaths of newborn babies, fights, screams, and attacks on guards might affect the safety, security, and health of male inmates. Efforts to control the women by starving and flogging them failed. Despite efforts by reformers, the flogging continued, because judges ruled that physical force was necessary to control inmates and make them obey, The public also believed that women criminals were more depraved than men and beyond redemption. Only a few people, motivated by religious impulses, attempted to help them.[6]

CORRECTION OFFICERS AND SUPERINTENDENTS: THEORY AND PRACTICE

Prison reformers in the United States adopted the theories and practices devised by Elizabeth Fry while she and other women volunteered to reform female prisoners in London in the early nineteenth century. She believed that women criminals could be reformed if they were separated from men and supervised and taught by virtuous and pious women. Once separated in an all-women's prison, female offenders required a structured program of discipline, cleanliness, education, work, and religious instruction to ensure their return to true womanhood. These ideas formed the theoretical and practical foundations upon which women's corrections developed.[7]

Reformers implemented Fry's program, first in juvenile facilities, then in homes for delinquent females, and finally in women's sections of penitentiaries. The first successful adaptation of her program took place in Sing Sing from 1844 to 1848, under the leadership of reformer/head matron Eliza Farnham, who established precedents for women's corrections. First, as a reformer concerned with female offenders, she moved from theory to practice and became a head matron. Second, she added a component to Fry's program; she attempted to simulate a homelike atmosphere in prison, with matrons setting examples as mother figures for their "errant daughters."[8]

One of the most illuminating documents to come out of Farnham's group of matrons is a book by Georgiana B. Kirby, who wrote about the years she spent with Farnham at Sing Sing. Her book is important because it provides insights into the theories, problems, and public understanding of women in corrections. She observed that educated women worked much better with the inmates than did uneducated women, because thay had the discipline and ability to control inmates. She nevertheless encountered criticism from some of her friends who held corrections work in low esteem: "It was natural that some of my old friends should be shocked on hearing that I had thus allied myself to the civilization we condemned."[9]

The Farnham approach, as described by Kirby, was the maternal one used by all professionals in that period:

> As I said, it had pleased us to love these low-down children of circumstances less fortunate than our own. We gloried in being able to lift a few of them out of the slough into which they had fallen, or in which they had been born, and to sustain them while they were trying to take a little step upward in the direction of the light.[10]

Farnham's success encouraged women reformers. They proceeded to gather information about incarcerated women; many instances of beatings and sexual abuse provided ample evidence to convince men in government and prisons of the necessity for a separate women's prison system. However, men seriously doubted whether respectable women should work in a prison environment with depraved females, and whether reformers had the ability to control and reform such females. The reformers stressed that the innate characteristics of pious, pure wives and mothers provided them with the strength and capacity required to deal with fallen women; only mothers could teach daughters true womanhood. This argument, together with the evidence presented, convinced legislators; they passed laws establishing a separate women's prison system and, in doing so, created a permanent place for women professionals in corrections.[11]

The first of these professionals, Superintendent Sarah Smith and her matron staff, started to work in 1873 at the Indiana Reformatory Institution for Women and Girls. Women's institutions had a common denominator: all were established as a result of efforts made by women's groups; all were planned and led by women who held to the basic theory of the unique capability of women to reform female offenders; and all incorporated Fry's program with the addition of the homelike atmosphere introduced by Farnham. Professional women in corrections reinforced traditional women's roles and ensured careers for themselves.

These reformers came from middle- and upper-class, white, Protestant families, and several had earned doctoral degrees. They may have deviated a little from societal norms when they became professionals in corrections, an area once reserved for men. However, because they worked only to teach their fallen ''daughters'' to return to true womanhood, they were permitted to enter the prison system. Although many of the reformers who worked did not become wives and homemakers in the traditional sense, they made the reformatories their homes and the inmates their children. Men in the prison system permitted women to enter the system because they knew and remained in their place. By establishing a matriarchy in corrections, women did not compete with men.

SUPERINTENDENTS

Women who led these prisons were all experienced in social work and reform. Detailed information is available on seven of the first group of superintendents from 1884 to 1932: they were well educated—three had Ph.D.s and one had a B.A. degree; two were married; all were white; all had experience as either nurse, teacher, matron, or social worker; four actively supported women's rights; and all were experimenters and innovators. At

Framingham, Massachusetts, Jessie Hodder began case study and work release programs; Dr. Miriam van Waters (Ph.D. in sociology) organized the Friendly Visitors, a community service volunteer group that is still found in many cities.[12]

Dr. Katherine B. Davis (Ph.D. in political economy) began a case study program and established a venereal disease clinic at Bedford Hills, New York. In 1911, with funds from John D. Rockerfeller, she opened a center for the study of the causes of female criminality. When, in 1914, she became the first female commissioner of corrections in New York City, she appointed a friend, Dr. Mary Harris (Ph.D. in Sanskrit and Indo-European comparative philology) as superintendent of the women's division of the workhouse. During Davis' four-year tenure, she introduced many reforms for all inmates and with Harris, made a number of changes that benefited women in particular. They replaced striped uniforms with gingham dresses, issued shoes that fit, engaged doctors to treat venereal diseases, and fenced in the courtyard so that women inmates, for the first time in the history of the workhouse, could go outdoors.[13]

The superintendents encouraged inmates to work and exercise outdoors as means of developing good work habits and relieving boredom and tension, and with the intent of reducing the level of homosexual activity. In addition to educational and work programs, they introduced the concept of self-government in order to promote a sense of responsibilty and citizenship among the inmates. The superintendents did their best with the small budgets appropriated to operate women's prisons. As a result, treatment programs for drug addicts and alcoholics were often nonexistent. Harris lamented the lack of such programs and the resultant high rate of recidivism: "Unless we have built within them a wall of self respect, moral integrity, and a desire to be an asset to the community instead of a menace, we have not protected society—which is ourselves—from the criminal."[14]

The first group of superintendents had to cope with problems that continue to the present: the lack of proper funding for rehabilitation programs and for salaries, and the difficulty of attracting mature, educated, concerned women to work in the institutions. In 1934, a doctor, discussing her observations at a women's facility, wrote that a superintendent would have a hard time attracting and hiring capable officers, because she could offer a salary of only $45 per month with room and board, and the officer had to live in the prison 24 hours a day, with 2 days off every 2 weeks and 2 weeks' vacation a year. She concluded:

> This is not tempting bait to a woman of ability and when one also considers the fear, which any normal woman may be expected to have, of entering "prison employment," because of the physical risks she thinks she may run, it is a marvel that women's prisons recruit such able matrons and staff members. The movies and *Anne Vickers* do not help in popularizing this line of work as a career.[15]

Many of the programs created by women such as Harris and Davis were inspired by the social programs of settlement houses. The settlement house, a nineteenth-century contribution to the need for social services in rapidly growing industrialized cities of the East and Midwest, provided a homelike setting for workers—usually white, middle-class women—who went out into the local community to perform their mission. Davis and Harris, like many women who eventually became active in corrections during the late nineteenth and early twentieth centuries, had once served in a settlement house. The concept of a home in which women lived and served others was easily transferred to prisons when the women became superintendents.

Ruth Collins, the first superintendent of the House of Detention for Women (HDW) in New York City, was typical of that group of reformer superintendents. She had also served as a juvenile worker in several cities, as head of the Women's Division of the House of Correction in Detroit, and as an administrator of the Social Service Division in the Bureau of Prisons of the Department of Justice in Washington, D.C. She operated the HDW with a social work approach, believing that women offenders needed education, cultural benefits, and time to think about how to change their lives. In an interview in the *New York World Telegram* in 1932, when she became superintendent of the HDW, Collins said, "If we cannot send them out generally prepared for a new and better start, it is our fault and we have failed them. A prison is a place for restoration rather than for punishment."[16]

At the time when women like Harris, Collins, and Davis were entering corrections as superintendents of prisons, it was extremely difficult for women with college degrees to obtain managerial positions in the private sector. Even at women's colleges they had a hard time becoming faculty members or administrators, so great was the general prejudice against placing women in positions of responsibility. Ironically, the one area where they had a right to leadership was in women's corrections, where law, civil service specifications, or custom usually excluded men. It was therefore common for women to remain in the corrections system for long periods of time because there were few outside opportunities. This may explain why so many educated and able women were willing to subject themselves to the many unpleasant aspects of the life of a women's prison superintendent: they earned less than men superintendents; they were not expected to marry and have families; the rural communities where most women's prisons were located expected a high degree of sexual morality and kept prominent women under the microscope of constant gossip; and, because of the rural environment, social opportunities were extremely limited.[17]

Only recently has this changed; as the civil rights movement has thrown down barriers and restrictions on employment, women have begun to enter areas of the economy once reserved for men. Now corrections professionals work as consultants or administrators in departments of correction and may even move into academe as faculty. For example, Laurel Rans, former superintendent of the Iowa Women's Reformatory (1967-72), became a consultant. In June 1979 she received an appointment as deputy commissioner of the Illinois State Department of Corrections. Dr. Katherine Gabel, a Ph.D. in sociology and an attorney, moved from superintendent of Arizona Girls' School to Smith College as dean of the School of Social Work and a lecturer in the Department of Sociology and Anthropology.[18]

Because of their education, participation in reform, and innovative contributions to corrections, these superintendents have gained the respect of both men and women in penal reform and in corrections. Some of them are taking reform one step further, actively supporting women's equal employment rights in corrections and in the community.

CORRECTION OFFICERS

Although superintendents are the most visible women in corrections, they are far outnumbered by the women correction officers, or, as they were usually called before the 1960s, matrons. From the nineteenth and early twentieth centuries, most of our information about them comes from reports, articles, and autobiographies of superintendents and a few autobiographies of former inmates. Kate O'Hare, imprisoned in 1919 for a federal offense under the Espionage Act, wrote of her experiences at the state prison in Jefferson City, Missouri. It was a men's prison with a special section for women; a male warden was in charge of a chief matron and subordinate matrons. O'Hare criticized the matrons, although she sympathized with many of the problems they faced:

> The matrons were required to live in the prison and were never, except on rare leaves of absence, out of the sights and sounds and smells of prison. They were prisoners to almost the same degree that we were, and they all staggered under a load of responsibility far too great for their limited intelligence and untrained powers. They handled human beings at their worst, and under the worst possible conditions, and saw nothing day or night but sordid, ugly things ungilded by the glow of hope or love.[19]

She also described the sadness of the lives of these women:

> These women who were our keepers had missed love and wifehood; they had nothing to look back upon or forward to. There is a sort of stigma attached to their work that makes the possibilities of love and mating for them very limited indeed. The ordinary social relations of normal life were impossible for them, and they lived in a very inferno of loneliness and isolation![20]

O'Hare's description of the problems of matrons both on the job and in their personal lives is one of the best available. She was able to understand and explain to her readers what it was to be a matron. She was explicit in her descriptions of the matrons' corruption and harsh treatment of the inmates, much of which, she thought, resulted from the stigma attached to corrections, which destroyed both inmates and matrons.[21]

Many of these problems still exist. The job of prison guard is still not considered proper women's work by the public, and within corrections, the status of women professionals is so low that they have been ignored in almost all books on corrections and studies of correction officers. Only a few studies have been done since the 1970s, but a major study, *Women Employed in Corrections,* conducted by the Center for Women Policy Studies, was published in 1983. (These studies will be discussed later in this chapter.)

Training is still often inadequate. Until the federal prison system instituted formal training at an academy in 1971, training for women officers normally took place in the women's prison at Alderson, West Virginia. New York City opened its academy and started formal training in 1957. New Jersey has a training academy, but it is not mandatory and officers may be assigned to it after they have been on the job for years. Although most states offer some type of training, many counties and cities do not; the officer is given a key and told to go to work.[22]

Correction officers must still face the problem of dealing with an extremely diverse group of women inmates, sentenced for a wide variety of crimes and often under serious emotional stress. Since most states have only one all-women's facility, if any, women are usually incarcerated in the one facility. The institution includes all females over 16, with every type of criminal history and security classification, as well as levels of education and skills, emotional maturity, and family experience and problems. Reports from state and federal facilities in the 1970s and 1980s have indicated an increase in the number of emotionally disturbed women coming into the facilities, perhaps as the result of drug abuse. Many of the inmates are in emotional turmoil.[23]

Geography plays a role in another problem, that of attracting and keeping a qualified staff. Because women's prisons are located in rural areas, it becomes difficult to recruit staff except from the local communities. Women from cities are reluctant to travel long distances to the prison or to move to an isolated community. The warden of the women's prison in New Jersey commented that he was "scraping the bottom of the barrel" of the civil service list.[24] Turnover of staff is high because women leave for other jobs as soon as possible. Recruiting from local communities often produces sharp differences in the race, religion, and life-styles of inmates and staff. Women's jails are easier to staff because they are located in cities. In addition, since the 1950s, it has been more likely that the staff in the jails will be similar to the racial and religious backgrounds of the inmates. In New York City, for example, the percentage of black staff and black inmates is about 80 percent; many of the staff have socioeconomic backgrounds similar to those of the inmates, often living in the same neighborhoods.[25]

Geographic location can also affect staff morale. For example, when the women's jail in New York City was moved from Greenwich Village to Rikers Island in Queens, morale dropped and several officers retired or resigned. In Greenwich Village the officers were within walking distance of public transportation, banks, and stores. It was easy for them to get to and from work, and to take care of their personal and family needs either before starting work or after finishing their tour of duty. These services were not conveniently located near Rikers Island; it became necessary for most of the women to have cars for transportation. Absenteeism rose as women took time off to meet their personal and family needs.[26]

Correction officers must also cope with the fact that they work in what is called the "locked-in culture." Like women in some other kinds of employment, correction officers must often work holidays or night shifts. However, when they do so, they are literally locked in the institution for the entire period of their duty. They may not leave the institution for any reason, and in that sense are as incarcerated as the inmates. After their eight-hour shift, they may be obliged to work an additional eight hours if an officer on the next shift fails to report for duty. If the officers remain for a few years, they tend to stay until retirement. Some officers become "job phobic" from the emotional stress and the locked-in culture.[27]

The isolation and harsh working conditions of prison life are therefore factors working against the entrance of women into corrections, but obviously women enter anyway. A major attraction seems to be money. In rural areas even low salaries are better than nothing. According to Elizabeth Gurley Flynn, incarcerated at the Alderson federal prison from 1955 to 1957 for violating the Smith Act, most of the matrons were white rural women from the immediate vicinity. They worked for the money, not from any sense of dedication; the turnover rate was high because many left for better jobs in cities and others quit when they married.[28]

However, it is not easy to generalize because conditions, salaries, and the women involved have changed since the 1950s. My interviews in the 1970s and 1980s with women working in jails and prisons in New York City, Los Angeles, Maryland, Pennsylvania, New Jersey, and elsewhere indicate that most of the women want job security, salaries, and benefits such as pensions, health (including maternity) insurance, and vacations. These reasons were particularly important to women with no skills and only a high school diploma or its equivalent. The Center for Women Policy Studies reported that women cited career opportunities and salaries, as well as interest in the work, as reasons for seeking employment in corrections.[29]

Salaries increased from 1979 to 1984, to an average of $13,938 to $18,804 a year, and included pensions, medical insurance, and vacations. For example, salaries in the Federal Bureau of Prisons increased from $11,712 to $15,497; in New Jersey from $11,365 to $17,523; and in New York City from $15,247 to $21,811. Additional pay for overtime and night shift duty could increase salaries as much as $5,000 a year. By 1984, however, almost all states and many cities required a high school diploma or its equivalent.[30]

Although salaries increased and benefits were included, poor working conditions and a negative image of correctional occupations make it difficult to recruit competent staff. Therefore, it is not surprising that college-educated and skilled women have turned their backs on careers as correction officers, preferring probation, parole, and law enforcement careers. During the depression of the 1930s, college-educated women took as many civil service examinations as possible, and many were appointed from the correction officers list. It may not have been their first choice, but it provided them with steady work and an income. Because of their education, they quickly rose through the ranks to become superintendents, as was the case with three women who became officers in the New York City House of Detention for Women in the late 1930s and early 1940s, a period when an estimated one-quarter of the officers had college degrees. Now, however, with other job opportunities available, few college-educated women are attracted to careers as corrections officers.[31]

DISCRIMINATION

There is a final set of problems associated with women in corrections, and it is encompassed in the word "discrimination." Major changes have occurred since the 1960s that have opened new areas of employment to women. Nevertheless, progress is uneven, and while the courts extend women's opportunities in one area, they may restrict them in others.

A recent form of discrimination stems from veterans' preference laws that mostly benefit men. Women have pointed out that veterans who score lower on civil service examinations than women receive jobs and promotions that should go to the women. In June 1979, the U.S. Supreme Court, in *Personnel Administrator of Massachusetts* v. *Feeney,* upheld the Massachusetts veterans' preference law, on the grounds that the law is not "gender-based" because it places both men and women at a disadvantage as individuals, even though it does benefit men as a class.[32]

A much older form of discrimination is, of course, racial. Before the U.S. Supreme Court decision in *Brown* v. *Topeka, Kansas Board of Education,* declaring racial segregation to be unconstitutional, racial segregation existed as institutional policy and practice, de jure in the South and de facto in the North.

Superintendents were white, as were most officers. Although black officers were hired, they were assigned to guard black inmates. It was not unusual for black officers, even those with college degrees, to be assigned the most menial and physically strenuous work available in the institution. For example, Elizabeth Gurley Flynn, writing of her experiences as an inmate at Alderson in the 1950s, stated that black officers and inmates were always assigned to the piggery. In the New York City House of Detention for Women (HDW), black officers and inmates were assigned to housing areas called ''black corridors,'' and black inmates worked in the laundry while white inmates worked in the kitchen. Three former HDW superintendents (from 1967 to 1978) agreed that segregation ended after the *Brown* decision, and racial discrimination ceased to be practiced. The new policy was implemented without resistance because, during the 1950s, a large group of black women became officers.[33]

Since the 1950s, noticeable changes have occurred in correctional staffs. Black women in particular have benefited from employment opportunities in the corrections system since racial segregation has ended. The number of black officers and administrators has increased, especially in urban areas. Black women have found that civil service employment offers them steady, full-time work, an income with benefits, and opportunities for promotion based on competitive examinations where racial discrimination does not interfere with advancement. This trend is particularly noticeable in women's jails in large cities, such as New York, Los Angeles, Chicago, and Washington, D.C.

Since the New York City Department of Correction employs about as many female correction officers as the state of California and more than any other department in the nation, (841 uniformed female officers of a total of 5,770 uniformed officers as of 1984), it offers an excellent illustration of the gains made by black women in the system.[34] After the *Brown* decision, many black women, several of whom had graduated from college, applied for positions as officers in the HDW. (It was renamed New York City Correctional Institution for Women when the HDW closed and the new institution opened on Rikers Island in 1971.) By the end of the 1950s, they constituted approximately 50 percent of the staff, and by the early 1980s the percentage had increased to approximately 80 percent. According to the department's Equal Employment Opportunity Report for 1983–84, of the 841 female officers, 663 were black, 101 were white, 76 were Hispanic, and one was Asian. (Of the five women in the warden, deputy warden, and assistant deputy warden group, four were black and one was white.) The first black woman was promoted to superintendent in 1969, the second in 1971. In 1980, Jacqueline McMickens became the first female chief of operations, the highest uniformed position in the department. She was responsibile for the implementation of policies and practices that concern security, personnel, and inmates in all the male, female, and juvenile facilities in the city. In 1982, Gloria Lee became warden of the

Bronx House of Detention, one of the largest and most dangerous jails for men in the city, and in 1983, she was appointed as one of the supervising wardens of the Rikers Island jail complex. In 1984, McMickens was appointed commissioner of corrections and Lee became chief of operations.[35]

Interviews with McMickens, Lee, and other black women in the system indicated that as employment opportunities opened for women in other areas, many white women left the penal system, creating a vacuum for black women to fill. As the system became identified with black women, both as staff and inmates, fewer and fewer white women applied for jobs. Experiences of black women in other large urban penal systems are similar to those of black women in the New York City system. However, in rural areas, white women still account for the majority of female officers and administrators. This pattern is in keeping with the demographic distribution of black and white people in the country. In 1983, there were 2,778 black, 5,425 white, 251 Hispanic, 37 American Indian/Alaskan, and 21 other women correction officers, for a total of 8,512 women officers in the nation.[36]

The major form of discrimination involving women is, of course, sexual. Whatever their race, religion, or ethnic identity, all women in the corrections system have encountered discrimination—some subtle, most quite blatant. For example, men have been permitted to be wardens of women's prisons. (Clara Waters became the first woman warden of a state prison upon her appointment to the Oklahoma State Reformatory in 1927.) Men were assigned to women's facilities in security, maintenance, and administrative capacities, but women were not assigned to men's facilities until the late 1960s—and then only to search female visitors for contraband. Not until the 1970s did women work in male institutions as correction officers performing all duties. Rarely did women work in the central offices except as secretaries or clerical workers. This held true even if the commissioner was a woman, as has happened twice in New York City (Katherine B. Davis in 1914–18 and Anna M. Kross in 1954–65), twice in Oklahoma (Kate Barnard in 1907–15 and Mabel Bassett in 1923–27), and once in Minnesota (Blanche LaDu in 1936–37).[37]

There can be little doubt that women's opportunities for employment in the prison system are limited. In the United States there is usually only one women's prison in each state, and a few states have none at all. Therefore, a sex-segregated prison system limits women's employment opportunities in three ways: only a small number of women officers can work in the prison system at a given time; promotions to supervisory and administrative positions are very limited and seldom available; and women are restricted to one prison in a single geographic area, with no opportunity to transfer to institutions in other areas of the state. In jurisdictions where integration has been implemented, women have certainly gained both employment and promotional opportunities. The most obvious example is in the New York City Department of Correction.

Since the 1970s, local and state departments of correction have been forced to comply with federal legislation forbidding employment discrimination based on sex. Title VII of the Civil Rights Act of 1964, which forbids discrimination on the basis of sex, gave women a legal basis on which to speak out against unfair practices and conditions in the corrections system. Title VII's real effects, however, were limited because it did not include employees of federal, state, county, or city governments; in 1972 it was amended, broadening the powers of the Equal Employment Opportunity Commission (EEOC) to cover all government agencies. Discriminatory practices were forbidden in all agencies receiving Law Enforcement Assistance Administration (LEAA) funds. This was restated in the 1973 and 1976 amendments to the 1968 Crime Control Act: no private, state, local, or federal agency would receive LEAA funds if sex-based discrimination were found. Since departments of correction all over the country relied heavily on LEAA funds, they made efforts to comply with the new laws.

When, in 1983, congressional appropriations for LEAA ended, other federal funding agencies took over the responsibility of withholding funds from programs, institutions, or government departments that discriminated against persons on the basis of race or sex; these were the Office of Revenue Sharing of the U.S. Department of the Treasury (Revenue Sharing Act of 1972) and the Office of Justice Assistance, Research and Statistics (Justice Systems Improvement Act of 1979). In addition, the Equal Pay Act of 1963 and the Pregnancy Discrimination Act of 1978 provided women with the means to take legal action in cases of discrimination.[38]

As a result, women correction officers have been assigned to male institutions and men to women's, in direct contact with inmates of the opposite sex. Gloria Lee was appointed warden at the Men's House of Detention, Bronx, New York; Janice Warne at the Albion Correctional Institution, Albion, New York; Arleene Love at the Deberry Correctional Institute for Special Needs Offenders, Nashville, Tennessee; Norma Gluckstern at the Pautaxent facility for emotionally ill inmates at Heightfield, Maryland; and Margaret Hambreck at the Federal Correctional Institution, Morgantown, West Virginia. At the same time, male wardens were appointed to three women's facilities for the first time in their history: the federal prison at Alderson, West Virginia; the state prison at Clinton, New Jersey; and the city jail in New York City.[39]

By 1979, according to a survey by CONtact, almost all states and several cities had complied with federal legislation and had assigned women to male institutions, although almost all placed severe limitations on where women could work and what they could do; most did not permit women to be in direct contact with male inmates or to work in housing areas.[40] CONtact conducted another survey in 1982 and reported that, of 44 states responding, only New Mexico did not employ women officers in male institutions; in the other 43 states, approximately 8.4 percent of the correctional staff in male facilities were women. The survey also reported that, as in 1979, limitations were placed on women officers because of inmates' right to privacy. Therefore women, in general, did not perform strip searches, and did not supervise inmates in housing and/or bathroom areas. Several states indicated that these limitations placed restrictions on women's right to employment and could prevent women from being promoted, since they did not receive the same work experiences as did male officers. Most of the states did not notice any negative impact from women working in male institutions but, rather, that women became "a positive addition to the prison environment."[41]

Only Delaware and California integrated male and female staffs from the start, with few, if any, limitations. The efforts of the California Department of Corrections were particularly notable. Prior to 1972, women did not work in a custodial capacity in male institutions. From 1972 to 1974, they were assigned to men's facilities only to search and supervise women visitors, so as to prevent the smuggling of contraband. As a result of pressure exerted on the director of corrections, Raymond Procunier, by the chief of personnel and by the only woman executive in the department, the policy of full integration of staff went into effect in mid 1974. Women who were accepted for nontraditional job assignments in male institutions received the training and supervision necessary for the job. As Arlene M. Becker, deputy director of the department, wrote: "The department cannot supervise the feelings and opinions of the managers, but it can supervise their behavior."[42] The male managers of male institutions were assured that women assigned to their facilities would do the same work and meet the same standards as men. This policy and Procunier's support have been crucial to the success of equal employment opportunity in California's corrections system.[43]

New York City began to end sex discrimination in 1978, when a new commissioner of correction, a woman deputy, and a woman assistant commissioner began to change policies. The next year the city personnel director deleted the word "superintendent," which had applied only to women in charge of the women's jail, from job designations and substituted the title of "warden" for both sexes. Sex-linked designations for all other titles were eliminated. After the changes were made, Gloria Lee became warden of the House of Detention for Men in the Bronx and Albert Nolen, acting warden of the New York City Correctional Institution for Women on Rikers Island. For the first time, two women officers were assigned to key positions at central headquarters, one to the Communications Control Center and one as chief of operations. However, for reasons of security and privacy, women officers were primarily assigned to the women's jail. By 1984, significant steps had been taken to integrate male and female staffs and to expand women's employment opportunities. In fact, women were appointed to most of the top administrative positions. Jacqueline McMickens became commissioner of correction, two women became deputy commissioners, three became assistant commissioners, and Gloria Lee became chief of operations. Men and women officers receive assignments on an equal basis and work in all capacities, regardless of the sex of the inmate. However, unless an emergency exists, strip searchers of inmates are conducted by officers of the same sex as the inmates.[44]

The federal prison system also changed its policy in its efforts to end discriminatory practices. Sylvia G. McCollum, of the Federal Bureau of Prisons (FBP) wrote, "The federal government is the largest single employer in the United States. What it does—and equally important, what it fails to do—in employment practices is critical."[45] As late as 1975 the FBP began implementing an affirmative-action program that included the Women's Program to advise the Equal Employment Opportunities Commission on issues concerning women in corrections, and the Upward Mobility Program to ensure that women have an opportunity for advancement in the system. The FBP acted to promote women to supervisory and training positions, as well as to integrate men and women officers into a single correctional staff in all but maximum-security penitentiaries.[46]

In March 1979, women officers in the FBP comprised 16.5 percent (345 officers) of the total correction officer staff. By January 1985, there were 419 women, but they comprised only 10 percent of 4,224 officers. Of the 419 women, 221 were white, 179 black, 18 Hispanic, and one Asian.[47] In March 1979, one woman, Margaret Hambreck, was a warden of a male facility, the minimum-security prison for young men at Morgantown, West Virginia. In addition, women were associate wardens at the women's facilities at Alderson, West Virginia, and Pleasanton, California. Both these institutions had male wardens. (The facility at Pleasanton became cocorrectional in 1980.) By January 1985, a trend backward toward more traditional assignments was noticeable, with Gwynne Sizer, the only female warden in the entire FBP, in charge at Alderson.[48]

In 1971, the FBP initiated uniform training for men and women. Sam Sample, in charge of training in 1979, commented that women who stay in corrections are the most persevering people in the world. They have to overcome enormous and subtle obstacles placed in their way by men in the system. He noted that there were fewer problems for women in federal cocorrectional institutions than in male institutions. He also noted that the location of the facility affects acceptance of women in male institutions, with women less likely to be accepted in rural areas than in urban areas.[49]

The roots of sexual discrimination go far back in history, with the embodiment of discrimination in law and policy. But in practical terms, discrimination is confronted by women most often in the personal views and biases of men, who compose most of the personnel in corrections. I have had considerable exposure to the views of both men and women officers and administrators, especially in the course "Women's Corrections" that I taught at the New Jersey Department of Corrections Training Academy. Since I was not responsible for assigning grades, the class discussions were open and unrestrained, sometimes even emotionally charged. These discussions corroborated impressions gained while working for the New York City Department of Correction as a project director of a rehabilitation program in the women's jail, and also while visiting other jails and prisons. Most men in corrections continue to see women in traditional ways: the good woman is the wife and mother who stays home; a woman working in corrections is suspect; a woman who works in a jail or prison for men is considered sexually loose or deviant.

Despite federal legislation, women who seek to integrate men and women into one correctional staff on an equal basis encounter hostility and resistance from male staff and from women officers as well. Those opposed to an integrated staff repeat traditional assumptions about womanhood, not facts, to prove their points of view; they base their arguments on traditional perceptions about stereotypical woman.

Ironically, many who favor an integrated staff resort to arguments based on stereotypical women; women are different from men: they are more humane, more sensitive, and more caring. In support of an integrated work force in penal institutions, integrationists, feminists, and several social scientists have stated that women would sensitize male workers and humanize the work environment, creating an atmosphere more conducive to rehabilitating inmates. In addition, they have included the theory that because women may have experienced discrimination based on sex or race, they would be more aware of the interests and needs of other oppressed people, the inmates. Norval Morris, of the University of Chicago Law School, claimed that women "will tend to reduce violence," and therefore aid in the rehabilitation of inmates.[50] After interviewing inmates in male institutions, Joan Potter wrote: "Women tend to be less abusive and more willing to talk, these prisoners say; moreover, their presence makes the artificial world of the prison seem more like the outside world."[51]

Although Morris, Potter, and others have expected that women who entered a male-dominated field would deviate from existing role expectations and introduce a feminine, more humane, role model, there are no empirical data to substantiate these assumptions. Rather, there is some evidence suggesting that women hired under the recent policy of staff integration, with assignments in male as well as female institutions, identify with the male model of guarding: one that adheres to the rules and is founded on suspicion and emotional distance from inmates.[52] In essence, three types of women officers and administrators are identifiable in corrections: the traditionalists, who have been in corrections a while and resist change, and want only to work with women in a female institution; the integrationists, many of whom have worked in corrections for many years and have fought to achieve equality with their male colleagues; and those who have been hired since the late 1970s and have experienced work only as officers under the new policy of integration. The latter group is more likely than the other two to see themselves as officers and to identify with male officers in terms of attitudes toward their job.

COURT DECISIONS

Given the strong feelings of male officers and administrators, it is not surprising that a reason for the opposition to the integration of women into the staff in male prisons and jails concerns security. Those opposed to a fully integrated staff argue that the presence of women increases security risks in three ways. First, women are not physically strong enough to control dangerous or violent male inmates, either on a one-to-one basis or in a riot situation. Second, women are objects and potential victims of rape, and this makes them vulnerable to sexual assault by inmates. Third, male officers feel compelled to protect female officers from rape and from other violent situations, thereby increasing danger to themselves.

These arguments persist despite the fact that male officers and administrators are unable to provide documentation to prove that female officers and administrators increase security risks in a male institutions. There are no studies to evaluate the ability of women to handle dangerous or violent situations in a male prison or jail. Therefore, there are no data to verify or refute arguments opposing women's right to work in male facilities on the basis of security concerns. Equally important, since the implementation of equal employment practices in the penal system, there have been no reports of actual incidents of violent confrontation or dangerous situations brought about by the presence of female officers and administrators or their inability to handle their jobs. Both male and female security staffs work unarmed, aware that other officers, fully armed, are prepared to come to the aid of anyone in trouble. Furthermore, although departments of correction are loath to report incidents of rape, of either officers or inmates, it is known that a number of male officers have been raped by inmates. But as of January 1985, no female officer had been raped by male inmates.* Despite the lack of data to support their argument, men in departments of correction have taken the security issue to court and have been successful in limiting the employment opportunities of women.

---

*On May 15, 1981, Correction Officer Donna Payant, a 31-year-old mother of three and wife of a correction officer, was strangled to death at the Green Haven Correctional facility in Stormville, New York by a 39-year-old inmate, Lemuel Smith who was serving two consecutive life sentences for murder. He was an inmate assistant to a chaplain and therefore had access to

Women officers were excluded from working in certain male institutions as a result of *Dothard* v. *Rawlinson* in 1977. The U.S. Supreme Court based its decision on the bona fide occupational qualification (BFOQ) exception to Title VII's ban on sex-based discrimination in employment. A provision in Title VII of the Civil Rights Act of 1964 states that it is not unlawful for an employer to hire someone on the basis of sex, religion, or national origin if there is a bona fide occupational qualification reasonably necessary to the normal operation of the particular job or business. The Supreme Court decided that in a male maximum-security institution, where women officers would be in physical danger and subject to rape, sex could be a BFOQ exception to Title VII and women therefore could be prohibited from employment in that institution.[53]

The possible long-range significance of *Dothard* v. *Rawlinson* requires some comment. Dianne Rawlinson, with a degree in correctional psychology, applied for a position as correctional counselor with the Alabama Board of Corrections (a correctional counselor is a prison guard). She was rejected on the basis of the board's height and weight requirements for the position; she was five pounds less than the required weight. She filed suit in federal court, basing her case on violations under Title VII. The federal district court ruled that there was neither a basis for height and weight requirements for a prison guard nor for a "no contact" rule against hiring women to work in a male facility; there was no evidence that women posed a security risk or violated male inmates' right to privacy.[54]

The Board of Corrections appealed to the Supreme Court and, in *Dothard* v. *Rawlinson*, the Supreme Court upheld the opinion of the lower court regarding height and weight requirements, but reversed the lower court's rejection of the "no contact" rule. Justice Potter Stewart, speaking for the Court, said that a guard's position fell within the BFOQ exception to Title VII because the male prisons in Alabama were so dangerous as to pose a security risk for women; they could be sexually assaulted. Justice Thurgood Marshall, in his dissenting opinion, argued that rather than punish women by denying them the right to employment, Alabama should be made to create a secure and humane prison system to ensure the safety of staff and inmates.[55] (Alabama was operating its prison system in violation of the Eighth Amendment and

---

the chaplain's office and phone. Smith called Payant, claiming to be a correction officer, and told her she was needed in the chaplain's office. When she arrived, he strangled her and placed her body in a garbage bin. Her body was found the next day in a landfill dump 25 miles from the prison. There was no indication of sexual assault. What happened to Payant had no relationship to the fact that she was female as all officers are expected to respond to a call for assistance from other officers. She was the first prison officer to be killed in the line of duty in New York State since the 1971 Attica riots, and the first known female prison officer to be killed in the entire United States.

was supposed to remedy that situation by order of the Court in *Pugh* v. *Locke*.)[56]

This was the first time the Supreme Court, or any other federal court, upheld an employer's right to limit or refuse employment to a person solely on the basis of sex, and the first statement by the Supreme Court on the scope of Title VII's BFOQ exception. The Court broadened the scope of the BFOQ exception to Title VII, whereas Congress had intended it to be interpreted and applied very narrowly.[57]

The integrationists have expressed concern that the *Dothard* decision will prevent them from reaching their goal. The decision can be used by their opponents to justify the security arguments by citing the need to secure the male institutions and to protect women, and by departments of correction to slow their personnel integration process. In addition, because broad experience throughout the system is a requisite for promotion, opportunity for advancement to administrative and supervisory positions in men's prisons will be severely limited if women are unable to work in men's institutions. The long-range implications of the *Dothard* decision have yet to be felt. That decision might be used as a precedent for limiting activities and employment of women in other fields, such as law enforcement, considered too dangerous for women.

Male inmates have also succeeded in limiting the employment opportunities of women officers through the use of litigation. Arguing that their right to privacy is violated if women officers are assigned to their housing areas or if women conduct body searches, male inmates have taken their cases to court and have, more often than not, won, especially in the 1970s. In New Jersey, the state attorney general declared that just as members of the opposite sex do not work in public bathrooms, so in the state's correctional institutions, members of the opposite sex should not work in the housing areas of inmates. In other cases—*Bonner* v. *Coughlin* in 1975, *Hodges* v. *Klein* in 1976, and *Frasier* v. *Ward* in 1977—the courts have supported inmates' right to privacy, basing their decisions on the Fourth and Eighth Amendments. In *In re Long* in 1976 and *Forts* v. *Ward* in 1978, the courts relied on the Fourteenth Amendment to ensure the protection of inmates' right to privacy. *Forts* v. *Ward* was the only case brought by women inmates against male officers. The inmates at Bedford Hills, New York, charged in a class action suit that the prison's 43 men officers violated the privacy of the 407 women inmates. However, the courts attempted to reconcile employment issues. In the *Long* and *Forts* cases, as well as in *Reynolds* v. *Wise* in 1974 and in *Meith* v. *Dothard* in 1976, the courts stated that women and men officers should be given selective work assignments so as not to interfere with the rights of inmates.[58]

The resulting problems are similar to those raised by the *Dothard* v. *Rawlinson* decision. Women can be denied assignments that are required or are advantageous for promotion. Furthermore, in order not to abrogate the privacy rights of inmates, departments of correction have assigned women officers to the limited number of posts in a male facility that do not necessitate direct contact with male inmates. This policy serves to exacerbate the hostility of male officers who claim that women receive the same salary but do not do the same work—the tough job of working directly with the male inmates.

Furthermore, restrictions placed by the courts, forbidding women officers to move freely in men's facilities, have raised the issue of whether women so restricted can be effective members of correctional staffs. Marvin Frankel, federal judge in the New York State District, issued a "knock first" rule for officers in the Federal Metropolitan Correctional Center in New York City. An officer must knock on doors to alert inmates that he or she is entering the housing area or toilet/shower area.[59] However, this alerting of inmates to the fact that an officer is coming can interfere with security. This is obviously a convenient argument for any person who seeks to prevent women from expanding their role in corrections. Yet men have been, and continue to be, in charge of women's institutions and at work as officers guarding women inmates. It might be asked how they can attend to the safety and security of these institutions if they are not free to enter all areas. The question is thus more complicated, and not just one of women in men's prisons.

Since 1970, there have been many lawsuits by male correctional personnel and inmates arguing that, for security or privacy reasons, women should be denied employment in male facilities. The women under attack are part of correctional staff, not treatment staff. Women have filed countersuits, claiming that they are denied equal opportunites for assignments with men that lead to promotions and higher pay. Departments of correction in cities and states, faced with the expense of lawsuits, are attempting to deal with these issues. Some efforts have been made especially since the 1982 decision in *Griffin* v. *Michigan Department of Corrections*. In that case the court ruled that male inmates have no constitutional right to privacy for their bodies, when that right is balanced against the objective of providing equal job opportunities for women.[60]

In 1983, the attorney general of New Jersey reversed previous policy and stated that all public employment titles were to be open to males and females. In situations where security or inmates' right to privacy conflicted with employees' right to employment, the employer might apply to have a BFOQ exception to Title VII established. However, and most important, Title VII's BFOQ provision would be narrowly construed and the burden of proof would be on the employer. One recent request for a BFOQ exception was turned down. The Camden County sheriff failed to prove that the job of lieutenant was too hazardous for women, and that it was not possible to make structural changes or to rearrange job duties in order to protect male inmates' right to privacy.[61]

Those who believe that the full integration of male and female prison staffs is a desirable goal also believe that there are ways in which the potential problems can be mitigated or eliminated without litigation. Security issues may be resolved if safe and humane prison conditions are established for staff and prisoners. An effective staff training program needs to be developed that includes courses in self-defense, crisis intervention, and riot control. Simulations of dangerous situations, such as fights among prisoners, attacks on officers, and prisoners taking officers hostage, would train both male and female officers to handle these emergencies alone or as a team. And, since both men and women are subject to rape in a male prison, a strong training program should benefit both male and female staff. Training proved to be a decisive factor in the ability of a female officer to break up a fight between two male inmates at the Metropolitan Correctional Center in Chicago. Despite her small size, 96 pounds, she performed her duties without any problem.[62]

The issue of prisoners' right to privacy may be resolved if new institutions are designed and structural changes are made in existing prisons that provide for the privacy of male and female prisoners, regardless of the sex of the staff; these might include shoulder-height partitions in front of toilets and showers. In addition, codes of behavior for staff and prisoners dealing with situations such as pat and body searches and nudity may prove to be a benefit for staff as well as prisoners. A statement of expected behavior will protect the privacy right of prisoners and reduce the possibility of legal action against staff for violation of this right.

One of the most promising attempts to date to solve this problem has been made in the California state prison system. According to Deputy Director Arlene M. Becker, the problems of searching inmates and supervising toilet and bathing facilities have been successfully solved. Women officers do not, as a general rule, do "skin searches" of male inmates, nor do men officers search female inmates. Screening has been put up in the shower and toilet facilities so that only the upper portion of the body is exposed; windows have been fogged. An inmate who follows the rules retains his or her privacy. Since this policy went into effect, inmates have had no complaints and officers have encountered no insoluble difficulties. Rather, male inmates have actually been better-behaved, less profane, and more concerned with their hygiene and appearance than before the women appeared. Male officers are also showing more respect for the privacy of inmates.[63]

If all positions are opened to qualified men and women, and a staff grievance process is implemented to deal with problems that may develop as men and women learn to work together in an integrated staff, then all will learn through experience that women can perform on an equal basis with men in all positions and at all levels of authority.

PERFORMANCE STUDIES

Very few studies have been conducted on women correctional staff and the effect female officers and administrators have on male staff and inmates.

One such study took place in Boulder, Colorado. From July 1976 to June 1977 the men's jail in Boulder was the subject of the most comprehensive study yet done of the effects of women officers in male institutions. The researchers questioned inmates and officers, both male and female, on issues of right to privacy, resentment among inmates and male officers, sexual frustration among inmates, and security and discipline in the jail. Ten women were hired to work in the county jail for men, performing all the duties of men officers except strip searches.[64]

The Boulder study reported that inmates, male officers, and female officers were satisfied with the results—that is, the experiment was a success. Specifically, the majority of inmates felt no invasion of privacy, no resentment at having to take orders from women, and no sexual frustration. They could not manipulate the women any more than they could the men, and did not feel any more protective of the women, whom they cursed as they did the men, until they realized that the verbal abuse had no apparent effect on the women's effectiveness as officers. Male officers did not resent working with women, and believed that the presence of women reduced tensions, brought a softening effect that reduced violence, and had the effect of "increasing the livability of the institution." Male and female officers alike thought women could be just as effective as men in the same jobs, except in stopping fights, where women were at a physical disadvantage.[65]

The matter of women's physical strength and ability to handle fights between male inmates is not so simple; affirmative-action policies have reduced height and weight requirements to enable Oriental and Hispanic men to qualify for corrections work, and some of these men are as small as or smaller than some women. The issue is therefore not size so much as training in self-defense and in handling fights among prisoners. Programs to provide such training do exist, but several have serious flaws in the way women are trained. In federal and state systems, men and women have been trained together since the 1970s. However, women are sometimes treated too harshly; the intent is to discourage them from seeking to work in a male facility. In other situations, women may be treated too leniently, often paired with other women in physical training in self-defense or breaking up fights; women thus get no training and experience in handling even simulated fights with men. If these inequalities in training could be eliminated, women officers would be much better able to cope with conditions in male facilities. And, most important, men might feel more comfortable and more trusting of the female officers with whom they work.

Cheryl Petersen, who conducted her study in 1977 while working as an officer in a male prison in Minnesota, also learned that male inmates and officers questioned women officers' ability to handle fights. However, inmates believed that women, because they tend to have a nonaggressive manner, were better able to break up fights than were male officers. Petersen reported a positive-to-neutral reaction to female officers from male inmates, and a hostile and negative reaction to female officers from male officers. Inmates stated that the presence of women improved the atmosphere in the prison, and 65 percent said they would protect a female officer but not a male. In other respects, they considered a female officer as a guard. Male officers expressed and exhibited hostility, first overt and then, as time passed, covert. Covert behavior involved sexual harassment, spreading rumors about women's sexual behavior, both with male officers and with inmates; even a pregnant officer was harassed about the identity of the father of the child. Male officers did not trust the women's ability to protect themselves or others, and believed women would become romantically involved with inmates. Petersen believed that the women's job performances suffered because there were no consistent and certain rules about inmate privacy or the duties of officers, male or female. Both men and women officers lacked guidelines, but men had a network for support and advice; women had no such network, no support from the men or administrators, nor experienced women as role models.[66]

THE NEW PROFESSIONALS

More so than women in law enforcement and the legal system, women in corrections are divided over their roles and goals. The women who seek equality of opportunity in the profession, the integrationists, want to be fully trained and prepared to accept any assignment in both men's and women's institutions. However, not all the women want equality of opportunity with men. The traditionalists want equal pay and benefits with men but not equal assignments, and prefer to work in a women's facility. They have no desire to participate in the physical training programs conducted at corrections academies. Furthermore, when working with men officers in a women's or a men's prison or jail, they assume the traditional women's role and expect men to do the heavy work. They provide a convenient example for men who claim that in reality most women do not want to change the old ways.

The new professionals, hired since the late 1970s, fall someplace in between the integrationists and the traditionalists. Most see themselves as officers in charge of guarding inmates, not as social workers, reformers, or mothers; they have a custodial approach to corrections rather than the "mother uplifting the errant daughter" approach. Equally important, this new professional identity exists whether the women work with female or male inmates. However, because they are locked in prisons and jails with inmates, many of the new professionals prefer to work only with women in women's facilities.

The burden on the women who want change is thus very great. They must deal with the opposing views of both women and men. Invariably they must be a cut above the norm, must work harder to prove themselves to the men officers and administrators, and must often get the job done without the help of colleagues. In fact, many have had male officers and administrators be less cooperative and create more trouble for them than have male inmates. And all the while they must act pleasant and not show resentment or insubordination. To do this, usually with the support of few women co-workers, creates a stressful working situation. The task is made more difficult by the low esteem in which the women are held by most men officers and administrators, and by the open opposition of these men to working with women. The integrationists face not only open hostility but also sexual innuendo, obscene gestures, and harassment from male officers, not male inmates.[67]

Women who do speak out face the risk of being punished, if only informally, by being transferred to another institution, by a lack of cooperation from male colleagues, or by constant reminders that they are not trusted because they are incapable of doing the same jobs as men. An outspoken deputy warden in charge of the training academy in New York City was transferred twice in one year. A woman in New Jersey who actively sought equality for women in the profession faced many obstacles in order to gain a position at central headquarters as an administrator. In an attempt to scare her away from the position, she was sent to supervise correction officers training at the firing range, where live ammunition was used, without advice or instructions.[68]

Perhaps these factors are responsible for the small growth in the proportion of women in corrections. In 1973 there were 5,181 (9.2 percent) women and 51,276 men officers, in 1979 there were 9,592 (12.7 percent) women and 65,768 men officers, and in 1983 there were 8,512 (11 percent) women and 70,011 men officers.[69] The feelings of women who seek equal opportunities and careers in corrections may at times match those of one officer who said:

> Corrections is a fascinating field . . . but there are days when I really wonder if this is the place for me. The department seems to be encouraging women to enter the system but that attitude hasn't filtered down yet to the "good ole" boys I have to work with. They watch every move I make and challenge everything I do if it's not exactly the way they would do it. Sometimes I feel more like one of the inmates than one of the staff. . . .[70]

While much has been done to reduce the level of sexual discrimination, a great deal remains. Aside from the strong biases that exist in the minds and hearts of men, there are specific inequities that persist. Women officers continue to be concentrated in women's facilities; only 8.4 percent of officers in male institutions are female. The small number of women in corrections, approximately 11 percent of officers and 1 percent of administrators, means that most of them are needed in women's institutions in order to comply with inmates' right to privacy as mandated by most courts. Although three federal district courts—in California, Oregon, and Michigan—rejected inmates' right to privacy when women's employment rights were at risk, court-mandated policies are often implemented slowly by unwilling correctional personnel. In addition, these policies must be won in court, one jurisdiction at a time.

Although it has been demonstrated that women officers are as effective and competent as men, women will continue to be kept from advancing within corrections as long as security issues can be used to establish a BFOQ exception to Title VII; the *Dothard* decision still stands. Without the requisite experience, women will not be eligible for promotion on the same basis as men. Veterans' preference laws will also keep women from being hired for and assigned to desirable positions, and even in an integrated system will reduce the possibilities of women becoming supervisors and administrators.

These court decisions on privacy, security, and veterans' preference have served to limit the number of women and, thus, to further isolate women who work in male prisons and jails. The result has been that women, in small numbers and in posts that prevent their contact with inmates, have had little discernible impact on humanizing the work place, changing the behavior of male officers, or facilitating the rehabilitation of male inmates. Thus, few of the positive effects of integrating women into an all-male work force, predicted by theorists, have in fact been realized or proven.

Even the "get tough on criminals" policy of the 1980s will not add appreciably to the number of women in corrections or to their career opportunities. Many new prisons and jails are being constructed around the nation; all are for males. The jails will have sections for women inmates. Although hundreds of new officers will be hired, as in the past, most will be men.

Women in corrections lack an organization, formal or informal, that can lobby for them. Women are excluded from the "old boy" network that binds male correction officers together. As in any profession, this network is the best way to familiarize oneself with the inner workings of the system and to make contacts that will help in securing assignments and promotions. Although the network is not tangible or formal in any given facility or system, its existence is essential to the officers in many ways.

One answer is for women to form an "old girl" network, as is generally happening in many professions, such as law enforcement and the law. But women correction officers have unique disadvantages in this regard. The number of women's institutions is small and the facilities are widely dispersed across the country. There has not developed any tradition of becoming vocal and active on corrections issues; support groups have not emerged even in large cities, where there may be many women in corrections. Unlike women in law enforcement and the legal profession, those in corrections are not as active and articulate on issues concerning their careers, nor do they have national or local organizations. Lacking support both within corrections and in the community, women in corrections who want equality often have to make that effort on an individual basis. The odds are against them.

SUMMARY

The position of women in corrections has improved considerably since the advent of women's corrections in 1873. Women have become commissioners, chiefs of operations, wardens of men's as well as women's institutions, and officers in male and female facilities. However, court decisions and male officers and administrators have acted to restrict women's career opportunities; women's desire for equal opportunities in employment in corrections has also been thwarted by their female colleagues. The results have been, according to one study, that:

> Occupational segregation subsumes a multitude of factors that work to the disadvantage of women employed in corrections. Women not only experience differential recruitment and placement; once in the field, their mobility and attainment also differ from men.[71]

The debate on the role and place of women in corrections reveals the tenacious hold that traditional values concerning women have on men and women in the courts, corrections system, and the community. Although the debate on women's place in the system continues, it is still primarily a topic of concern and discussion within the system itself, receiving little attention from social scientists. What little we know of female correctional staff comes mainly from autobiographies of matrons and superintendents and from former inmates, literature that is tainted with bias and subjectivity. Only a few studies have been conducted, and they have dealt primarily with attitudes about women working in male facilities.

Women seek employment in the penal system, by and large, for the same reasons that men do: the system offers individuals without highly developed skills and with no more than a high school education or its equivalent a reasonable income, benefits, and opportunities for advancement. However, women must struggle against the traditional stereotypical view of women held by those who founded the women's corrections system. In order to create a place for women in the male-dominated field, the founders argued for the establishment of women's prisons staffed only by women, emphasizing traditional views of the role and place of women in society. These arguments have proved to be the most difficult to overcome because they are so pervasive in society and so readily accepted by women and men alike.

Ironically, to counteract the arguments of those opposed to women's equal role in corrections with men, those in favor of an integrated corrections system have promulgated a view based on their own version of stereotypical woman: women are more humane and sensitive than men, and therefore are more able to humanize the work place, thereby contributing to the rehabilitation of male inmates.

The absurdity of arguments invoking stereotypical images should be apparent to all. Not until such arguments have been laid to rest can there be establishment of a rational policy dedicated to the development of well-trained and effective staffs of men and women in the penal system.

NOTES

1. Carroll Smith-Rosenberg, "Beauty, the Beast and the Militant Women: A Case Study in Sex Roles and Social Stress in Jacksonian America," in *Many Pasts: Readings in American Social History, 1600-1876,* edited by Herbert G. Gutman and Gregory S. Kealey (Englewood Cliffs, N.J.: Prentice-Hall, 1973), pp. 287-305; Eleanor Flexner, *Century of Struggle: The Woman's Rights Movement in the United States* (New York: Atheneum, 1971), pp. 23-70, 179-215; David J. Pivar, *Purity Crusade: Sexual Morality and Social Control, 1868-1900* (Westport, Conn.: Greenwood Press, 1973), pp. 50-73; Alice Felt Tyler, *Freedom's Ferment: Phases of American Social History from the Colonial Period to the Outbreak of the Civil War* (New York: Harper Torchbooks, 1962), pp. 227-462; Allen F. Davis, *Spearheads for Reform: The Social Settlements and the Progressive Movement 1890-1914* (New York: Oxford University Press, 1967), passim; Barbara Welter, "The Cult of True Womanhood: 1820-1860," in *Our American Sisters: Women in American Life and Thought,* edited by Jean E. Friedman and William G. Shade (Boston: Allyn and Bacon, 1973), pp. 96-123.

2. Smith-Rosenberg, op. cit,. pp. 288-96, 300-02; Pivar, op. cit,. pp. 18-43; Estelle B. Freedman, "Their Sisters' Keepers: An Historical Perspective on Female Correctional Institutions in the United States: 1870-1900," *Feminist Studies* 11 (1974): 82-83.

3. Smith-Rosenberg, op. cit., pp. 288-95; Pivar, op. cit., pp. 24-32.

4. Smith-Rosenberg, op. cit., pp. 300-01.

5. Richard Hofstadter, *The Age of Reform* (New York: Vintage Books, 1955), pp. 174-86; Philip Klein, *Prison Methods in New York State: Studies in History, Economics and Public Law* (New York: Longmans, Green, 1920), p. 45.

6. David W. Lewis, *From Newgate to Dannemora: The Rise of the Penitentiary in New York, 1796-1848* (Ithaca, N.Y.: Cornell University Press, 1965), pp. 94-97, 155-59, 162-64, 173-75; Klein, op. cit., pp. 41-45; Freedman, op. cit., pp. 77-79; Clarice Feinman, "Imprisoned Women: A History of the Treatment of Women Incarcerated in New York City, 1932-1975" (Ph.D. diss. Department of History, New York University, 1976), pp. 22-40.

7. Lewis, op. cit., p. 160; Freedman, op. cit., pp. 79-80.

8. Freedman, op. cit., p. 80; Klein, op. cit., pp. 225-26, 374; Lewis, op. cit., pp. 237-41; John F. Richmond, *New York and Its Institutions, 1609-1872* (New York: E. B. Treat, 1972), pp. 317-20, 457-60; Georgiana B. Kirby, *Years of Experience: An Autobiographical Narrative* (New York: AMS Press, 1971), pp. 190-211.

9. Kirby, op. cit., pp. 194, 199-200.

10. Ibid., pp. 225-26.

11. Freedman, op. cit., pp. 86-88.

12. *Notable American Women 1607-1950: A Biographical Dictionary* (Cambrige, Mass.: Belknap Press, 1971), vol. I, pp. 439-41; and vol. II, pp. 197-99, 277-78; Burton Rowles, *The Lady*

at Box 99: The Story of Miriam van Waters (Greenwich, Conn.: Seabury Press, 1962), pp. 31–33, 260–70.

13. Feinman, op. cit., pp. 49–53; Mary Harris, *I Knew Them in Prison* (New York: Viking Press, 1936), pp. 28–34, 43–49; Women's Prison Association, *Annual Report: 1915,* pp. 34–35; *1917,* p. 30; and *1929,* p. 15.

14. Harris, op. cit., pp. 43–49, 382–401.

15. Ellen C. Potter, "The Problem of Women in Penal and Correctional Institutions," *Quarterly Journal of Corrections* 1 (Fall 1977): 13; Harris, op. cit., pp. 88–91; Florence Monahan, *Women in Crime* (New York: Ives Washburn, 1941), pp. 43–44.

16. Feinman, op. cit., pp. 71–72; Davis, op. cit., pp. 23, 187; Prison Association of New York, *Annual Report 1933,* p. 42.

17. Potter, op. cit., pp. 13–14.

18. "Profile," *Quarterly Journal of Corrections* 1 (Fall 1977): 7–9.

19. Kate R. O'Hare, *In Prison* (Seattle: University of Washington Press, 1976), p. 162.

20. Ibid.

21. Ibid., pp. 161–63.

22. Interview with Marie D. Miller, county training supervisor, New Jersey Department of Corrections Training Academy, December 13, 1978; Interview with Sam Samples, staff training development, Federal Bureau of Prisons, June 22, 1979; New York City Department of Correction, *Annual Report: 1950,* pp. 28, 30; *1952,* pp. 3, 25; *1953,* p. v; *1955,* pp. xv–xvi; *1957,* pp. 11–13; *1958,* p. 78.

23. Judy Sammon, "Campus Look Is Sharp Contrast to Reality of Penitentiary Walls," *Quarterly Journal of Corrections* 1 (Fall 1977): 47; interview with Sherry MacPhearson, Professional Services, Correctional Institution for Women, Clinton, N.J., May 3, 1979; interview with Essie O. Murph, superintendent, New York City Correctional Institution for Women, January 16, 1976.

24. Interview with Philip Dwyer, superintendent, Correctional Institution for Women, Clinton, N.J., May 1 1979.

25. Interview with Murph, January 16, 1976; Clarice Feinman, "An Afro-American Experience: The Women in New York City's Jail," *Afro-Americans in New York Life and History* 1 (July 1977): 202–03.

26. Interview with Murph, January 16, 1976; Feinman, "Imprisoned Women," pp. 163–65.

27. Interview with Miller, December 13, 1978; interview with Devora Cohn, director of labor relations, New York City Department of Correction, May 4, 1979; interview with Jean Wolfe, research analyst, California Department of Corrections, July 9, 1979; interview with MacPhearson, May 3, 1979.

28. Elizabeth Gurley Flynn, *The Alderson Story: My Life as a Political Prisoner* (New York: International Publishers, 1972), pp. 94–95.

29. Jane R. Chapman, Elizabeth K. Minor, Patricia Rieker, Trudy L. Mills, and Mary Bottum, *Women Employed in Corrections* (Washington, D.C.: U.S. Department of Justice, National Institute of Justice, 1983), p. 62.

30. Diana N. Travisono, ed., *Vital Statistics in Corrections* (College Park, Md.: American Correctional Association, 1984), pp. 12, 23; information from Cathy Morse, public relations officer, Federal Bureau of Prisons, February 11, 1985; information from the Personnel Department, New York City Department of Correction, March 1, 1985.

31. Letter from Mary K. Lindsay, former superintendent, House of Detention for Women, New York City, to Clarice Feinman, February 25, 1974; interview with Murph, January 16, 1976; interview with Florence Holland, former superintendent, House of Detention for Women, New York City, April 8, 1974; interview with Jessie L. Behagen, former superintendent, House of Detention for Women, New York City, April 20, 1974.

32. *New York Times,* June 10, 1979, p. 20E.

33. Flynn, op. cit., pp. 97, 99; interview with Murph, January 16, 1976; interview with Holland, April 8, 1974; interview with Behagen, April 20, 1974.

34. New York City Department of Correction, *Equal Employment Opportunity Report 1983–84;* Edward Hershey, "Big System, Big Strides," *Corrections Today* 47 (February 1985): 66.

35. New York City Deptartment of Correction, *Equal Employment Opportunity Report 1983–84*; Ibid.; interview with Murph, January 16, 1976.

36. Travisono, ed,. *Vital Statistics in Corrections*, p. 18.

37. Allen F. Breed, "Women in Correctional Employment," in *Women in Corrections*, edited by Barbara H. Olsson, (College Park, Md.: American Correctional Association, 1981), p. 38.

38. Cynthia Sulton and Roi Townsey, *A Progress Report on Women in Policing* (Washington, D.C.: Police Foundation, 1981), pp. 16–21.

39. Interview with Samples, June 22, 1979; interview with Cohn, May 4, 1979; interview with Dwyer, May 1, 1979;"Profile," "N.Y. Women Inmates Sue State over Posting of Male Officers," *Quarterly Journal of Corrections* 1 (Fall 1977): 107; *Corrections Digest* 8 (April 13, 1977): 10; "Men and Women," *Crime and Delinquency* 22 (January 1976): 7–8.

40. *Corrections Compendium Survey Book 1979* (Lincoln, Neb.: CONtact, 1979), pp. 78–83.

41. "Female Correctional Officers," in *Corrections Compendium* (Lincoln, Neb.: CONtact, 1982), pp. 5–10.

42. Arlene Becker, "Women in Corrections: A Process of Change," *Resolution* 1 (Summer 1975): 19–21.

43. Ibid.; interview with Arlene Becker, Deputy director, California Department of Corrections, May 18, 1979.

44. Interview with Cohn, May 4, 1979; interviews with Gloria Lee, supervising warden, New York City Department of Correction, February 10, 1976, and August 11, 1983; interviews with Jacqueline McMickens, chief of operations, New York City Department of Correction, March 10, 1976, and August 11, 1983.

45. Sylvia G. McCollum, "The Federal Government and Affirmative Action: A Default of Leadership," *Resolution* 1 (Summer 1975): 11.

46. Interview with Samples, June 22, 1979.

47. Information from Morse, February 11, 1985.

48. Ibid.

49. Interview with Samples, June 22, 1979.

50. Norval Morris, *The Future of Imprisonment* (Chicago: University of Chicago Press, 1974), p. 109.

51. Joan Potter, "Should Women Guards Work in Prisons for Men?" *Corrections Magazine* 6 (October 1980): 30.

52. John Lombardi, "The Absence of Suicide in New York City's Women's House of Detention" (Ph.D. diss., Department of Psychology, Rutgers University, 1979).

53. Susan L. Reisner, "Balancing Inmates' Right to Privacy with Equal Employment for Prison Guards," *Women's Rights Reporter* 4 (Summer 1978): 243–50.

54. James B. Jacobs, "The Sexual Integration of the Prison's Guard Force: A Few Comments on *Dothard* v. *Rawlinson*," in *Women in Corrections*, edited by Barbara H. Olsson, (College Park, Md.: American Correctional Association, 1981), pp. 58–59.

55. Ibid., p. 59.

56. Ibid., p. 81, fn. 65.

57. Ibid., pp. 59–60.

58. Reisner, op. cit., pp. 243–50.

59. Gillian Sacks, "Prisoner Privacy and Equal Employment Opportunities" (unpublished paper, University of Connecticut School of Law Special Research Project, 1979), p. 14.

60. Elaine Ballai, "Should Female Correction Officers Work with Male Prisoners?" *New Jersey Corrections Quarterly* 1 (June 1984): 1, 4.

61. Ibid., p. 1.

62. Jacobs, op. cit., p. 79, fn. 46.

63. Becker, op. cit., p. 21; interview with Becker, May 18, 1979.

64. Peter J. Kissel and Paul L. Katsampes, "The Impact of Women Corrections Officers on the Functioning of Institutions Housing Male Inmates" (unpublished paper, National Institute of Corrections Jail Center, Boulder, Colo., 1979), pp. 1-8.

65. Ibid., pp. 27-32.

66. Cheryl B. Peterson, "Doing Time with the Boys," in *Criminal Justice and Women,* edited by Barbara Price and Natalie Sokoloff (New York: Clark Boardman, 1982), pp. 437-60.

67. Interview with Becker, May 18, 1979; interview with Miller, December 13, 1978; interview with Cohn, May 4, 1979; interview with Samples, June 22, 1979; interview with Wolfe, July 9, 1979.

68. Interview with Cohn, May 4, 1979; interview with Miller, December 13, 1978.

69. Chapman, et al., op. cit. p. 27; Travisono, ed., *Vital Statistics in Corrections,* p. 18.

70. Chapman et al., op. cit., p. 63.

71. Ibid., p. 119.

PART IV

CONCLUSION

Undo what man did for us in the dark ages, and strike out all special legislation for us; strike out the words "white male" from all your constitutions, and then, with fair sailing, let us sink or swim, live or die, survive or perish together.

(Elizabeth Cady Stanton, "Address to the New York State Legislature 1860," in *Feminism: The Essential Historical Writings,* edited by Miriam Schneir [New York: Vintage Books, 1971], p. 121.)

All I ask of our brethren is, that they will take their feet from off our necks and permit us to stand upright on that ground which God designed us to occupy.

All history attests that man has subjected woman to his will, used her as a means to promote his selfish gratification, to minister to his sensual pleasures, to be instrumental in promoting his comfort; but never has he desired to elevate her to that rank she was created to fill. He has done all he could to debase and enslave her mind; and now he looks triumphantly on the ruin he has wrought, and says the being he has thus so deeply injured is his inferior.

(Sarah M. Grinmke, "Letters on the Equality of the Sexes and the Condition of Woman 1837," in *Feminism: The Essential Historical Writings,* edited by Miriam Schneir [New York: Vintage Books, 1971], p. 38).

7

WOMEN IN THE CRIMINAL JUSTICE SYSTEM: CONCLUDING OBSERVATIONS

Legally mandated change may, in time, alter policies and practices, but it usually has little effect on altering culturally mandated attitudes and values. Consequently, despite antidiscrimination legislation and judicial decisions that have led to expanded employment opportunities for professional women in the criminal justice system and to improved conditions under which incarcerated women live, there has been little change in societal beliefs about the proper role and place of women. Whether they be criminals, law enforcement officers, lawyers, judges, or correction officers, women have been perceived and treated in accordance with a deeply ingrained, widely held stereotype, the madonna/whore duality. It has been taken for granted by most people over the course of Western history that women are basically different from men in certain socially defined ways, and that they must therefore be treated differently from men. For the most part it has also been assumed that this difference implies inferiority, so that different treatment has really meant protection and relegation to roles that men did not regard as important enough to perform themselves. Women were ready sources of offspring, physical satisfaction, adornment, cheap labor, and entertainment. Paradoxically, these same inferior beings were often placed on a pedestal as the incarnations of probity and virtue: in Europe in the cult of the Virgin Mary, in the United States in the cult of true womanhood. Women were somehow both weak and vulnerable, yet pure and worthy of the highest regard.

This view of women, at the same time condescending, genuinely admiring, and callous, is reflected in the history of women who have become professionals in the criminal justice system.They have been expected to adhere to "womanly" roles within the system, in keeping with their "womanly" ability. As long as they have remained in their prescribed roles, they have been accepted in the system. For example the earliest U.S. women to enter corrections and law enforcement would seem to have been departing from the straight path of womanly virtue, according to which nothing was to be done that brought them into contact with the dregs of society or with unseemliness of any kind. But in fact they avoided most criticism because they did not depart from clearly defined, traditional womanly roles; they were sisters and mothers, not "guards" and "cops." Both the reformers and, later, the first paid professionals used the madonna/whore duality to argue that women criminals required their own separate institutions where a staff composed entirely of moral women would uplift the fallen to their proper place in society. Over the next century women carved out a small system of their own from which men were mostly excluded.

From the men's point of view, too, this was an agreeable arrangement. Segregation reduced the opportunities for women, and thus eliminated direct competition between men and women for jobs, money, and status—the things men valued most highly. Women of great ability were given free reign within the women's system but were not allowed into the men's system, where the rewards were highest. Therefore women were automatically excluded from the top of the pyramid. They quickly saw this disadvantage but, until much later, had no choice but to accept the arrangement.

The intellectual and psychological basis of the arrangement was widely accepted, and was so unquestioned by most women and men, and by persons in authority, that full integration with full equality was impossible. This was especially galling to women lawyers and judges, who were not so completely segregated as women police and correction officers, and could often see very clearly how the duality limited their freedom to rise according to merit. Unlike women in law enforcement and corrections, women who entered the legal profession did not ask for separation or proclaim their unique ability to protect and reform women and children. Rather, they assumed the right to practice law on an equal basis with men. Therefore, from the start, men lawyers viewed women lawyers as competitors, and constantly placed obstacles in their paths to keep the women from sharing the rewards of the profession: status, wealth, and power.

In the period after World War II, changes began that would produce the first serious challange to the prevailing views. Middle-class women began entering colleges and professional jobs in unprecedented numbers; the civil rights movement of the 1960s raised fundamental questions of human freedom that could not be ignored; federal legislation and court decisions raised the possiblilty of social change through goverment action; and the women's movement provided the growing number of activist women with psychological support, theoretical arguments, and publicity. Out of all these simultaneous developments came calls for the end of segregation and descrimination against women in the criminal justice system, on the argument that the old duality is not a true perception of women but a myth, a relic of the past that should not govern the present. The future, it was argued, should not be a continuation of the past and the present, but something new and different, based on equality of opportunity between men and women.

Such an argument has its pitfalls, of course, since it not only gives women equality but also strips them of their old "privileges" and "protections." This is one of the prices of true independence and true adulthood, and it is unsettling to many people, even to quite a few women. Instead of the comfortable values of the often romanticized past, there is the uncertain promise of better things to come. And there is no guarantee that the day of full equality will ever come. It thus is not surprising that women who favor integration and full equality have met with enormous resistance, and will continue to do so.

There is a mistaken belief that women have "made it." Even many of the new generation of women, exposed to the publicity given to the individual women who have succeeded in their chosen careers, have been deluded into thinking that equality of opportunity is, indeed, a fact of life for all women. In reality, only a small minority of women have benefited from equal rights legislation. Only a small number of women have succeeded in entering employment areas that were once the territory of men only. Most women continue to be employed in jobs traditionally associated with females and, as a group, earn less than men do even when they are in the same field doing the same work. At the end of 1984, the Bureau of Labor Statistics reported that job discrimination was still so pervasive that it would be years before women would reach parity with men in the work place. Women were still primarily in low-income, low-status jobs; two-thirds held clerical, sales, service, or government positions. Furthermore, women earned, on average, less in comparison with men in 1980 than they had in 1970.[1] In fact, women constitute the fastest-growing group living below the poverty line in the United States.

Professional women in the criminal justice system know that full equality is not a reality, and that they must continue to work hard to reach that goal. Their efforts may meet with increased opposition in the 1980s, for there are signs that one result of the more conservative political climate may be less vigorous enforcement of antidiscrimination legislation. The Equal Rights Amendment was not ratified, the Republican Party platform for the 1984 presidential election did not mention the amendment or women's rights, and national support for civil and women's rights is weak compared with what it was in the 1960s and 1970s. Women in the criminal justice system must also deal with other problems that serve to hinder their full participation in the system, such as financial crises, tax revolts, budget cuts, court decisions upholding veterans' preference laws, the *Dothard* decision, and the subtle and overt opposition of some women as well as many men in the system. Nevertheless, despite this more hostile climate, there is reason to hope that the situation for professional women will improve. Legal precedent has been established, and women's groups are still active on behalf of all women. And women themselves, though their representation in policy-making positions is small, continue to exert pressure on the system to alter both policy and practice thereby enabling women to expand their employment opportunities

Clearly, the position of professional women in the criminal justice system has improved, but the gains made by women have been unevenly distributed. On the whole, women who work most closely with criminals have achieved the least. The *Dothard* decision, the only federal court decision to have limited women's rights to employment opportunity by referring to the BFOQ exception in Title VII, remains on the books and in the minds of policy makers in corrections. There is no doubt that corrections is the least highly regarded component of the criminal justice system, not only by the public but also by legislators. Budgets are not sufficient to provide adequate staffs or proper training, the working conditions are poor, and the locked-in culture affects almost all officers. Women in corrections are not well organized and have no national organization to act or speak on their behalf in the corrections system, the legislatures, or the media. In the few areas where women in corrections have been active and where a strong women's support group exists, the gains have been impressive. The position of women in the New York City Department of Correction provides a clear example.

The situation is a little better for women in law enforcement, who are more involved with the public when on patrol and as members of rape, juvenile, and domestic violence task forces. The public, especially women victims, have come to accept and depend upon women law officers in times of trouble. In addition, female law officers have their own national organization to speak on their behalf. However, they must still resort to legal action to achieve employment and promotions in some cities and states, and very few are in supervisory positions.

Lawyers and judges have the best position of all women in the criminal justice system. They are the best-educated and most articulate, are well organized, and, often, are politically well connected. Their work is not physical, they do not wear uniforms or carry weapons, and therefore they avoid the taint of being called "unwomanly" or "masculine." They are also able to share the generally high status associated with a nationally recognized profession. Within the profession, however, the position of women is more ambiguous. Until recently they were few in number and usually restricted—by custom, not law—to the least lucrative aspects of law practice. Only since the mid 1970s have they made real, if limited, progress toward equality of opportunity. One women, Sandra Day O'Connor, is a U.S. Supreme Court justice, and others are state supreme court justices. Yet true equality eludes them all. O'Connor told her female colleagues that they all had to work harder than male judges to be accepted, so that other women might become judges.

It might be said that criminals are at the other end of the system; and among criminals, there are few signs of improvement and little hope of the future equality of women with men. Somehow the word "equality" seems inappropriate for persons who have been taken out of society and put behind bars. Students of U.S. history and the criminal justice system are well aware of the double standard that has existed for women offenders in the system. White, propertied, and conforming women have been viewed and treated as potential madonnas and subsequently have been given preferential or chivalrous treatment. Lower-class, minority women have never been considered madonnas worthy of honor, protection, or deference. They have been disproportionately visible among the accused, convicted, and punished; they have been viewed and treated as whores. The unbalanced scales of justice have been obvious to many, and have yet to be balanced.

There are many theories put forth by professionals in the criminal justice system to explain why women commit crimes and what the future of that criminal pattern might be. Here, too, traditional views have been tied to the madonna/whore concept, with its notion of a fall from grace and its emphasis on domesticity as the vehicle for rehabilitation: and little has changed in this regard. Theories designed to explain the nature of female crime are no more rooted in fact now than they were a century ago, despite the accumulation of volumes of statistics and data. Always, it seems, some researchers go out of their way to find exotic causes for criminal behavior of women, such as the women's movement, when many of the causes are apparent in poverty, ignorance, drug and alcohol addiction, and lack of opportunity. As long as women face sexual and racial discrimination, high unemployment, and a limited range of jobs that, for the most part, pay poorly, they will constitute a large group at or below the poverty level. Those who become dependent on drugs or alcohol will be caught in an especially vicious bind, since their addiction will reduce their ability to work and will make the petty crimes of larceny and prostitution the most accessible means of livelihood.

Perhaps the reluctance to recognize these facts is simply a way of avoiding a painful truth that women have been, and continue to be, discriminated against in the economic arena. It is far easier to blame the women's movement for everything, even new forms of criminal behavior (which in fact do not exist), than to look inward for the causes. The reluctance to face reality about women's criminality may serve another function: to reinforce the myth that the nonconforming woman is dangerous and criminal, the whore.

Similarly, many highly emotionally charged reasons have been given for denying women in law enforcement, the law, and corrections full integration and equal opportunity. The intensity of the madonna/whore duality argument is obvious in statements describing the women who want equality: unwomanly, sexually suspect, loose, physically weak, emotionally unstable, unreliable, and endangering the lives of correction and police officers, and the legal cases of clients.

The intensity and emotionalism of the issues raised against women began in the 1960s, when many moved to achieve equal status in the criminal justice system and went to court to obtain that right; the intensity and emotionalism is thus directly related to women's challenge to men's control of the system and its rewards. This relationship becomes clear when we remember that, during World War II, when competition for jobs was not an issue, there was little effort to keep women out of nontraditional employment, so-called men's work. The controversy came to prominence only after the war, when men returned to civilian life and employment.

This is not the first time that rationalization has been utilized to justify one group's near monopoly of wealth, power, and status. And the emotionalism of the recent debate over the women's movement and the issues concerning the role of women in society and in the criminal justice system strongly suggests that the traditionalists well know how high the stakes are. With such high stakes, the struggle for equality will be long and arduous, and the goal elusive. If the past is any gauge of the future, those components of the criminal justice system that contain the most educated, most articulate women will make the greatest strides toward equality of opportunity; the other components will lag behind, trailed by the criminals.

Although gains have already been made by the professional women, full equality will not be a reality in the near future. Despite their differences, women in the system continue to be bound by the persistence of traditional beliefs concerning their womanhood that deny them full acceptance and equality in society and in the criminal justice system. Dr. Jeane J. Kirkpatrick, during her tenure as U.S. representative to the United Nations, succinctly described the problem thus: "Sexism is alive. . . . It's alive in the United Nations, it's alive in the U.S. Government—and it's bipartisan."[2]

NOTES

1. *New York Times*, November 25, 1984, pp. 1, 32.
2. Ibid., December 20, 1984, p. B3.

INDEX

ABOUT THE AUTHOR

CLARICE FEINMAN is Associate Professor of Criminal Justice at Trenton State College, New Jersey. She has been director of a rehabilitation program at the New York City Correctional Institution for Women and consultant to the New Jersey Department of Corrections Training Academy.

Dr. Feinman has published in criminal justice and history. She is the coeditor of *Criminal Justice Politics and Women: The Aftermath of Legally Mandated Change,* published by Haworth Press in 1985. Her articles and reviews have appeared in *Crime and Delinquency, Afro-Americans in New York Life and History, Crime and Justice: A Historical Review, The Prison Journal,* and *Women and Politics,* and in a number of edited books.

Dr. Feinman holds a B.A. from Brooklyn College and an M.A. and a Ph.D. from New York University.